SYSTEMA
AWARENESS TRAINING

Robert Poyton

Copyright@ 2019 R Poyton

SECOND EDITION

All rights reserved

The moral right of the author has been asserted

No part of this book may be reproduced in any form or by any
electronic or mechanical means including information storage
and retrieval systems, without permission in writing from the author.
The only exception is by a reviewer, who may quote short
excerpts in a review.

The author and publisher take no responsibility for any illness or
injury resulting from practicing the exercises described in this book.
Always consult your Doctor prior to training or if you have any medical issues.

Published by Cutting Edge

ISBN:978-1-64669-000-8

DEDICATIONS

With respect and gratitude to Mikhail Ryabko,
and Vladimir and Valerie Vasiliev,
for their generosity and guidance.

Thanks to all my colleagues and students
and everyone who helped
in the production of this book.

ABOUT THE AUTHOR

Robert was born in the early 1960's in East London.
He trained in Judo and boxing as a child and at age
18 began training in Yang Family Taijiquan.

For many years he studied the Chinese Internal Arts in depth.
In the 1990's he set up his own school and began cross
training in several styles.

Robert has trained extensively with with Mikhail Ryabko and Vladimir
Vasiliev in both Moscow and Toronto. In addition he has arranged
numerous UK seminars for Mikhail, Vladimir and other instructors.

Robert now trains solely in Systema and runs regular classes
in the UK and teaches seminars throughout the UK and Europe.
He has been featured in numerous martial arts books and magazines
as well as producing his own magazines and training films.

Outside of training, Robert is a professional musician and currently
lives in rural Bedfordshire with his wife and a small menagerie.

*"Rob Poyton has been training and teaching Systema since 2000.
He is a dedicated and talented instructor, knowledgeable on
all of the key components of Systema.
Rob presents his teaching in a clear and structured manner
through his classes and reading materials."*
- Vladimir Vasiliev, October 2019.

"Then the eyes of the blind will be opened And the ears of the deaf will be unstopped."

— Isaiah 35:5

CONTENTS

CHAPTER 1: INTRODUCTION
Basics 12
Science 16

CHAPTER 2: VISUAL AWARENESS
How the Eye Works 19
Stick Catching Drills 26
Reaction Drills 30
Low Light Work 38
Camouflage 43

CHAPTER 3: TACTILE AWARENESS
The Homunculus 64
Pushing Drills 66
Sticky Hands 69
Blindfold Work 79
Using Equipment 88

CHAPTER 4: HEARING & SMELL
The Amygdala 96
Sound Drills 97
Moving Quietly 102
Working with Smell 106

CHAPTER 5: THE SIXTH SENSES
How Many Senses? 109
Balance 114
Pain Control 120
Proprioception 123
Cross Body Drills 127
Developing Intuition 131

CHAPTER 6: PERSON TO PERSON
Body Language 139
The Three Fs 142
Reptile Brain? 147
Pacifiers 148
Eye Access Cues 154
Personal Space 163
The OODA Loop 166
Fight Indicators 172
Muscle Reading 176
Cold Reading 177
Misdirection 181
Pickpockets 184

CHAPTER 7: SITUATIONAL AWARENESS
Guidelines 189
Integrated Awareness 194
Positioning 197
Verbals 200
Home Security 202
Vehicle Security 205
Preparing for Violence 207

CHAPTER 8: CONCLUSIONS
Are You Here? 212
Changing Perception 214
Social Systema 216
Habits, Fear, Phobias 217
Know Yourself! 219

CHAPTER ONE
INTRODUCTION

If you do an internet search for "self defence advice" one of the things that tops almost every list is "awareness". *Be aware of your surroundings*, we are advised. *Keep an eye out for bad guys. Plan your route when walking home.*

These are all strong points and certainly important when thinking about self defence in its broader context (personally I'd avoid anyone who teachers solely physical techniques as "self defence.")

But how do we apply this advice? How do we develop good situational awareness? And do awareness skills go beyond not walking down a dark alley? The answer to the latter is yes and the answer to the first question is - *Systema*. I'm presuming that most readers of this book are familiar with Systema. In case you are not, I will give a very brief over-view, then encourage you to research, or even better attend a good class, to find out more.

Systema is the modern name given to a particular type of training method developed in Russia over the last seventy years or, drawn from deeper historical roots. It is often labelled as a "martial art" but is quite different in approach from the Oriental styles such as Karate and Kung-Fu. At it's heart, Systema revolves around four pillars of *breathing, movement, posture* and *relaxation*. Think of it as an "operating system" for the human body. It teaches us to move efficiently and naturally, to respond intuitively and be adaptable in our physical and psychological response to situations.

Systema was primarily developed for military use by close-protection and other special operations units. Since Glasnost, these previously secretive methods became known outside of Russia. But its potential extends way beyond military application, into all areas of life and activity. So today, as well as being practiced by military professionals and martial artists, Systema has also been embraced by athletes, dancers, movement enthusiasts and "regular" people looking to improve their over-all health and well-being.

So what can Systema offer us specifically in terms of awareness? First, let us consider that awareness can be split into two areas, external and internal.

EXTERNAL AWARENESS

At its most fundamental level, Systema teaches us to have good posture and to be calm. Both of these are of great use in maintaining general awareness of our surroundings. If our posture is contorted, we cut down the amount of information coming into the brain. If we are stressed, agitated or aggressive, we tend to go into "tunnel vision" mode. Similarly, being overly tense reduces our sensitivity, both on a tactile and an emotional level. Being calm allows us to both transmit and receive.

On a more specific level, Systema training teaches us to be aware of tension in other people. This can be overt physical tension or more subtle emotional tension. Each is important in managing any type of

confrontation or stressful situation. In addition, working with various items, particularly sticks and other weapons, develops a very good sense of spatial awareness and distancing. Rather than fixed stances, Systema relies heavily on movement as its defensive base, so this ability to be in "the right place at the right time" becomes ingrained in experienced practitioners.

INTERNAL AWARENESS

The engine of Systema is breathing. I have trained in a range of martial art and meditation disciplines over the years, but none, for me, touches the breadth and depth of Systema breath work. From very simple starting points, Systema breathing takes us deep into our "internal" world.

On a basic level, this means simply being aware of our breathing. From there, we can influence and monitor our psyche and our physical state. Further exercises give us a range of tools for monitoring our levels of tension, posture and ease of movement. We learn to become comfortable in what we do, even in uncomfortable situations.

This is one of the prime differences for me from previous breath training. Most forms of meditation work from positions of quiet and comfort. Systema puts us squarely in the real world, the here and now and teaches us inner control in all types of situation. Emotional control is very important in any potential confrontation. It may be an argument at work, a potential fight, or personal dispute,. In each case, going off at the deep end is unlikely to improve the situation.

Beyond this, Systema also helps with deeper set issues. We all suffer stress and trauma throughout our lives. If left unresolved, these issues often sit deep inside our bodies, usually in the form of internal tension. Systema has methods to unlock that deep tension and so release the associated traumas. Much work has been done with military veterans along these lines and many others have felt the benefit of Systema's healing aspects. Hopefully this process also brings a knowledge of how such problems develop and so give us the tools to avoid them in the future.

On a wider level, the general mindset engendered by good Systema training should bring us an appreciation of life - our own and others! We look to foster an atmosphere of support and community in classes that carries out into regular life. Understanding our own shortcomings and issues makes us more receptive and sympathetic to others. We may grow to recognise, for example, that aggression is often a mask for fear and a cry for help. That's not to say we may not need to take some kind of action, but any actions are tempered by understanding and a root desire to help others.

This, then, is the aim of this book. To give you a range of Systema drills and exercises that will help to develop and nurture your awareness across these different areas. Quite often it is not so much about teaching you awareness as it is reminding you that you have it and "waking it up" again! Modern life has a tendency to dull some senses, Systema is a great antidote to that!

This book is not comprehensive, for two reasons. First, there are only so many pages available! And second, this book reflects my current level of understanding and ability. For deeper levels and other ideas and advice, I point you to the numerous good Instructors out there as well, of course, to my teachers Mikhail Ryabko and Vladimir Vasiliev. Also, some of the drills may be familiar to you and some of them have been covered, to an extent, in my other books. But I hope

their inclusion here gives you a new perspective on those drills, as even the most basic System exercise contains many layers of work.

I suggest you read through the book, then pick a couple of drills or exercises to practice at a time. If you have a group, you can work with them. Most of the drills involve two or more people, though there are some solo exercises too. Feel free to adapt and develop the drills as you see fit, to suit your own particular circumstances. In some cases I present the basic drill and give some ideas for variations.

In terms of intensity, always gauge the level of participants, especially for some of the more challenging drills. Make sure you give them the tools to cope before throwing them into any exercise. Always be aware of safety. And just one other thing, a personal thought - don't put people through any drill you have not experienced for yourself, particularly the more psychologically challenging ones. Lead from the front! If you don't have a group or class to train with, you can work through all the solo drills. Hopefully, at some point, you can work with some friends, or perhaps start up your own training group. Support and advice is always on hand from Systema HQ.

Overall, try as much as you can to embed the principles from training into your everyday life. In this way "awareness" becomes something you are, rather than something you do, in a very natural way, appropriate to the environment and situation. I hope you will also find that increased awareness brings an increased appreciation of life and all its wonders! As for the bad things, see them as opportunities to grow. Learn to put things in context, be measured in all things and above all - keep breathing!

BASICS

There are certain principles that are fundamental requirements of Systema training and should be present in all activities. Whether engaging in solo or group training, we should always be mindful of these requirements.

THE FOUR PILLARS

Systema is built on four major principles - the Four Pillars. They are relaxation, form, movement and breathing. The practitioner should understand the role of each in any type of exercise or drill. Although we often separate them for ease of learning, we should remember that in reality there is constant inter-action between all of these principles. We should also bear in mind that there is a psychological as well as physical aspect to each principle too. Here is a brief run-through of each.

RELAXATION

In our activities we are looking to accomplish any given task with just the required amount of tension. If we look at fitness training in general, it is not uncommon to see people doing fast squats with red faces and hunched up shoulders. People get the pulse elevated and so feel they are achieving something. Unfortunately, all they are often doing is increasing tension within the body with a corresponding risk to health.

For the most part we are seeking to perform any exercise or movement with the minimal amount of tension. For a push-up this means relaxing the shoulders, holding the body straight and keeping just enough tension in the hands to maintain the structure. Think of the body as a bridge, it has to be strong in the right places, but if the whole structure is tense and immovable it will fail under load.

Some exercises call for us to tense specific muscles or the whole body. The purpose of these exercises is usually to help us release accumulated tension, or in order to help strengthen a particular part of the body. We try and avoid moving under tension - or at least moving fast. Slow movement under tension can be useful for some things but should always be done with care.

Get into the habit during the day of regularly checking yourself for unwanted stress. Over time, you will get a feeling for controlling your tension This in itself is one of the great benefits of Systema, as stress is a leading cause of numerous ailments.

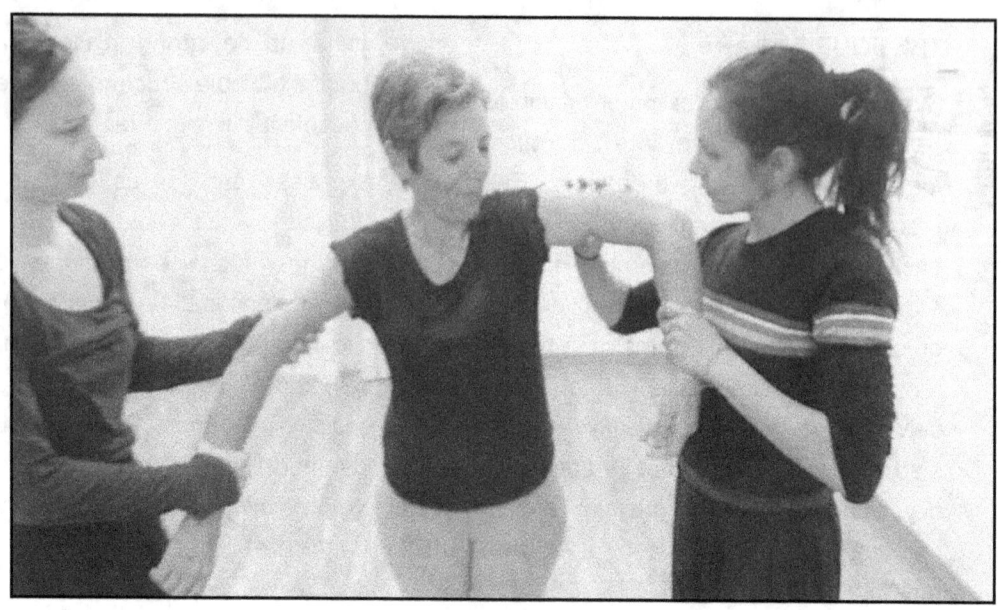

FORM

By form, we mean good posture and practical knowledge of your body on a bio-mechanical level. As unwanted tension is released, you will find ways of using or organising your body structure with greater efficiency. To return to our push-up example, you will find that with correct form you are able to "rest on the bones" rather than use tense muscles to support your body weight. Exactly the same principle applies to standing or sitting. Achieving this in static posture is one thing, doing so in solo movement is another. Adding in pressure from outside in the form of a partner or equipment, adds in another level of challenge.

If you want to get a feel for good basic posture, simply stand upright and relax the body, without slouching. Imagine you are holding a stick across your shoulders (or actually use a stick.) Your shoulders and hips should be level, it is surprising how many people carry one side higher than the other. Check in a mirror or have someone correct you. Your head should not lean or jut forward. To get this feeling, place your hand on the crown of your head, grab some hair (if you have some!) and pull lightly upwards. You should feel the neck stretch slightly and the chin tuck in a little. This is the optimum position for the head. The spine too should be straight, with no leaning or kinks. Think of the spine as an antenna, with the head atop. The better its shape, the more information it can take in and relay.

There are many resources available to learn about bio-mechanics and sports science. It is good to get a sound scientific understanding of how the body operates, as well, of course, as all the corresponding information on psychology and the like. However we must remember that intellectual understanding is always a support to physical work and can never replace "body knowledge".

MOVEMENT

With relaxation and good posture comes free movement. We can now explore our range of motion, develop strength in different vectors, improve how we walk, run, climb and so on. Freedom of movement brings with it a sense of liberation. It is hard to be "uptight" when the body is free and relaxed. This takes us back to a time when we were children. Watch how young kids move, often with very little tension and no preconceived ideas, judgements or mental blockages.

The notion of "playfulness" is an important and powerful aspect of Systema training. Even the most challenging exercises should be approached with a focused but playful mindset rather than the *suffering* mindset. Research has shown that new neural pathways in the brain are formed much quicker through play than through repetition. For more on the concept of *Play Fight*, I recommend you look up Bruno Caverna of *Formless Arts* who is doing excellent work in this area.

BREATHING

Fundamental to every aspect of Systema training. If you have not done any breath work before, I advise that you consult the many resources available from Systema HQ that go into greater detail, but here are some basic methods to use when training.

Unless otherwise directed, the procedure is to inhale through the nose and exhale through the mouth. People typically exhale upon exertion, which is fine, but is is also good to get used to inhaling on exertion too. When you first start out it is advisable to practice breathing in a safe and comfortable position. If you have any blood pressure or other health issues, always check with your healthcare professional prior to training.

thing should be comfortable, not over filling or completely emptying, unless otherwise directed. Learn to breathe smoothly and to the requirements of the situation. In this way you will develop a deep awareness of your breathing and how it relates to every other activity.

The most basic level of breathing awareness is Circular Breathing linked in with selective tension. Get into a comfortable position and begin an even inhale-exhale cycle. Relax and slow the breathing a little. Now, as you inhale, tense a limb or muscle group, as you exhale, relax it.

Cycle round the body - legs, arms, back, shoulders, face, etc. Remember, you only tense one part at a time.

However, to finish, inhale and tense the whole body, exhale and relax a few times. This simple routine is the foundation for all breathing exercises and I encourage you again to explore all the other resources available on Systema breathing. Be mindful of your breath through all the following exercises and use it to adjust your psychological state.

SCIENCE

The science presented in this book is at a basic level. I really just want to give you an over-view of how our senses work. Once again, I encourage you to undertake your own research in the areas of behaviour, Fixed Action Patterns, Limbic Response and so on.

The important thing is to understand how intellectual knowledge can be applied to physical work. I think people often overlook the fact that Systema has undergone extensive testing and development to reach us in the form it has today. It was forged in the most extreme circumstances by professional warriors. That field

development was supported and refined by a huge amount of Soviet scientific research, many aspects of which are only recently being "discovered" by modern sports science.

It is possible to train without worrying about any of the science at all. Simply do it! Personally, I like to have a little information on the hows and whys and I also find that some scientific explanation gives a useful model for teaching.

I also like getting advice from the experienced. Those who have been through extreme situations often have great insight into the physical and psychological aspects of their work. Even on a mundane level, it's interesting to get practical tips on being efficient in any activity. Military friends have shared some field methods, for example. My wife is a trained police hostage negotiator, so picking her brains on communication skills has been eye-opening (negotiating which TV channel to watch is fun in our house).

Living in a rural area and speaking to local farmers has taught me a lot about the countryside. A friend who runs a large security company has shared his experiences of working with dogs and close protection work. We are lucky to have access to a wide range of people in the Systema community. From the operational experience of teachers, to the sharing of life experiences from our fellow students, in short, be open to learning from everyone and everything around you. This is another level of awareness and one that takes Systema way beyond being just a "martial art."

CHAPTER TWO
VISUAL AWARENESS

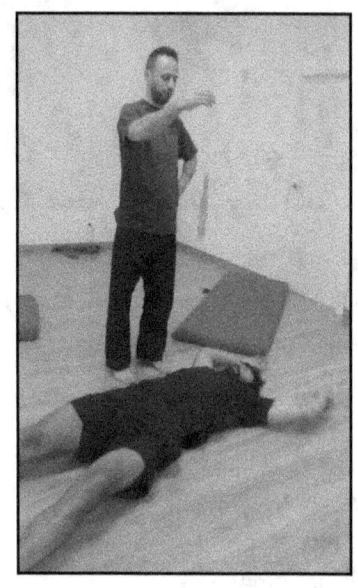

This is a function of our visual and vestibular systems. We will begin with a look at how the eye works, then detail some good exercises for general eye health and for developing good peripheral vision. Following the training drills, we will also discuss low light vision.

HOW THE EYE WORKS

Light from the sun or an artificial source, travels in a straight line, bounces off objects and into our eyes via the pupil. Depending on the amount of light coming in, the iris changes the size of the pupil to let more or less of it in. This prevents damage to the eyes, by stopping too much light entering when it is bright, and also maximising the amount of light entering when it's dark.

The light then passes though the lens, which focuses it onto the retina, the back surface of the eye. The lens changes shape according to distance to keep the light focused on the retina. A thicker lens bends light more than a flatter lens.

So the lens changes shape as we look at near or far objects to keep them in focus, what is known as *accommodation*.

For many people, light from an image is not perfectly focused on their retina. Depending on severity, this can lead to a person needing to wear glasses. A short-sighted person can see things close-up, but has trouble seeing things further away. A long-sighted person struggles to see near objects, but can see distant objects.

The retina transforms the focused light into an electrical impulse, which travels to the brain via the optic nerve. The image we receive on the retina is actually upside-down. Our brain turns it around so we don't get confused!

ARE YOU RIGHT OR LEFT EYED?

Our brain uses our eyes to work out the distance of an object in front of us. This is not to say that two eyes are essential to seeing – people who are blind in one eye still manage perfectly fine. What you may not know, however, is that our eyes normally grow to become different strengths, and much like people are right-

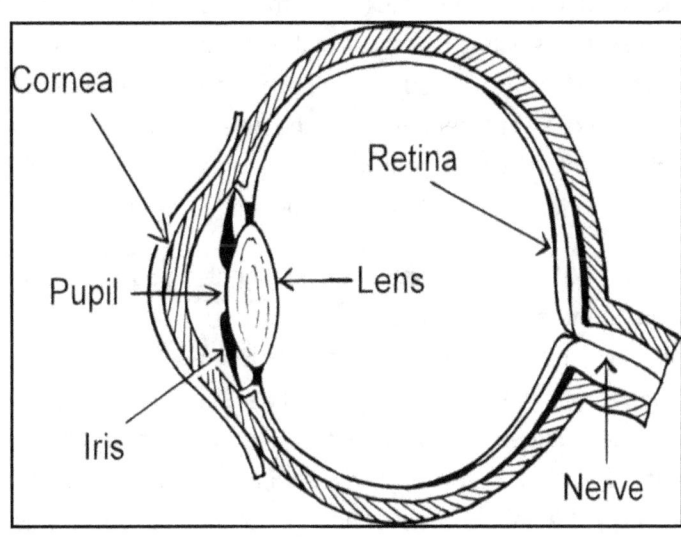

or left-handed, they are often also right or left eyed. Here's how you can find out which you are.

Make a circle with your thumb and first finger. With both eyes open look at an object on the wall and centre it inside the circle. Close one eye, and then the other. Note what happens. When you closed your left or right eye you should find that the object jumps outside the circle. If the object moved when you closed your left eye, then you have left eye dominance. If the object moved more when your right eye was closed, then your right eye is dominant.

About 80% of the population are right-eyed, and a very small percentage seem to have no eye-dominance at all. Even when both eyes are open, the dominant eye is giving priority information. This is useful to know if you take part in any activity that involves shooting at a target (eg archery or darts). Left eyed people should shoot with their left hand, and right eyed people with their right hand, in order to improve their aim.

EYE MOVEMENT

One last thing to consider before we begin our exercises are the different types of eye movement. There are four basic types: saccades, smooth pursuit, vergence movements, and vestibulo-ocular movements. Each has its own function and knowing this, we can build our drills around that particular function.

Saccades are rapid eye movements of the eyes that abruptly change the point of focus. That may be small movements, such as you are doing now while reading, or larger movements - such as when you are outside and gazing around at your surroundings. Saccades occur reflexively whenever the eyes are open, even when fixated on a target. They also occur when we are asleep, in the sleep stage known as REM or rapid eye movement. Saccadic eye movements are described as ballistic because the saccade generating system cannot respond to subsequent changes in target position during the course of the eye movement. So if the target moves again during this time (which is in the order of 15–100 ms), the saccade will miss the target, and a second saccade must be made in order to correct the error.

Smooth pursuit are much slower tracking movements designed to keep focus on a moving target. Imagine watching a car driving past. These movements are under voluntary control, in other words the observer can choose whether or not to track the target (saccades can also be voluntary, but are usually made unconsciously.) It is interesting to note, though, that only highly trained observers can make a smooth pursuit movement in the absence of a moving target. Most people who try to move their eyes in a smooth fashion without a moving target simply make a saccade.

Vergence is the simultaneous movement of both eyes with targets located at different distances from the observer. When a creature with binocular vision looks at an object, the eyes rotate around a horizontal axis so that the projection of the image stays in the centre of the retinas. To look at a closer object, the eyes rotate towards each other (convergence). For an object further away, they rotate away from each other (divergence). For convergence simply focus on the tip of your nose! This convergence is a reflexive visual response to a near object.

Vestibulo-ocular movements work to stabilize the eyes relative to the external world, so compensating for head movement. This reflex response prevents images from "slipping" on the surface of the retina as the head changes position. Imagine fixing your gaze on an object and moving the head from side to side; the

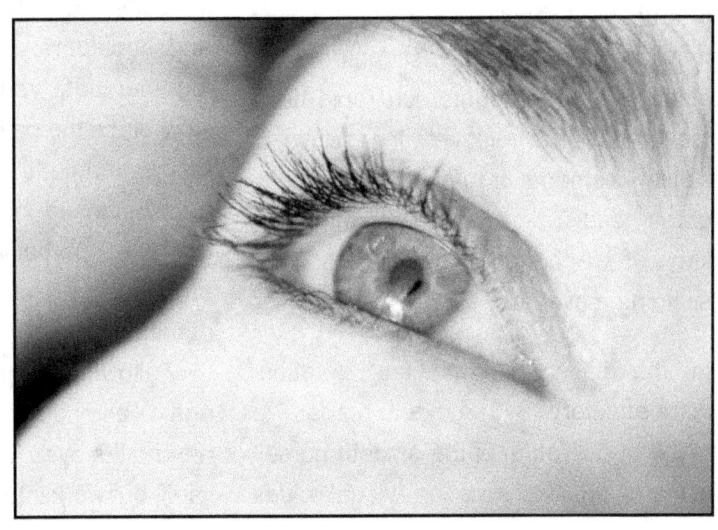

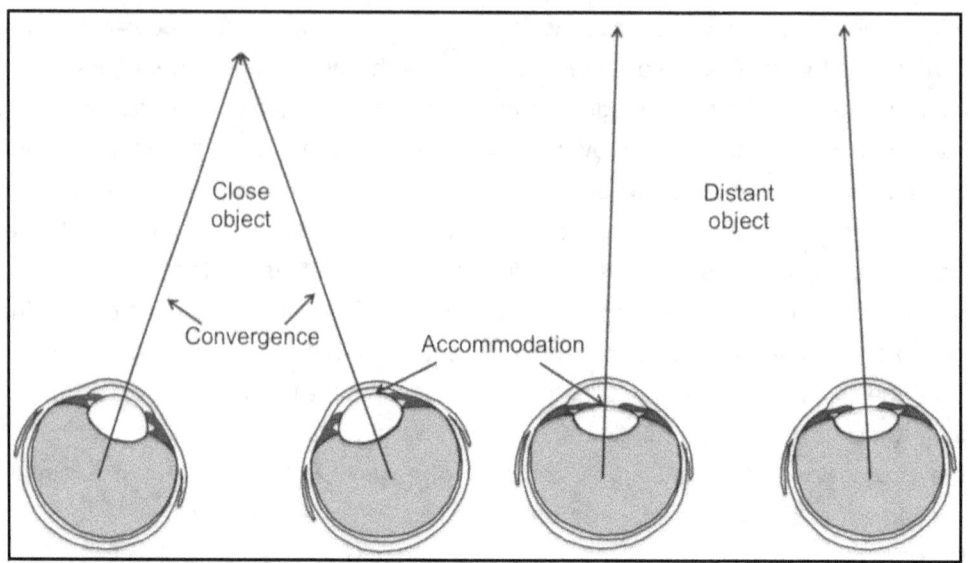

eyes automatically compensate for the head movement by moving the same distance in the opposite direction, so keeping the image at more or less the same place on the retina.

Our vestibular system also provides the leading contribution to our sense of balance and spatial orientation. It detects brief changes in head position and produces rapid corrective eye movements. While the vestibular system operates well to counteract rapid head movement, it is relatively insensitive to slow movements or to persistent rotation of the head. This is useful information to know if we are in a situation of fast, spinning movement.

In the case of consistent rotation, compensatory eye movements are a result of activation of the smooth pursuit system, which relies on visual clues rather than information from the vestibular system.

Before going into our drills, let's take a look at some exercises to help improve eye function.

EYE MASSAGE

Sit in a comfortable position. Focus on your breathing, begin to slow it down. Let the body relax, particularly the head, neck and shoulders. Rub the palms briskly together until you develop some heat. Now place the palms over the eyes. You can experiment with keeping the eyes open or closed. Allow the heat to envelop the eye, particularly all the muscles around the eye socket. Hold for a couple of minutes.

Following this, rub the hands together again and begin to gently massage around the eyes. Do not press on the eye itself, but work into the sockets, under the eyebrow and down the sides of the nose. When finished, sit quietly for a few minutes with eyes closed.

DIRECTION CHANGE

Sit upright. Look straight ahead. Without moving your head, look to the left. Focus on what you see. Then look right and focus. Move your eyes side to side five times. Repeat this three times.

Without moving your head, look down. Focus on what you see. Then, look up. Focus on what you see. Repeat three times. Without moving your head, look straight ahead. Then, look down and to the left. Focus on what you see. Then, move your eyes diagonally and look up and to the right. Focus on what you see. Repeat this exercise five times. Then, look straight ahead and do the same exercise looking down and to the right and then looking up and to the left. Repeat the whole cycle three times.

FOCUS CHANGE

Sit down and hold your index finger close to your eyes. Focus on the finger. Now slowly move your finger away from your face, maintaining focus.

Look away for a moment, into the distance. Then focus again your outstretched finger and slowly bring it back towards your eyes. Look away and focus on something in the distance. Repeat three times.

NEAR AND FAR FOCUS

Sit and hold your thumb up around 25 cm from your face. Focus on it for 15 seconds. Then find an object roughly five metres away, and focus on it for 15 seconds. Return your focus to your thumb. Repeat five times.

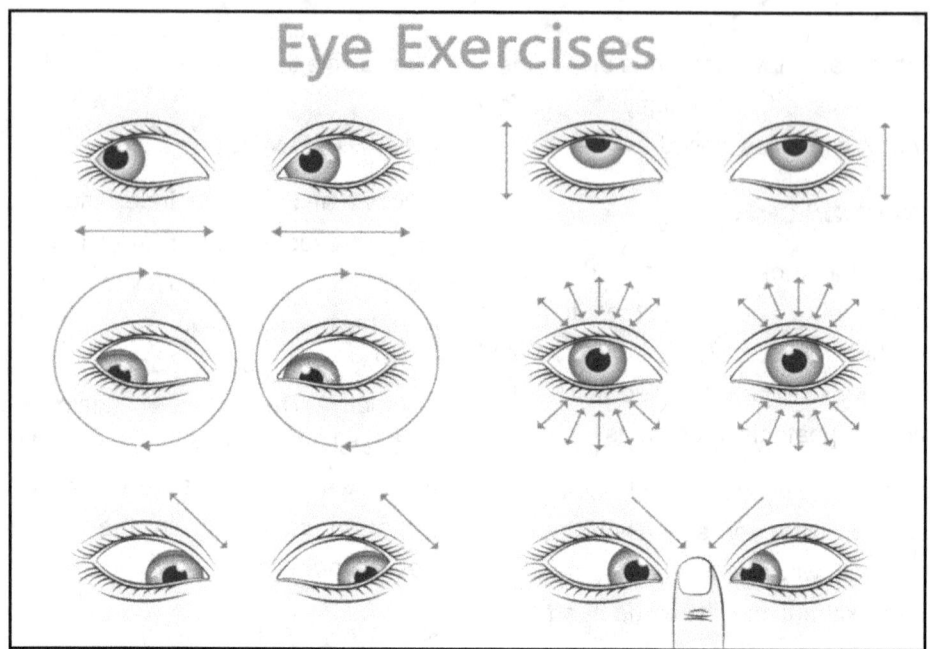

FIGURE EIGHT

Sit down, pick a point on the floor about three metres in front of you and focus on it. Trace an imaginary figure eight with your eyes. Keep tracing for 30 seconds, then switch directions.

THE 20-20 RULE

Human eyes are not supposed to be glued to a single object for extended periods of time. If you work at a computer all day then practicing the 20-20-20 rule may help prevent digital eye strain. To implement this rule, every 20 minutes, look at something 20 feet away for 20 seconds.

PERIPHERAL VISION

Also sometimes called side vision, this is the ability to see objects and movement outside our direct line of sight. Peripheral vision is the work of rods, the nerve cells located largely outside the macula (centre) of the retina. These rods are also responsible for night vision and low-light vision but are insensitive to colour. Our survival once depended on the quick response of our peripheral vision. A detailed picture, such as is created by our central vision, is useful in situations where we have time to focus on details. But peripheral vision helps us to quickly see and respond to danger. Here's how it works.

Whenever you look at something, you use your central vision to focus on the detail, and peripheral vision to gather information about the surroundings. At the back of our eyes we have two types of light-sensitive cells, cones and rods. Central vision uses the area densely packed with cones. Cones are sensitive to colour and need plenty of light to function well. Peripheral vision uses mostly rods and almost no cones. Rods are sensitive to movement and quickly pick up changes in brightness. They also function well in lower light conditions.

The differences continue as signals travel to the brain. Some signalling cells are sensitive to colour but not so much to contrast, whereas other cells signal respond faster to low-contrast stimuli. In the brain's vision centre (the visual cortex), more neurons will analyse a stimulus picked up by our central vision compared with the same stimulus picked up by our peripheral vision.

All of this leads to us having a colour-sensitive, high-resolution central vision and a fast-working, movement sensitive peripheral vision.

TESTING YOUR PERIPHERAL VISION

Many eye and brain disorders can cause peripheral vision loss and other visual field abnormalities. Eye care professionals use something called visual field tests in order to detect blind spots and other visual field defects, which can be an early sign of problems.

For the sake of our training, we will describe a basic method of testing our peripheral vision. Of course, should this test highlight problems, we advise that you seek further testing from a qualified professional. The same principle holds for all of the exercises in this book. Systema

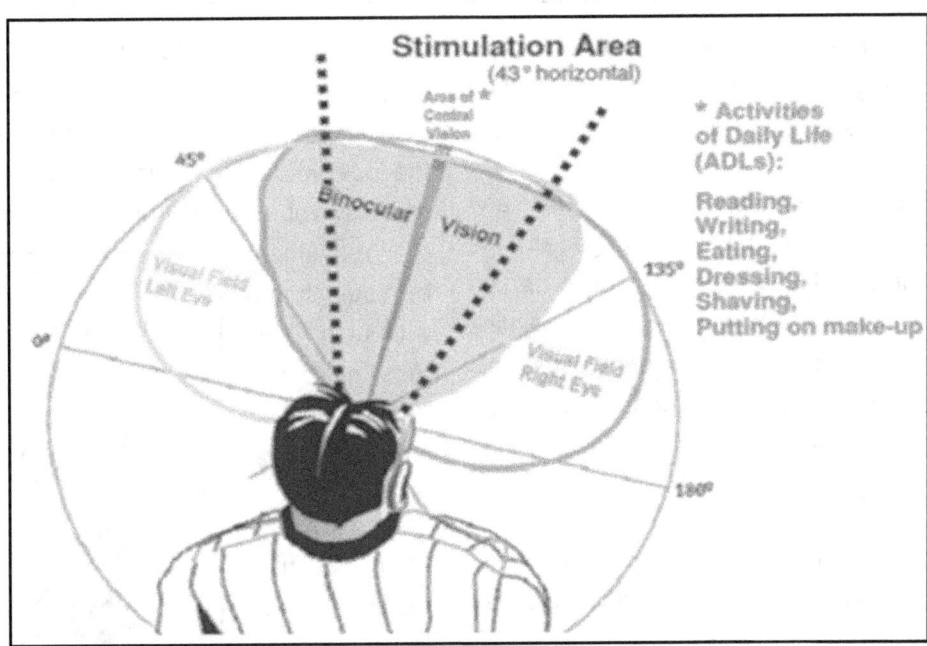

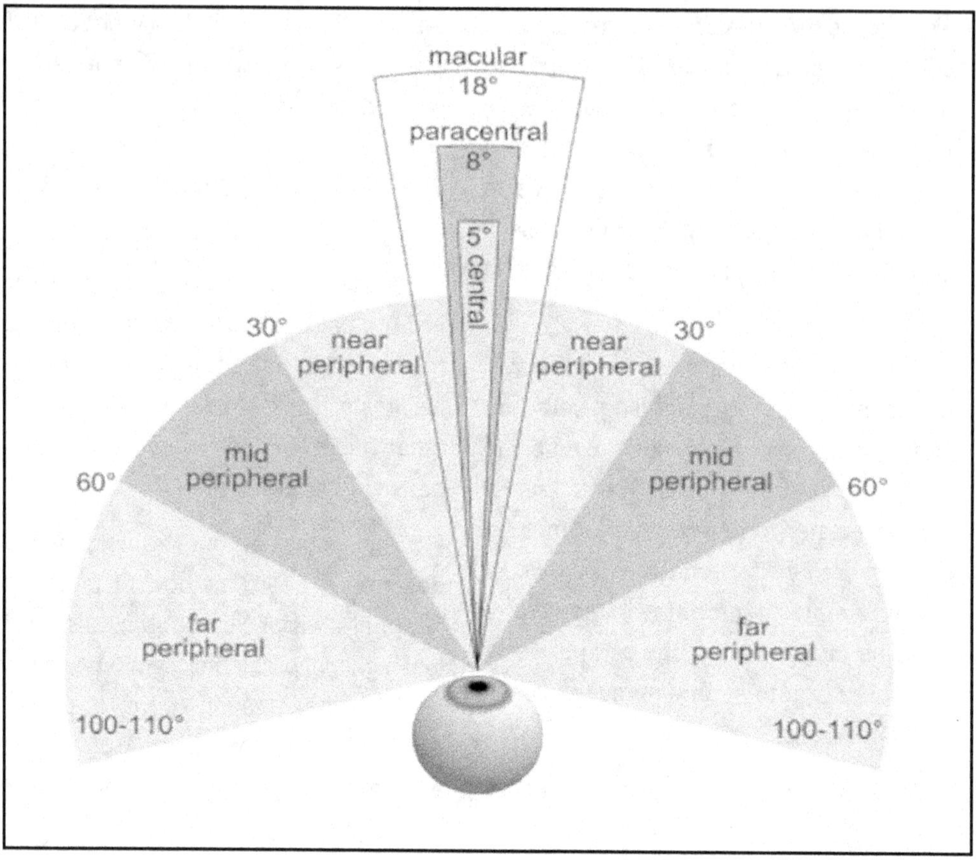

[Diagram: field of vision showing macular 18°, paracentral 8°, 5° central, near peripheral 30°, mid peripheral 60°, far peripheral 100-110°]

is a great tool for self-diagnosis and for picking up minor issues before they become major ones.

Stretch out a hand in front of your face and raise your thumb. Focus your gaze on the thumb nail and keep it in focus as you slowly move it towards your nose. Notice how the background is out of focus. This is *tunnel vision* and the nearer your thumb gets to your nose, the less background detail you can see.

Do the "thumbs-up" again but this time, look beyond your hand and focus on an object on the other side of the room. Now keep your eyes focused on this object as you again move your thumb slowly towards your face. If you're doing this correctly you will see that you can track the movement of your thumb without actually focusing on it. This is called *small peripheral vision*.

After you've tried this, go

back to the first step again. This time, move your thumb quickly towards your nose. The faster you go, the more difficult it is to see anything but your thumb. Now try the small peripheral vision test again. You should find that no matter how fast you move your thumb, you can still track it while looking at the object on the far side of the room.

The next step is to try *wide angle peripheral vision,* also called *soft focus.* Position the thumbs-up sign as before and again look towards the other side of the room. However, this time don't focus on anything, just let your eyes relax into a sort of day dreaming state. You'll be able to see everything in the space taken in by your eyes including, of course, your thumb, no matter where it is or how fast you move it.

Now, place both thumbs up in front of your face. Maintain soft focus beyond the thumbs and slowly move them out to the sides. Notice how far you can track the movement of your thumbs while still looking forwards. You should be able to take your arms out to around 90 degrees each side and still be able to track the thumbs. Once you have run through these exercises, you can put your thumbs away! Next, without moving your eyes, try "looking" left, right, up and down etc. With a bit of practice you will be able to mentally "see" any object in this "globe" without having to "look at it" although it will be out of focus.

Using this method of observation while walking down the street or in a bus or crowded room will make you much more

aware of your surroundings. Later, we will see how this can help us to anticipate other peoples movements. For now, however, let's take this idea of peripheral vision into some work with sticks.

STICK CATCHING EXERCISES

We will now run through a series of stick catching exercises that will help sharpen our vision and reactions. The first revolve around catching and throwing the stick, so let's start with a few guidelines. T h e sticks we use are the "standard" Systema training sticks. A metre or so long, broom handles or similar are fine. The sticks should be blunt at each end.

The aim of these exercises is to throw a stick *to* a person and not *at* them! Bearing that in mind, throw the stick in such a way that it is easy to catch, ie upright rather than like a spear. Unless directed otherwise, try not to hold onto the stick for too long. Catch it, throw it. The aim is to cut down on thinking time and tap into our

sub-conscious reactions. You can experiment with either returning the stick with the catching hand or switching hands to throw.

Speed and number of sticks are the two main variables in these drills. Always start at a comfortable pace and pick up speed as required. If the sticks are being dropped often, bring the speed back down.

Always be aware of the space and people around you when working with the stick. Watch out for light fittings especially! These are great drills to run outdoors in a good, open space. Start with good visibility, later on you can work in low light conditions.

Of course, you can run these drills with any object - a ball, a training knife, etc. However a sticks are a good starting point as they are easy to see and catch.

STICK PAIRS

Start by working in pairs with one stick. Keep quite close and throw the stick back and forth between you. Work on the spot at first, then begin to slowly walk around. Keep the pairs spaced out across the training area. Once comfortable, increase the distance and move faster.

STICK PAIRS, GROUP

Work the pairs drill but this time the pairs are mixed in amongst each other as they throw to each other. Work the same progression as before. Begin with static partners, then moving. The pairs should move around the group while keeping watch on each other.

STICK CIRCLE

A group of around six people stand in a circle. Begin with one stick. The stick holder throws it to any other person in the circle. Keep the pace steady and be very clear who you are throwing the stick to. You are not trying to trick anyone or catch them out!

When ready, introduce another stick into the circle, so now there are two being circulated. After another period of time, introduce a third stick. Remember, make your target clear and keep calm. We find that as the intensity increases, the stick throwing can become a bit rushed and ragged. So this is also a good drill for developing "professional mindset." Keep calm, stress brings tunnel vision! If things get too hectic, drop back to two or one stick.

MOVING CIRCLE

The same drill as above, but this time the circle is moving. You can start by moving

to the sides, all going either clockwise or anti-clockwise. Then everyone can walk in a random direction, while keeping within "stick range." As before, add in extra sticks as required. When practicing this one, get used to throwing the stick to where the person is going to be rather than where they are. You can also work at passing the stick up close.

HALF CIRCLE

A group of around six form a half circle in front of the catcher. We begin with one stick again. One of the group throws the stick to the catcher, who must immediately throw it back to any one of the group.

There is an extra rule in this drill. If the stick is dropped / falls to the floor, then it is up to a member of the group to pick it up and "return it to play". The catcher does not pick up sticks, even if they fall close, but must constantly be ready to catch.

After a time, introduce two sticks, then three. You can add in several other variations - experiment with distance and spacing of the group. You can also try with a static or moving catcher (going side to side.)

Once again, if things get too intense, dial the speed down or decrease the number of sticks. The catcher must try and be aware of the movements of the whole group. Maintain a soft focus and have the hands ready to catch. Take care again that everyone throws the stick in a controlled way and not in "panic mode".

REACTION DRILLS

Sticks are not the only tools we can use to work our sight reaction. Tennis balls are easy to use. You can work all the previous stick drills with TBs. Here are some other ideas, for using them, too.

DODGEBALL

One or more people (the targets) stand against the wall. At least double their number take position a distance away and throw TBs at the targets. The progression is as usual. Start with just a few TBs, then increase the number. The throws can be quite soft at first, working up to full speed and power. It is good if the throwers are spread out too, in order to really work the target's peripheral vision.

The target's job can simply be to dodge, or to catch and throw back. Obviously, be aware of any breakables in the room before running this drill! It's very easy to add in variations with this drill, depending on space, numbers and environment. For example, split the group into pairs. One must try and hit the other with the TB while moving through and around the whole group.

To add in another layer, have someone target the thrower - so they have to not only track the target but also be aware of their own attacker. Add in some cover and you have another layer of possibilities.

OVER THE SHOULDER

The previous exercises mostly worked peripheral vision on a horizontal level, but how about up and down?

The catcher stands, with hands ready. The thrower stands behind, then extends a hand over the catcher's shoulder and drops a tennis ball. The movement should be quite slow at first and the dropping hand held high. After a time, increase the speed. The next variation is to take the hand over the catcher's head rather than the shoulder.

Following this, the thrower takes a step back and throws the ball over the head or shoulder. It should be thrown in such a way that it arcs over the catcher and can be caught without too much reaching out.

This can be quite a difficult exercise, so at the start you might also want to give a spoken cue, say a 1-2-3 count before dropping the ball.

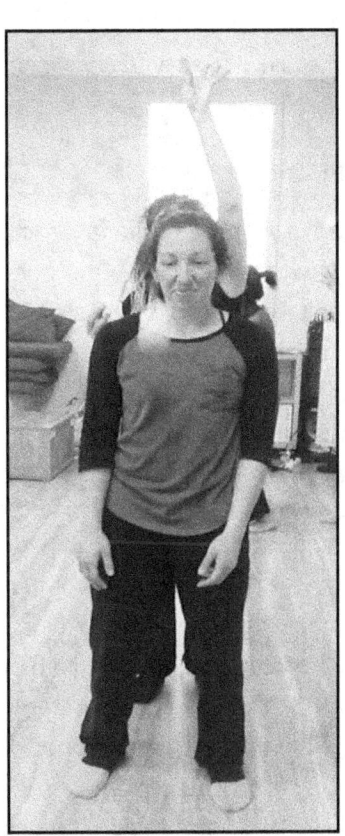

Another variation is to change the start position. Try throwing the ball from below. So the thrower crouches behind the catcher and tosses the ball upwards. This is the static version, it is easy to add in some movement as another variation. Simply walk in a straight line to begin, then more randomly as you progress.

WALL BOUNCE

A variation of the over the shoulder throw, is for both partners to stand facing a wall, with the catcher a little closer to it. The thrower tosses the ball over the catcher to bounce off the wall.

The catcher must catch the ball after the bounce, before the ball hits the floor. Once again, it is easy to work in variations of distance, etc

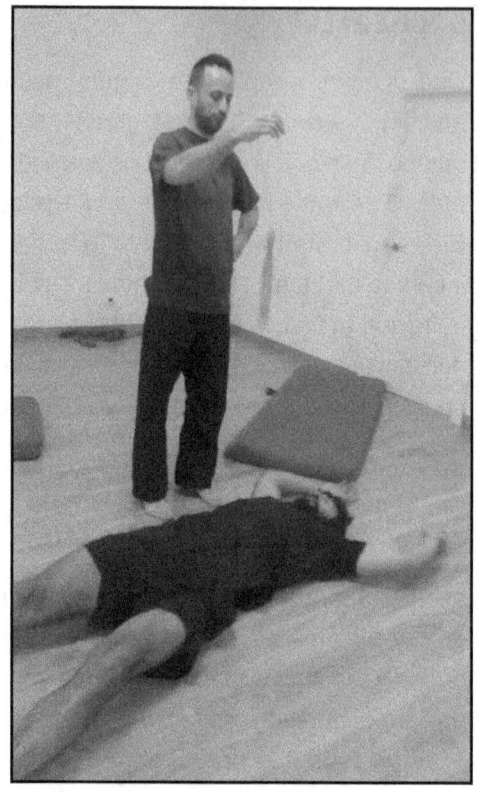

KNIFE DROP

This is a simple drill that takes little space and is worked in pairs. One person lays on their back. The other stands beside them and holds out an object. You can use a TB to start, or you can work with a training knife. Rubber or wood is a good start.

The holder counts to three, then drops the object. The person on the floor must move to avoid the falling item. After a while, repeat but now the count is just "one" and drop. After another while, there is no count, the object is just dropped. T h e other variation in this exercise is the height at which the object is held. Obviously, held higher gives more time for the person on the floor to react.

PAD HIT

This reaction drill uses a focus pad. The hitter stands with eyes closed. Hands can be at sides or in ready position. The holder positions the pad , then calls "Go!" The hitter must open their eyes and hit the pad as quickly as possible.

There are some variations. Use two pads, requiring two hits. Rather than a verbal trigger, use a slap or push with the pads. In this way you can see how this drill can start to combine visual, tactile and audio stimuli to elicit a response.

ROPE DODGE

This is another group exercise and requires the use of a long piece of rope or string. Two people hold each end of the rope, stretching it across the width of the training space. The rope starts at one end of the space and the holders run with it to the other end. The group position themselves in the space. As the rope approaches, the group must either fall/duck under it, or jump over it.

The holders should vary the height of the rope each time. It can be held level, or each holder can have the rope at a different height so that it is sloping. Another factor you can vary is speed. The holders can start at walking speed and work up to full sprint, with no pause at each end.

STICK EVASION

We go back to the stick for the next series of drills. This time we are also working in a measure of evasion. These drills are particularly useful as a starting point for learning to defend against weapons. They get us used to angles of attack, footwork and positioning and also the ability to "read" an attack as it develops.

We are using the same type of stick again. You may wish to start with a light stick as some contact may be experienced to begin with!

The first set of drills are worked in pairs, and we are keeping things pretty much on the spot. Always begin with slow, clear movements. It is important at first that the stick wielder be clear in the angle of attack and not try to catch the dodger out. That can come later! Be sure you work at the correct distance. The dodger should be in contact range of the stick strike but not too close to the wielder.

FIXED TRAJECTORY

The stick wielder begins by moving the stick in one of the following trajectories:

- downward /over shoulder strike
- side to side, head height
- side to side, waist height
- side to side, knee height

- forward thrust and back
- an X shape, upward and downward

The dodger stays roughly in place and has to dodge the stick. So for the head height swing, for example, you might squat under the stick and let it pass over your head. Run through each pattern for a while at slow speed. Once the dodger is comfortable, repeat and increase the speed. If the dodger starts to get touched by the stick often, drop back to a slower speed. A couple of tips for the dodger:

- watch the body movement of the stick holder, particularly the shoulders, this will give you a clue as to where and when the strike is coming.
- don't try and dodge the stick so much as move into the space where the stick isn't.
- keep your breathing working and the body relaxed. Make a note of where any fear/tension comes into the body and work (breathing or movement) to get rid of it.
- even though you are working against just once person, keep your gaze soft. Avoid tunnel vision, especially when the drill speeds up.

FREE TRAJECTORY

Once comfortable with the above drill, the wielder can move from fixed to free trajectory. The aim is still purely to avoid the stick and not worry about moving "tactically".

For the stick wielder, this is a chance to explore free movement with the stick. Try all the previous movements, combined with figure eights and changing height. Work to keep the stick moving smoothly, monitor your own tension and breathing.

THE HOOVER DRILL

You can easily work the same type of drill on the ground. The dodger sits of lays on the floor. The wielder can either swing/strike with stick, or place one end of it on the floor and "hoover" around. The dodger must avoid contact once again. Experiment with large movement (rolling out of the way, etc) and small movement (keeping on the spot.)

STICK IN THE MIDDLE

This is a group drill, using the free movement developed in the last drill. The stick wielder stands in the centre of a circle formed by the group and begins making free movements with the stick. The aim for the group is to touch the stick wielder in some way.

If a person is touched by the stick, they must retreat back to the edge of the circle. The wielder can aim for people, or can close eyes and work blind. Work slow to start, especially if you have a heavy stick. This drill tests the awareness of both the group and the stick wielder.

GROUP STICK

From here you can easily move into working with more sticks. Using the fixed or free trajectory drills, work two stick wielders onto one dodger,. You could try giving everyone in the group a stick, each becoming wielder and dodger and so on. Just always keep an eye on safety.

STICK GAUNTLETS

This is another group exercise, with three levels of difficulty. The set up is the same each time. The group forms two rows, facing each other. The rows should be slightly staggered, so that you are facing a gap opposite. Space out fairly wide at first, you can decrease the gap to make the drill more challenging.

Each person in the row has a stick. The dodger starts at one end of the row and has to move down to the other end, avoiding contact with any of the sticks.

For the first level, the wielders simply hold the sticks static out in front of them. The dodger can move in any way necessary to get through the gaps.

For the second level, each stick wielder makes one fixed movement with the stick.

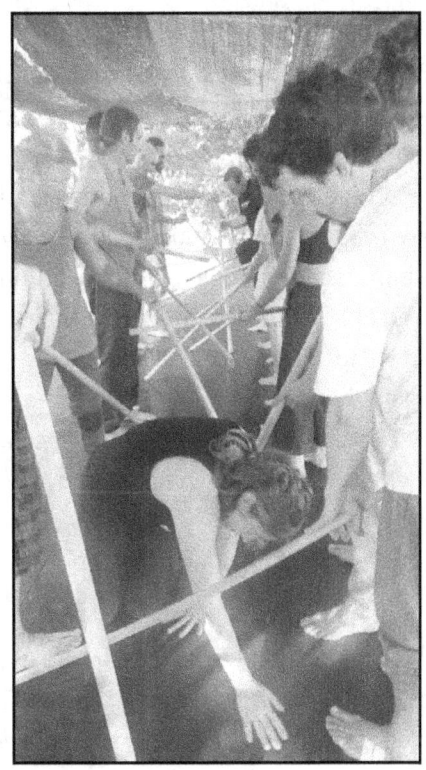

It may be a simple thrust, or a downward strike. Simply keep repeating the same movement. The dodger must once again negotiate the gauntlet, avoiding contact with the stick.

It is important to note that the stick wielders are not actively trying to hit the dodger as such, they are just doing a movement. For this reason, it is sometimes good to have the wielders close their eyes. This discourages both tracking the dodger and also pulling a strike that may hit. The wielders can change their movement between dodgers. Again, start slow and with a little space between the wielders. You can increase intensity as required.

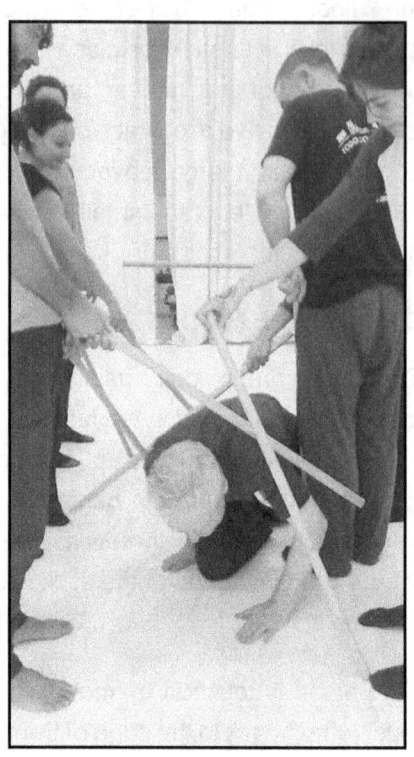

The final level is wielders working freestyle with the sticks. You can either apply random movements, or actively try and touch the dodger as they come through. Try not to track too much, though, give a clean "strike." To keep things running smoothly, each dodger slides their stick down to the far end of the row before going through. They simply pick the stick up once through and take their place as a wielder. The rows will naturally move down as you go, so you may have to pause and reset back at the original position.

For the dodger, there are two ways to go through. The first is to observe trajectory of the sticks, position yourself and go. This means there will be short pauses in your movement. The second way is to let go a little, observe on the fly and adjust on the move. This takes a little more psychological relaxation but it is possible to travel the length of the gauntlet in one, smooth movement. As ever, breathing is the key!

WALKING DRILLS

These are another Systema staple and can be worked at several levels. Let's first look at the basic sight-orientated versions, we will return in a later chapter to the more "internal" versions.

PAIRS

The most basic version of the drill is where

one person walks towards another. The aim is simply to avoid contact with the walker. At first they should give a nice, straight line of movement. Later the movement can be a little more freestyle. Of course, you can also vary the speed from a slow walk to a full sprint. At this stage the target is simply reacting to the approach of the walker on a visual level.

ZOMBIES AND DALEKS

These drills work in groups of six or so. One person is designated the target, the others are the walkers. The aim is the same as the pair drill, except this time the target has to contend with a group of walkers. So keep the vision soft, don't get fixated just on what is front of you and keep your evasive movement soft and relaxed.

Next step up is for the zombies to become daleks (a *Dr Who* reference for any non-Brits!). Each walker extends and arm out at shoulder height and forms a fist. The walker must now dodge fists and bodies.

Intensity can be graded as before, speed, distance and free movement can all be varied to suit. Once again, at this level we are working primarily from a visual perspective. If you want to combine drills, give some of the walkers sticks or training knives to wield too, but don't let the exercises get too messy.

OBSTACLES

A further variation on the above drills is to add in obstacles. Work around furniture, on uneven terrain, in woods,etc. You can also try working in low light or night conditions.

LOW LIGHT WORK

Our eyes take around 30 to 45 minutes to fully adapt to low light conditions. Night vision utilises our rod cells. As we mentioned before, these cells only see black and white and have poor resolution but they are very sensitive in low light circumstances. Our ability to adapt to darkness also depends on other factors, such as age, and any existing eye conditions. However there are some things we can do in order to see the dark!

The best way to prepare is to let yourself slowly acclimate by relaxing in perfect darkness for 20 to 30 minutes. To adjust to the darkness more quickly, wear an eye mask, or close and cover your eyes, to give your eyes a chance to adjust before entering a darkened area. Even an eye-patch can help, protecting one eye from light for 20 to 30 minutes will accustom that eye to the darkness.

Another preparation is to gently massage your eyes. Close them tightly and use the palms of your hands to apply slight pressure. About 5 or 10 seconds into the massage, the normal blackness turns to white for a few seconds. When the white fades and the blackness returns, open your eyes and your night vision will be improved. Some people also find it useful to squeeze their eyes tightly shut tightly for five to ten seconds when coming into a dark area.

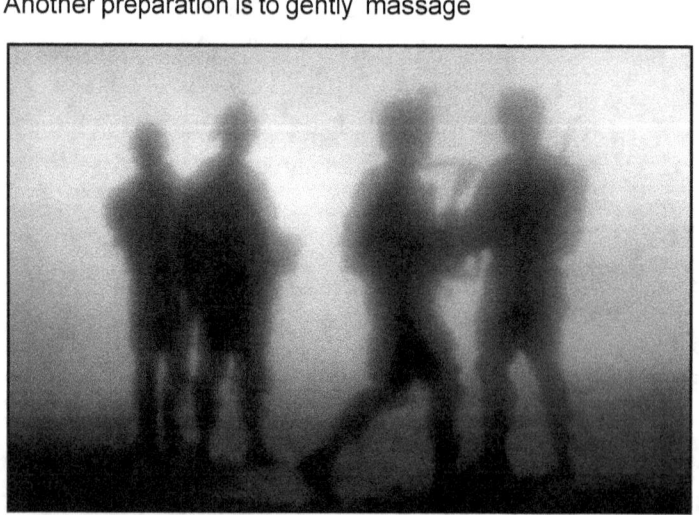

A method often used by aviators before night flying is to wear red-tinted glasses or goggles. Rod cells don't pick up the colour red, so twenty minutes of wearing red tinted glasses before you go into the dark area will help you to detect motion around you more quickly.

Once your eyes are accustomed to the dark, be sure to never look directly at a light, even a dim one. Looking at the light means that we use cone cells rather than the rods. It also forces your pupils to contract and so diminish your night vision. So if you have adapted to low light and someone shines a torch in your face, you will have to wait 30-45 minutes for your eyes to adjust again.

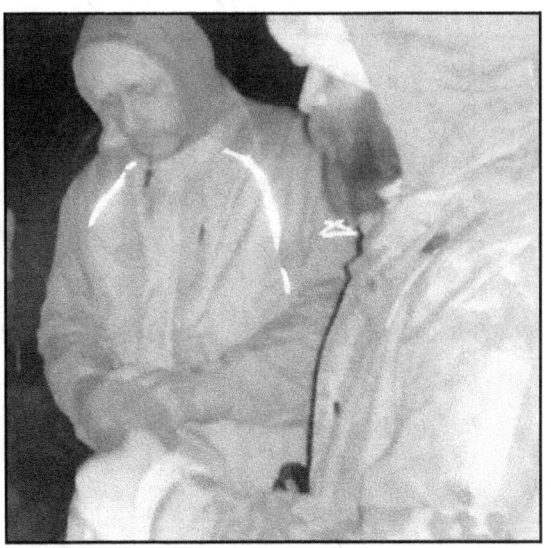

For this reason "torch discipline" is an important factor in low light activities. Always keep your beam dipped and never shine it on someone else's face. Head torches are particularly notorious for this - you call someone who is wearing one, they turn to reply and give you a full light blast! Be aware! If you can't avoid looking at a light source, try covering or closing one eye as you do so, this will help.

When in the dark, use your peripheral vision. Focus your gaze to the side of any object, or just off-centre of the direction you are going. Using your peripheral vision engages those rod cell, helping to detect movement and shape much better than by looking at something directly.

The night sky provides a source of light. If you position yourself as low as possible, the light from the night sky provides enough contrast to assist the rod cells. This way, you can use the sky not only to illuminate objects but also to reveal opponents by creating a silhouette.

One common situation where we use night vision is while driving. You can take steps before getting in your car to enhance your vision as you drive at night. As just mentioned, try to avoid looking directly at an oncoming light source. If someone comes around the bend with their high-beams on, protecting one eye will prevent you from getting "flash blindness" in both eyes, allowing you to more easily adjust back to the darkness. When driving, look at the white line off to the right but still on your side of the road. This allows you to maintain a safe course, to see movement around you with your peripheral vision and to avoid looking directly into oncoming high beams.

Another tip is to dim your dash lights to a low but safe level to help your vision while driving at night. Also, use your mirror's

"night" setting, this will help reduce glare from vehicles behind you. Keep your headlights, wipers, and windscreen clean. Spots on the windscreen can become sources of glare when you are driving at night.

LOW LIGHT DRILLS

Of course, any of the drills here can be carried out at night / in low light conditions. There are also some more specific drills that take advantage of low light conditions.

NAVIGATION

The first step is simply to get people used to moving in the dark. You might be outdoors, or use an indoor space with the lights turned off. Give people a straightforward route to follow at first. It might be a track through the trees, for example, or to cross a field to a particular landmark. You can then make the route more complex, as well as add in tasks and obstacles. People can work solo, or in pairs / groups. We like to work these types of drill at our camps, where we have access to woods as well as open spaces. If you have right of way or local landowner permission, you can work a much longer route, maybe even covering a few miles. Always be aware of safety issues and local laws and inform all the participants of them too.

HIDE AND SEEK

Once people are used to moving in the dark, start giving them specific tasks. One that everyone is familiar with is hide and seek. Send the hiders out into the training area, give them a few minutes, then unleash the hunters. Keep things very simple to start, no camouflage or extra tasks, simply have the hiders take as much advantage as possible of their surroundings, the hunters are simple trying to spot them. It might be handy to have a referee or two on hand.

The next stage is to give the hiders a task. They may have to get to a certain point, for example, or carry a "wounded" colleague from A to B. Now the game also becomes about stealth and concealment, more on those later!

One piece of advice - be doubly sure that everyone is aware of the boundaries of the training area! We had a guy once at camp who went outside the of the training area to hide and was happily tucked up in his bush for well over an hour! Being outside the boundary, no searcher went near him and he also failed to hear the whistle signalling endex. By the time he wandered back, he'd missed most of lunch too!

URBAN SETTINGS

Don't feel confined to woodlands. Though it can present certain difficulties, low-light urban drills are also a possibility. Part of the game now becomes avoiding detection by anyone around, not just your fellow students! Ed at our Leicester group once invited me up for an night time urban session. Part of it involved travelling through a large park near the centre of Leicester. Periodically, security and police cars would slowly drive by and we were told to hide from them. I asked Ed if he'd got permission for us to be in the park after dark. "Not exactly," was the reply. So avoiding the patrols became another aspect of the drill. I'm pleased to say no one got caught!

I'm not advising you try the same but I'm not denying it was a good drill either! Be sensible, but sometimes adding a little "real" danger into the work gives an edge to what become "run of the mill." Other aspects of that overnight session involved finding a place to rest sleep and other evasion-type drills.

BEHIND YOU!

Let's turn things around a little, and have the hider being the active person. This is another drill that's a little like the old childhood game of Statues. One person

(the target) stands in a particular spot and closes their eyes. The hider starts from some distance away. Their job is to get as close as possible to the target. Periodically the target announces "Looking!" and opens their eyes for a quick look around. If they see the hider, that person has to reset to start positions. If the hider is not seen, the drill continues until they are seen or get within a specified distance of the target.

A referee can be useful in this drill. The target does not move if they think they spot someone, they merely point. The ref can then go to that spot and confirm, or not, the sighting. Of course, stealth and camo can easily be incorporated into this drill too.

FOX AND HOUNDS

You can make these drills more active by incorporating a hunting element. For tracking, send a person out into the training area along a set trail. At some point along the trail, the fox has to hide. The task is now for the hounds to follow and try and spot the fox's hiding place. The hide should not be too far off of the track at this stage.

This is more of a passive track, to increase intensity, let both fox and hounds work off the track completely. The hounds now work as a group to sweep the area. This can also be a good team work drill as the hounds must be coordinated.

You can run this with the fox static once hidden, or have the fox moving through the area. Once again, tasks can be added in - capture the flag, for example, or escape to a particular place.

PAPERCHASE

A favourite at our camps, and a drill that I learned from Konstanin Komarov at one of the Toronto Camps (they have some serious woodland over there!). You will need a group, some paper (we use cheap paper napkins) and some safety pins. You can run this as a team event or everyone for themselves. I'll explain the latter, then you can easily adjust it to suit.

First, determine the playing area, set the boundaries. Woods are best again. Set a central safe zone, this is the start point. Gather everyone in the safe zone and pin a napkin to everyones back. The group disperses. Once the game starts, the aim is to collect as many napkins as you can. In other words, sneak up on someone and rip the paper from their back. If your paper is taken, you are "out", so raise your hands and immediately move straight away back to the safe zone. There, you get a new piece of paper and are sent out again. The winner is the person at the end (set whatever time limit you wish) who has the most pieces of paper.

Depending on the space, you can have people move freely, or limit them to a path or set course. You can set two or more teams, have free for all and so on. Just one other tip, I find the use of a whistle is good for the ref in these type of drills. One blast to start, two to stop. Impress upon people that on the stop signal they should stop immediately and return to the safe zone (it keeps things moving quickly and is also good in case of any emergency situation.)

A STAB IN THE DARK

For a variation of the above, give everyone a white T- shirt and a marker pen and go for stabs rather than grabs. The winner is the person with the least marks! When stabbed, you again return to the safe zone with hands up. A person with hands raised is not considered a target!

Depending on the nature and experience of the participants you can add in many more variations as you see fit, always bearing health and safety in mind, of course.

CAMOUFLAGE & CONCEALMENT

I mentioned camouflage a couple of times, so let's take a look at its main principles. Camouflage is typically, though not exclusively, a function of sight, most often in a military or hunting context. It is the art of concealing something that you don't want to be seen. That may be a sniper, it may be a building or it may be a group of bird watchers!.

Camouflage can go beyond the obvious uses. It may be used in undercover operations, in surveillance, in masking our true intentions and so on. Camouflage often brings to mind things covered with leaves and branches but it can equally be

applied in an urban setting. For the purposes of this book, we will cover some basics of camouflage and show how it can be used to help develop observational skills. Obviously this kind of work requires an appropriate venue and some preparation. For this reason it usually forms some of our work at our outdoor camps, an ideal setting to practice hide and seek! In this chapter will will consider the visual aspects of camouflage, later we will discuss some of the other factors involved. For now, let's begin with the basics, the Eight Essentials.

SHADE

This relates to the colours and patterns of kit and clothing in relation to the local environment. Colours or patterns that don't blend well or severely contrast with your environment, will get you seen.

Browns and greens are the most common shades for outdoor camo. Avoid black as it does not occur significantly in nature, and so stands out, even at night, when the eye sees in shades of blue or purple.

Do not think that bright colours are useless in camouflage. A friend sometimes uses a hi-viz vest and clip board to gain access to urban sites, for example, it's all about blending in! In an outdoor setting, any foliage added must also match your environment, and be changed as it dries out and alters colour. Likewise, if digging in, spoilage will more than likely be a different colour to the surface soil and should be hidden.

SHADOW

There are two aspects to shadow - casting a shadow that may be seen, and using natural shadows to hide in or move through. Be aware that at night, shadows register as a shade of blue and not black! Also, our night vision is helped by being in shadow as the pupil of the eye enlarges to take in more light.

SHAPE

The wrong object in the wrong place at the wrong time, will always draws the eye! Even if standing still, a person shape where a person shape should not be will most likely be easily spotted. Objects out of context, for example a mound on flat ground, are also a giveaway.

SHINE

Reflections will betray you, especially in bright sunlight, or artificial light. Ensure that any potentially reflective kit is dulled down or covered. Glasses, sights, metallic surfaces should all be checked. They can be covered, shaded with a brim, etc.

SILHOUETTE

The classic error that demonstrates this principle is known as "sky lining." This is where the distinctive human profile stands out black against a bright sky, even a night sky, which is always paler than the foreground. Likewise, if kit or clothing is the wrong colour for the background, you will be silhouetted and seen. So always be aware of background to avoid making a silhouette. Also consider breaking up the distinctive head and shoulders outline of your body. Attaching some local vegetation, scrim (synthetic foliage) or hessian or burlap (sacking) can help. Be sure it is not too regular in shape though, as that will also stand out.

SOUND

Sound can travel along way, and even a low resonant voice will be heard, even if not understood. A slightly higher pitched whisper works best, as it can only be heard over short distances.

Kit can also make a noise. Check your gear for clinking metal, sloshing water, and so on. Check by jumping up and down to see what noises come from your kit, then fix it as best you can. If you have to carry kit that rattles, move slowly to reduce the noise. Consider terrain too, twigs and dry leaves are difficult to traverse quietly, so be careful when choosing a route. Bodily noise can also be an issue, coughs, sneezes and other even less savoury sounds!

SPACING

If working in a group, be aware of your spacing. Evenly spaced people look unnatural, like trees in a neat plantation. Make gaps uneven and irregular in line.

As you move, vary the spacing so you don't form a moving pattern.

SPEED

As we mentioned before, the human eye is very good at registering movement. To avoid detection, keep movement to a minimum and when travelling move slowly. That also includes any gesture you make, such as hand signals. Even turning your head to look around should be done slowly.

CLOTHING AND KIT

So let's look at putting these principles into practice. Why you are hiding and what you are there for is the first consideration. Building an elaborate hide is no use if you have to be on the move. Consider who you are hiding from. If you are bird watching, then think what is most likely to alert a bird to your presence.

Movement is probably the key factor in that case.

The next factor to think about is your kit and clothing. Does it blend in with the surroundings? You may be wearing something with a camo pattern, but is it the appropriate pattern for your surroundings? Also for the season - autumn camo is quite different from spring, for example. In a military setting, it is no use having a great camo outfit, then carrying a shiny gun. Likewise all webbing, radios, watches, etc should be checked.

In the wild, foliage is often used to increase concealment. It is best to gather local foliage as it will blend in much more. Broken twigs and branches have a lighter end that may stand out. Again, arrange the foliage to look natural.

CAMOUFLAGE DRILLS

In most cases we can simply add camouflage into any of our Hide and Seek type drills. But here's a couple of other ideas to help you grasp the basics of camouflage and concealment.

CAN YOU SEE ME?

Choose an outdoor area with a very obvious boundary line. For example, where a wood edges onto a field. Split the group into a few hiders and the rest as spotters. The hiders go to the area and have a set time to conceal themselves, say twenty minutes, just within the border of the woods. Now bring the spotters in. They walk in the field, parallel to the tree line, a set distance away, to see if they can spot the hiders. When they think they have spotted one, they sit directly opposite that place. You can then have the hiders reveal themselves.

Hiders must make best use of cover and foliage, etc. Also, try not to hide in places that are too obvious. If you want, you can give the hiders more time to build some type of hide. A very quick and portable hide, is an old umbrella! Open it and strip away the fabric until you are left with the handle and bare spokes. Now attach foliage to the spokes, bearing all the previous principles in mind. To use, go prone and position the umbrella in front of you. It can be surprisingly effective!

BLENDING IN

This is a drill for any time you are in a crowd. A few of us often do this at the larger seminars. You can also try it in a supermarket while out shopping with your partner but I will not be held responsible for any ensuing domestics! The aim is simply to disappear and appear. So in the seminar setting, we try to sneak up on each other. See how close you can get, or how long you can stand just behind someone before they notice.

In a shop, see if you can "melt away" and re-appear a while later. Or, for the truly brave, try sneaking groceries into someone else's shopping trolley (again, I take no responsibility for ensuing problems!).

HIDING IN A CROWD

While all the usual principles apply, here's a few more suggestions for hiding in a crowd or working in an urban setting.

Be aware of your distinguishing features - do you walk with a noticeable limp, are you extremely tall, do you have a scar and so on. Work to minimse any such feature. Think about your clothing. If people are actively searching for you, remove your jacket, turn it inside out if reversible, or swap with someone else. This was a common tactic "back in the day" as the police were often working to visual descriptions, of which clothing is a big part.

There are urban camo patterns, of course, but consider again the circumstances. Urban camo will stand out a mile if you are walking down a regular high street! In those cases, you want to be wearing what the local people are wearing.

Tourists tend to stand out in most areas, likewise undercover regular police who get the clothes wrong. I remember how undercover police in certain clubs could always be spotted as, despite wearing the latest fashion they always had very well shined shoes!

Accessories or additions are another thing to consider. In urban settings, this may be something like a clipboard. I once worked in a central London office where, one day, two guys dressed in brown overcoats and carrying a clipboard walked in, lifted two computers "for repair" and walked out! No one questioned them, because they "looked official."

In a crowd, stand near people with bright clothes. They

will tend to draw the eye, while you will fade a little into the background. Monitor your body language. Tense, jerky movement will draw attention. Move at the same speed as those around you. Hunch a little. Don't keep looking round to see if you can spot someone trying to spot you.

If you are static, have a reason to be static. Stand at a bus stop. Chat on your phone. Use doorways as cover. Hats, glasses and similar items can help obscure features. But they must fit in both socially and in terms of weather. A winter coat on a hot day will not help! Loners can stand out more. If there is a large group, tag along. Chat to someone, make it look as though you are part of the group.

Consider the flow of foot traffic and why and where people are going. Someone pushing the wrong way against a crowd walking through the tube stands out. Become an "invisible person". Sad to say, there are some people that many in a crowd will not see, don't want to see, or ignore. The homeless, for example, or perhaps a street sweeper, someone who is "part of the furniture."

DIGITAL CONCEALMENT

We live in a digital age and, CCTV and surveillance aside, most of us interact via social media and the like. Outside of everday activites, this is a specialised

area and so beyond the scope of this book. But there are a few hints and tips to help keep you safe.

Basic security - this means keeping your passwords and PINS secret and non-obvious. Many use a pet name or a date of birth, then freely give such infoprmation out in social media fishing posts such as "type your pet name plus maiden name here to get your Star Wars name!" So be aware of any type of post or communication asking for personal details.

Be aware of your settings too. There was a recent case of someone having problems with stalking-type behaviour, who had all their FB settings set to Public. People publicly post on-line when they are going on holiday, photos of their latest gadgets and so on.

Streetview on Google can be another concern. Armed with your postcode, people can now zoom in and look all round the exterior of your property, in many cases. There is a little publicised option where you can have your property view blurred.

In short, I always assume that anything I put on-line is viewable. All we can do, to some extent, is control how many people can view. Do you share your credit card details in e-mails? How secure are those mails? Several times in the news we hear of even big companies getting hacked and customer details being taken. Being online is largely unavoidable, if you want a bank account and other normal things but just consider it the same envrionment as if you were out in the street. Do you know who you are talking to? What information are you giving away? And so on.

CCTV and similar is there to protect us - at least on one level. However, you do not have to be a criminal to be concerned at its increasing intrusion into our everday lives - although many of us now happily buy devices for the home that monitor our conversations!Even cameras and microphones on our laptops and phones can be remotely acessed now! Again, be aware of this and, if you feel the need,

take steps to protect your prrivacy. When out, see if you can spot surveillance. On the plus side, if you get into difficulties, move into an area covered by CCTV.

I realise that some people may regard all this type of training and activity as a bit too "secret squirrel", or playing at being spies, or even a bit paranoid. The first point I'd make is that some people who train with us rely on such skills daily in their professional lives, in a variety of roles. That aside, it does no harm to be at least aware of these skills. People can suffer from stalking, they may have to avoid a violent partner, perhaps they have been targetted by some bad people. In such cases,a little knowedge can go a long way.

Besides any of that, these "games" can be fun, and I make no apology for that. A few times our group has been chided for "playing kids' games" or been asked

"what's that got to do with martial arts." It shows a lack of understanding to me, not to mention, perhaps, a sign of taking yourself a bit too seriously. But each to their own. Let's round out this chapter by looking at observation.

OBSERVATION

If camouflage is the art of concealing, observation is the art of seeing. Not looking! Looking is fleeting, it is a quick scan. Seeing is taking that information in and analysing it, to understand and assess what is is we are actually looking at. Again, how you observe is dependent on circumstances and purpose. Let's think of some of those to start.

We may be observing in order to navigate. By the position of the sun or stars, local conditions, or even by looking at a map! It may be that we are observing in order to commit something to memory - a vehicle registration plate, a face, a series of numbers. Perhaps we are looking out over the exterior of our property after being awoken by a suspicious noise at night.

As we drive, we are constantly observing the road ahead for signs, watching traffic lights, other vehicles, etc (at least I hope so, don't text and drive!) We may be observing the patrons of a bar or club as we work on the door. Perhaps we are looking for something, specific - car keys, wallet, spectacles (check your head, or down the side of the sofa!). A teacher has to be observant of their pupils, to detect signs of bullying, or other issues.

In short, there are numerous examples of using observation, some on a daily basis. We can sharpen our skills by adhering to some simple guidelines. The first is to be attentive. Our vision, in particualr, is very easily distracted. A bright colour, something shiny, some movement, all will catch the eye. You may have seen on-line those videos that ask you to count the number of passes in a basketball match. You may get the passes right but did you notice the dancing bear in the background? I didn't and thought it was a trick video at first - but there the bear was on the replay! So, tip number one, pay attention!

The second tip is to not only look at what is there, but what is not there. In other words don't just look for things tha are out of place but also things that are missing. Either may be an indicator that something is not right.

Context is the next consideration. Types of behaviour, mannerisms, objects and so on may be perfectly normal in one context but not in another. Again, if something doesn't fit it could be an indicator.

Expectation is something else to watch out for. Be sure to interpret information as it is rather than how you think it should be or how you would like it to be. This is particualrly important in person to person communication, more about that later!

Also, you can learn to scan a scene quickly, but then zoom in on any pertinent details. Depending on the situation, you may also want to keep an overall , periperhal vision view going as well as taking in specific detail.

One last thing but perhaps the most important, is to consider the role of the Four Pillars in observation. Good posture means we keep the spine straight. Think of the spine as an antennae. When it is in optimum position it can pick up information from all round. If bent or distorted, information gathering is compromised. Tension, particularly emotional tension, can also affect our ability to process information. It leads us to react with anger, or might mean that we pre-judge people based on prejudice. Breathing is key, as usual, so get used to taking some calming breaths before any observation work.

Consider all the above and get into the

habit of generally being more observant in day to day life. Look up from your mobile phone more! So having establised a few guidelines, let's look at some specific drills.

TAKE A WALK.

Go for a twenty minute walk in your immediate neighbourhood. Leave your phone at home! Simply walk around and observe, perhaps you will notice some things you have not seen before. If your attention begins to wander, have a quick burst-breathe and return to the exercise. After a while, see if you can judge when the twenty minutes are up without referring to your watch. Or, if you have the time, don't give yourself any time limit, just wander around!

Of course you can do the same while out jogging or cycling (road safety allowing). This exercise is also useful for setting a "base line" of your immediate area. You will then quickly notice anything that looks out of place.

PEOPLE WATCHING

Pick a spot where you can sit for a hile. An outdoor table at cafe, for example. Simply observe both the surroundings and the people moving through it. Make a quick assessment of everyone you see - I doubt you will ever know if you are right or not, but it's good practice. Try not to be conspicuous - if someone notices you looking at them, be less obvious!

RUNNING COMMENTARY

A variation on the above drill, that you can practice walking, driving, etc is to maintain a running commentary. It doesn't have to overly detailed at first. "Lady walking a dog, man at bus stop reading a newspaper,"and so on, is fine. Comment, also, on your own actions. "Checking mirror, indicating, shifting gear now, pulling away from the kerb." If you

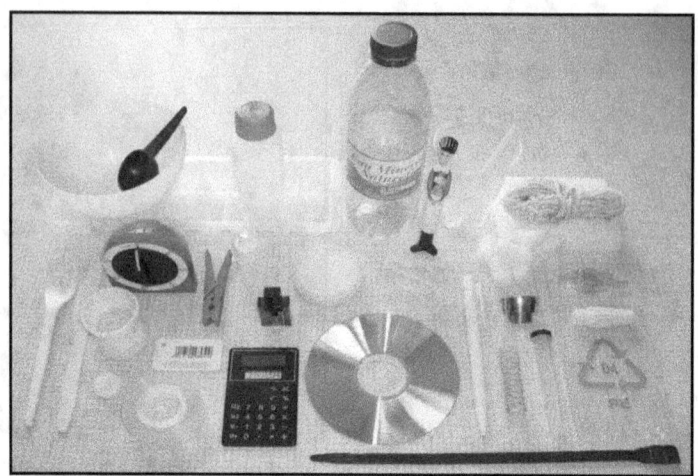

have a passenger who is happy to join in, you can also either commentate to them, or run a joint commentary. If it's a regular route, also commentate on anything different from the norm.

NOW YOU SEE IT

A staple drill for observation, one that we've probably all done at some time. A cover is removed from a table to reveal ten items. Viewers have a set time to observe, then the cover is replaced. Viewers must now list the ten items on a sheet of paper. For variations, make viewers add a brief description of each item, eg colour or what is written on it. If you want to be sneaky, say there are ten items but place out nine or eleven!

WHAT'S IN THE ROOM?

A similar drill to the table test, but moving. Viewers walk through or around a room for a set time. Then they move to another room and can either list items or answer a series of questions. For example:

- what colour were the curtains?
- what was the title of the book on the table?
- how many chairs?
- what time was on the clock and so on.

Of course you can again have them add in more detail, plus the odd trick question. A variation is to have everyone leave a room, make some changes, then bring them back in and see if they can spot the differences.

WHAT COLOUR SOCKS?

For the above drills, people know they are taking part in an aexercises and so will be more observant. To get that awareness working in a less conscious way, start asking questions during or at the end of training. People must give a quick answer. Examples might be:

- what colour socks am I wearing

- how many people are in the room?
- what is the tattoo on Dave's arm?
- what colour is the external door to the building, and so on.

WHAT'S MY LINE?

An interesting one where you have a large group of people new to each other, is to ask them to observe each other and see what conclusions they can come to. Think Sherlock Holmes! Does a person have rough hands, perhaps showing manual labour? Do they move with the grace of a dancer? What age are they? What background? It's a very good way to begin to teach people to quickly assess someone and to develop "gut instinct." More about this later on.

WHO'S CARRYING?

Another activity for small groups. Four people exit the room. One of the four now conceals a training gun, or whichever object you prefer, on their person. The four now come back into the room and walk around it. The aim for the rest of the group is to spot which person is carrying the gun. You can add many levels into this, more movement, drawing the gun, etc but this base level is a good start for observation. Look for tension, changes in posture and an "I'm so innocent!" expression!

YELLOW CAR PUNCH!

Now, to be fair, this one actually was a kids' game that I grew up with and used to play with my brother on long car journeys. When out in a car (passenger, not driving), the first to see a yellow car has to shout "Yellow car!" and punch the other player on the arm. I'm sure you can work out all sorts of variations for this one but please - nobody is allowed to punch the driver!

SCAVENGER HUNT

Another drill that we usually run outside. Set people off through a patch of woods or open ground. They have a list of items that they have to find. These could be thing you might expect to be in the area, or items that are totally out of place. At one camp not one person spotted the tin of soup hanging from a tree branch! Add pressure by

setting a time limit, working low light, running inteference, etc.

SCAN THE ROOM

When you walk into a place, particularly for the first time, get used to giving the room a quick scan. It might be a bar or club, it might be a work environment or sporting event.

Keep your scan brief, try not to look as though you are scanning. Make a quick assessment of those present, does anyone stand out and, if so, why? Don't hold eye contact, it marks you out and may be seen as a challenge. Scan on the move too, don't stop and gawk! I find after a while this becomes a natural habit, particularly in places where you think there may be trouble - forewarned is forearmed!

THE ASSASSINATION GAME

This was an activity popular on US university campuses since the mid-80s. I never played it but can see how, with any modifications required for local conditions, it would become a great tool for developing observation skills.

The basic idea is that each player is secretly given another player as target and must work to "assassinate" them, usually by use of a water pistol, marker pen or similar. Safe zones are set up, along with other guidelines. When a player eliminates their target, they get the victim's target, or are assigned a new target. The winner is the last person standing. Obviously, given current security concerns, I would not advise that you run a game like this on public property. However, if you have private facilities and are be interested in this type of game, I suggest you take a look on-line at the various rule sets available.

URBAN STEALTH

A scaled down version of the

Assassination Game are urban Fox and Hounds type drills. One person or group has to track another through a set area without being noticed. This will likely be quite an involved drill as you will need referees as well as participants. You should also consider local security and legal concerns.

For the trackers, adapt to local conditions. At night time, avoid brightly lit areas where possible. Use other people as shields. Hide in a crowd. Use clothing, hats, glasses, etc to disguise not only your face but your body shape. Adjust your walk, too. In short, apply all the principles of camouflage exactly as you would in the woodland setting.

OUTDOOR TRACKING

Another outdoor, mostly visually based skill is tracking. We can think of this as the art of following a person or animal by observation of the sign it leaves. That may be footprints, broken foliage, droppings and so on. Of course, a master tracker will fully utilise all senses and this is another huge subject, worthy of further study in itself, especially when it comes to recognising specific animal tracks, local weather conditions and so on. For the purpose of this book, let's take a look at the main principles.

Be present - to be truly aware and effective you have to be in the here and now. If necessary, before starting any tracking work take some time to slow down and clear the mind (see later drill).

Slow down - take your time. Observe everything. Don't just look, see. Use peripheral vision, then focus in as you need to.

Stop - don't be concerned about coming to a halt and sitting quietly for a bit. This gives you the time and space to fully observe your surroundings.

Be quiet - your mind should be quiet and so should your movement. I'm reminded

of an incident at camp a few years back. We were moving through woodland, our local guide was taking us to see a large badger set and hopefully spot a few of them. As we drew close, one member of the group pointed and loudly exclaimed "there it is!". We didn't see any badgers that night....

Be comfortable - you may be tracking on a wonderful, pleasant spring day. You may be tracking in the freezing cold. Either way, learn to be comfortable in your environment. That means suitable clothing, it also means not letting adverse conditions affect your emotional / psychological state. That doesn't mean you ignore potential dangers and get hypothermia but it does mean just getting on with the job!

Listen to nature - so much of our Systema work is learning to listen to our body. Likewise, when working in nature we should listen to what it tells us. That may be a sudden change in wind direction. It could be which side of the tree has moss on it. Have you ever been in a situation where birdsong suddenly stops? What do you think that might indicate?

Nature is in total and constant communication with itself, across all the senses. A deer will pick up your scent. Certain types of seed snag onto your clothing. A wise man once said to me, "When you go into the forest, everything within half a mile knows you are there. Yet you are totally unaware of the tiger hiding ten feet from you." Listen to what the world tells you - we are all part of the network!

Recognise signs - there are numerous resources available should you wish to study specific animal prints and signs. In general terms, though, learn to spot not only prints but other signs of where someone or something has been.

Broken vegetation is an indicator that something has been through this way. Damped down undergrowth may show someone has been laying here. Regular animal movement produces trails, some

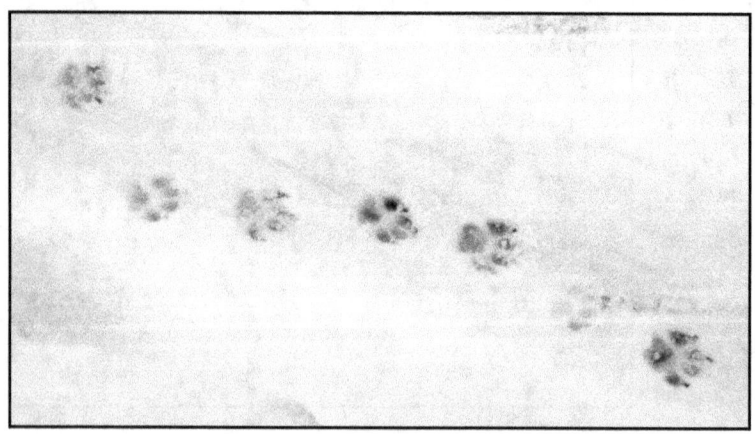

obvious and some more subtle. Learn to see and use them, they may provide the best route through the local terrain.

Left items are another thing to watch out for. That might be droppings, fur left on a bramble, litter or dropped items.

PAPER TRAIL

Those are some basic tracking principles let's look at working them into some simple drills. Again, we usually work these outdoors in woodland but with a little imagination there is nothing to stop you adapting to other environments.

The easiest tracking drill is to have someone set a trail by leaving very obvious trace. This may be sheets of A4 paper pinned to trees, for example. From there you can progress to less obvious signs. Pine cones are good option, they are natural and harder to spot. The setter can either finish the whole trail or, as we mentioned before, you can add an element of chase by letting the searchers loose earlier. Whatever you use as sign, please remember to take it with you once done. Our aim outdoors is always to leave little or no trace that we have been there!

FOLIAGE TRAIL

The next stage is to use only what is already there to set the trail. This may mean breaking stems of grass or small branches,etc. Please do not be too destructive to the landscape!

FOOTPRINTS

Another variation is to work with actual tracks. This is reliant on having soft ground, of course. Footprints give a clear indication of direction - unless your setter is doing some crafty backwards walking!

You could also work with two or more setters, so the trackers must

differentiate between the different prints. Perhaps your pet dog might like to take part and leave some imprints or muddy paw tracks!

I'M SO DIZZY

I mentioned earlier the question of how our sight relates to balance, so we will finish this chapter with a look at dizziness. This is also a function of our inner ear and general balance "sense", which we will cover more later. But let's first look at the visual aspect of balance.

The first drill is a common party game using dizziness to simulate being drunk! The set up is for a person to place their forehead on some object - the handle of a bat, for example - and quickly spin around for a minute or so. Then they stand up and try and walk in a straight line. We can work that way, or we can have a person close their eyes and spin them. Then give them a simple task, work against grabs, for example.

Speaking of alcohol, I have known of sessions where students had a few drinks first to get some of the effects of working under the influence. All under supervision, of course. I also hear they now having something called beer goggles, special glasses that you put on that scramble your sight and balance. Might be worth checking out! Back in my day, beer goggles meant something else entirely, but let's not go there!

AVOIDING DIZZINESS

Think about how some professions have to deal with dizziness. Dancers and pilots spring to mind. What methods do they use to maintain poise?

Spotting is the most common. To try it, stand on the spot and begin spinning around. Visually focus on a specific unmoving point in front of you, perhaps a spot on the wall. Keep your eyes and head steady while your body turns until you can't see the spot anymore. At that point you have to quickly whip your head around to find the spot again.

This is okay in some situations but not if you are moving around.

For that we use the rapid head turn. This time, imagine your head can go north, south, east or west. Let's call facing forward north. Start to walk and as you go, turn your steps in a little so that you are rotating as you walk. As the body turns, the head moves N,E,S,W as you go, pausing very briefly on each turn. The head turn should be quick. Get this right and you'll find you can run and turn quickly without getting too dizzy.

Incidentally, scientists have recently discovered that years of training enables ballet dancers to suppress signals from the balance organs in the inner ear. Brain scans revealed differences in the cerebellum and in the cerebral cortex, showing how training can suppress sensory input, so making dancers resistant to feeling dizzy. Food for thought!

CHAPTER THREE
TACTILE AWARENESS

Our second area of awareness is tactile - the sense of touch. This is a sense we are using constantly. We can close our eyes, block our ears but, extreme medical conditions aside, we cannot switch off our sense of touch. If you ever had to wear an itchy jumper as a kid you will know what I mean!

The sense of touch is a function of the nervous system. The human nervous system is a complex collection of nerves and specialized cells (neurons) that transmit signals between different parts of the body. We can think of it as the body's electrical wiring system. The nervous system has two components: the central nervous system (CNS) and the peripheral nervous system (PNS). The CNS comprises the brain, spinal cord and nerves. The PNS comprises sensory neurons, ganglia (clusters of neurons) and nerves that connect to one another and to the CNS. There are also two divisions in terms of function: the somatic, or voluntary, component; and the autonomic, or involuntary, component.

The autonomic nervous system regulates body processes that work without conscious effort - blood pressure and rate of breathing, for example. The somatic system consists of nerves that connect the brain and spinal cord with muscles and sensory receptors in the skin, and so is more relevant to our work in this chapter.

Neurons send signals to other cells through thin fibres called axons, which cause chemicals known as neurotransmitters to be released at junctions called synapses. The synapse then gives a command to a cell. That entire process typically takes only a fraction of a millisecond. Signals travel along an alpha motor neuron in the spinal cord at around 268 mph, said to be the fastest transmission in the human body.

Sensory neurons react to physical stimuli such as light, sound and touch and send

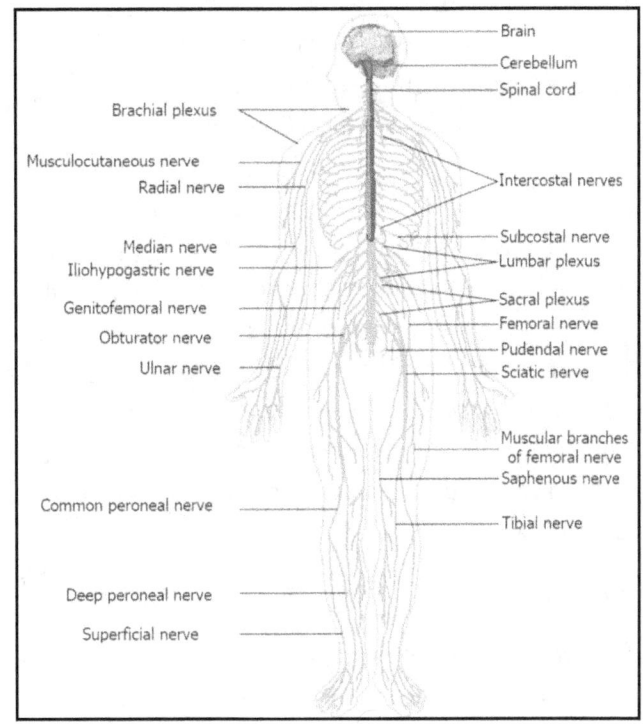

feedback to the CNS about the body's surrounding environment. Motor neurons, located in the CNS or in peripheral ganglia, transmit signals to activate the muscles or glands.

So, we know that the nervous system is involved in receiving information about the environment around us (sensation) and generating responses to that information (motor responses), but there is also a third function. Sensory input needs to be integrated with other sensations, as well as with memories, emotional state, or learning (cognition). Some regions of the human nervous system are termed integration or association areas.

The process of integration combines sensory perceptions with higher cognitive functions such as memories, learning, and emotion to produce a response. Stimuli are compared with, or integrated with, other stimuli, memories of previous stimuli, or the state of a person at a particular time. This leads to a specific response being generated. This could lead us on to a whole other area, the realm of Fixed Action Patterns and similar! However, for now, I want to keep our attention focused purely on the idea of touch. So let's look at the model known as *homunculus*.

HOMUNCULUS

The term homunculus is Latin for *little man*. It is used in neurology to describe

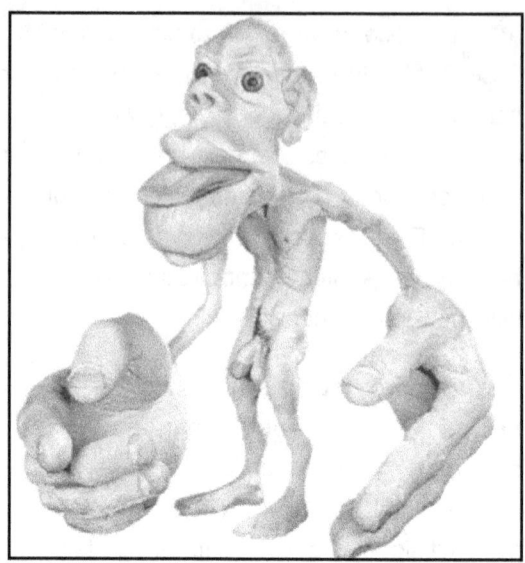

the map in the brain of sensory neurons in each part of the body (the sensory homunculus). In other words, it is a representation of how the brain sees the body. All body parts have an area of the brain devoted to them. If, for example, you bang your elbow, the area dedicated to the elbow within your brain will 'light up'.

In 3-D form, the sensory homunculus is represented as a sculpture of a strangely proportioned human being. In short, the larger the size of the body area in the sculpture, the more "brain space" they occupy. We can see, then, that the hands are extremely important and deliver a lot of sensory information to the brain. Our arms and legs, much less so.

How is this relevant to us? Well, the brain has 'plasticity' meaning that the sensory cortex is very adaptable. If you are a violin player, chances are that the part of your sensory cortex dedicated to the fingers of the left hand are larger than normal. It has even been shown that London taxi drivers have a bigger hippocampus (part of the brain used in navigation) than non-taxi drivers!

You'll often hear people talk about *muscle memory*, but you can see from this the importance of functionality when training - not merely in the muscles but also in the brain. The more we train well, the larger and more attuned that area of the cortex will become. This also goes some way to explaining phantom pain post amputation, as the sensory cortex still has a virtual representation of the missing limb. It also shows that the amount of pain you are suffering does not necessarily relate to the size of the tissue damage sustained.

A HEALTHY NERVOUS SYSTEM

Given that our nervous system is deep within us and largely sub-conscious, can we work to keep it healthy? Most suggestions for doing so fall in line with general advice on keeping healthy overall, though there are some specific actions you can take to directly influence nervous system health. They are:

- monitor your eating patterns and make sure to eat semi-regularly so as to not deplete the glucose your neurons use for energy

- maintain a balanced diet that includes good levels of B-12 and D vitamins, as well as healthy fats

- avoid smoking and drinking excessive alcohol

- keep a solid sleep schedule, as sleep helps strengthen circuits within the nervous system which can help with memory

- exercise your nervous system and brain with activities like writing by hand or playing mind games and puzzles

- take part in exercise that is appropriate for your body; aim to exercise at least three times a week.

- maintain a healthy weight as many conditions, such as diabetic neuropathy, are closely linked to obesity.

- avoid, or limit, environmental factors that can cause nerve damage, such as repetitive motions or exposure to toxic chemicals.

More recent research has shown that neurological health depends as much on signals sent by the muscles to the brain as it does on directives from the brain to the muscles. Published by Dr. Raffaella Adami in *Frontiers in Neuroscience*, the study discovered that: "people unable to do load-bearing exercises, such as patients who are bed-ridden, or even astronauts, not only lose muscle mass, but their body chemistry is altered at the cellular level and their nervous system

adversely impacted,"

The research showed that using the legs, particularly in weight-bearing exercise, sends signals to the brain that are vital for the production of healthy neural cells, essential for the brain and nervous system. Cutting back on exercise makes it difficult for the body to produce new nerve cells, some of the very building blocks that allow us to handle stress and adapt to challenge in our lives.

"Neurological health is not a one-way street with the brain telling the muscles 'lift,' 'walk,' and so on," says Adami. "It is no accident that we are meant to be active: to walk, run, crouch to sit, and use our leg muscles to lift things," Or, as we might say, *to do Systema!*

TRAINING TOUCH

So let's begin with some tactile sensitivity drills. Initially, these are purely to work our basic "feeling." The ability to detect, interpret and respond too some form of physical contact. As always, begin slowly!

BASIC PUSHING

A stock Systema drill and one that we do almost every class. One person stands and pushed, with fist or open hand, by their partner. The push can be fairly gentle at first, but should be strong enough to elicit a response. The receiver can react in one of two ways.

Whole body - as the push comes in you maintain posture and absorb the force by moving your feet.

Isolated body - as the push comes in you move only the part of the body affected. So, if the shoulder is pushed, you roll the shoulder.

In both cases try to maintain posture or, if it breaks, restore it a quickly as possible. Exhale on the push at first, as this will help relax the body.

To start, keep the tempo steady. Be sure to push on all areas of the body, particularly where you can see any tension. Allow the receiver to recover before pushing again. The receiver can experiment with closing the eyes, so they are then relying completely on the sense of touch. Over time, tempo and strength of push can be increased. You can also increase the number of pushers to two. Think also about pushing with the foot, knee or shoulder, it doesn't have to always be the hand.

Just another note for the pusher too - be sure to monitor your own posture, breathing, etc throughout the exercise. Make sure you are not over-extending, this also is a good drill for developing your comfortable range when working against another person.

BUILDING RESPONSE

We can turn this rather one-sided exchange into a back and forth drill quite easily! Now, the receiver has to take the push and use their response to bring out their own push. At a simple level, if you push on my shoulder, I lift it a little, rotate the waist, then take that movement through to my opposite hand to push. Work continuously but also keep the movement smooth. Try not to add in extra speed at this stage. Allow your body to naturally respond rather than over-thinking the process.

As with the first drill, it is easy to increase tempo, add in an extra pusher and work with eyes closed (both partners). Please bear in mind that this is not a "competition" drill is such, the aim is to develop a smooth back and forth response.

PUSH WARS!

Now this drill is more of a competition. The aim of the game is to push your partner off balance. We can do this from the previous set-up, but here is a way to try this drill that really works the upper body. Partners take a wide stance, way out beyond shoulder width. You face each other, no more than arm's length apart. You are allowed to push / pull the body or the arms. The feet do not move. Standing in this awkward position means you cannot use your legs to absorb force so well, meaning the upper body has to be much more relaxed. For variation, take the same stance but side-to-side with feet touching. If one partner is not enough of a challenge, try working against three! For this version, four people stand facing each other in a circle, with feet touching those of their neighbour. You can keep the stance a little closer in this time.

The game is the same as before, try to unbalance the other people in the group. You can reach across, or work against the people to your sides, it is a free for all! Remember, the feet are to remain in place. After a while, keep the same relative position, but everyone faces outwards. Feet are still in contact. For this drill, remember our "response training" from the previous exercise. Try, as much as you can, to recycle an incoming push or pull into an outgoing one.

WEAPONS PUSH

Let's go back to our very first drill and add in something extra. This time, rather than push with hand or foot, we use an object or weapon. One person stands as before, the other person now applies pressure with the end of a stick, the point of a knife, etc. Once again, we start at an even tempo but with a firm push. The person reacts in the same way, with either whole or isolated body movement. The extra levels can be added in too - eyes closed, more than one pusher, etc.

If we want to build in a response aspect, we can either use the incoming force as before, to power a return push or strike. We can also work to disarm, taking the stick or knife from the other person. At the level of "touch exercise" this can become a nice, back and forth flow drill and is a good foundation for later weapons defence work.

Just a word on what you use. A stick is a fairly neutral item, it can be any length. A knife obviously poses more difficulties. At first, a wooden knife is okay. Do not use rubber ones, they are useless for this work. The best to use is a metal knife. It does not have to be sharp, a butter knife will do to start. You can also use a blunted blade or, when ready, a live blade (with appropriate caution, of course).

You can experiment to test this for yourself - the feel of rubber, wooden, blunt and sharp blade is very different, physically and psychologically. It is very important that we prepare our bodies for real life conditions as best as possible. If the body is a little "asleep" it needs to feel the danger in order to provoke a good response. The touch of a rubber knife barely registers as anything, let alone danger!

Always remember that these drills are to develop attributes (in this case touch sensitivity), they are not "knife defence" as such, though, of course they play a role in developing defence skills. If you have a person who is particularly nervous of contact with the knife, have them close their eyes and take some slow breaths. Then begin the work slowly. The point is to remove fear based tension, not to increase it.

STICKY HANDS

Many martial arts use some form of sticky hands type training. It is an excellent method of developing touch sensitivity for the hands and forearms. After all, this is

the part of the body that most often comes into contact with an opponent, be it in grappling, striking or defending. The main aim, initially, is to develop the ability to deflect, to feel our partner's structure and balance through the arm and to be able to change position with ease.

BASIC TOUCH

The first level is to have both partners contact at the palm - one or both hands. The drill is simply to maintain contact as we move.

Partner A initiates the movement, moving the hand, walking, changing level, etc, and Partner B follows. Then we swap roles.

Finally, neither partner leads or follows, both simply move. Keep the palms in contact throughout. Keep the touch light and constant, slow and steady at first, speeding up as required.

You can work the same drill with other parts of the body in contact. Palm to shoulder, perhaps. Or elbow to elbow. Don't be afraid to experiment. One or both partners' eyes closed is another option to explore.

DEFLECTING DRILL

This drill goes back to our Basic Push. We start in the same way, with out partner pushing with fist onto the body. We move away, as before, but this time add in a deflection. Allow your nearest hand to come up under the push and, as the body moves away, lightly brush the push aside. The key points here are to work only at contact, to move from the body and to keep the deflection very light. The more tension, the more information you give your partner about your intentions.

With this drill it is very easy to begin working in some wave-type movements, from which it is we can build in a response, born of the original attack. To add some variation, switch to pushing with the feet and deflect with the hand, or by raising and turning the leg a little

REDIRECTING

This is a more vigorous version of the above drill. To start we will work in a set pattern, to establish the principle. Then, we can work more freestyle.

Partner A pushes Partner B's left shoulder with their left hand (so going across the body.) Partner B yields by rotation, as before. However, as the left shoulder rotates, the right hand comes up to gently take A's left elbow. Don't grip tight, just cup it. Now, as you continue the rotation, turn to the left and take a few steps. You should find yourself leading Partner A away for a short distance.

Remember, you are not pulling them by the elbow, you are simply guiding or "helping." The stronger the push, the more steps you take. Let the energy of the push disperse naturally. At this stage, there is no need to add in any other movement though, of course this type of work is a prelude to locks, throws and counter-strikes.

Once you have the basic idea, start to experiment. Work right hand push to left hand shoulder and work inside the arm, for example. Try coping with a double push, or being pushed from behind. In each case, the aim is to blend, merge and re-direct.

PUSHING HANDS

I am borrowing the name here from other arts. Many arts, such as Taiji, have Push Hands, the Systema approach is a little different. But let's start with a basic set up. Partners stand opposite each other and make contact at the wrists. Hands can be both outside, both inside, or one of each. Begin to slowly move the arms around. The first requirement is to maintain contact, as per our earlier drill. But now you can also start pushing.

The aim is to push your partner off balance. Try to "feed in" to your partner's core through their arms. If their arms are tense, you will find this is quite easy. If the arms are relaxed, then it is more of a challenge. Of course, when pushing you must guard against giving your partner your own tension, which they can use against you. You may also add in pulling too, but for now stick to working just with the arms. You may decide to have the feet static, or both be stepping.

The difference between this and other Push Hands methods is largely in the concept of' "root and sinking." Some styles work a lot on developing a strong ground connection, on moving the body from the lower centre (just below the navel) and on developing a strong stance. For Systema, we should instead think about "floating". Our centre is in the chest/heart area. The feet are not sinking into

your hands, though. Have both partners sit and work the same exercises with your feet. Stick, push, deflect, as before. You can also work legs from standing position - clasp forearms and raise one leg to stick, push, etc to your partners. As you progress, add in kicks, trips and sweeps.

HIT HANDS

First we push, then we hit!

the ground but gliding across it. In some ways, this is more of a challenge, as we must work with a much softer body, rather than relying on our stance. That is not to say you never use stance, but only if the situation requires that you are"immobile", not as a matter of course. Mobility, in all its aspects,is key to Systema training.

So this is our basic pushing set-up. From here you can begin to add in pushes to arms and body, even the legs. You can work in arm and wrist locks. You can even add in trips and throws if you wish. Just be sure not to lose sight of the drill, which is to develop tactile sensitivity! Use the exercise to develop the skills, then integrate those skills into your more regular sparring work.

Don't feel you have to confine this work to

This works from the same set-up as above, but this time we try to hit our partner. At first, just try to tap the chest. So, wrists join as before, begin to circle, then tap the chest. The trick, of course, is not to telegraph the strike in any way. We normally do this on two ways. We either tense prior to striking, which our partner should see or feel through the touch. Or, we break contact to hit. If we are quick, we may get away with this. But if our partner is quicker, then as soon as we break contact they will hit us!

So we have to maintain a balance between light contact and preparing to hit. Our strike then, should be formed out of relaxation, not jerky or twitchy speed. Another thing to consider, once we begin working on targets other than the chest, is how we can use our partner's arms to access their body. With pushing, we do this by feeling

or creating a line of tension up the arm, into the shoulder and from there into the core.

With a strike we can use the line or structure of our partner's arm in order to "slide in" and apply the hit. This is nice as it means we maintain contact as we hit. This gives less information to our partner but also allows us to receive information at the same time. As ever, start slow and build up speed and targets. Be careful how you apply power if working faster. Keep the hands relaxed and apply only surface strikes.

GRAB AND ESCAPE

Now change the push into a grab. As usual, we begin lightly and build up intensity. So our partner feeds in a grab. It might be an arm around the neck, a bear hug type move or trying to grab the wrist. We allow the grab to touch but, as soon as it does, we move to escape. Against a push we can work in a fairly straight line but now we may also need to change direction and level. We can still also use isolated body movement.

As an example, our partner approaches from behind and places an arm across our shoulders in order to position a choke. As soon as we feel this we may rotate the shoulders, duck under, then step away, so not allowing the grab to "bite".

The key is to work quietly and calmly so as to develop the sensitivity. If you find yourself being grabbed often, then ask your partner to slow down a little, particularly as they touch.

Keep good form as much as you can but if you have to break it (such as when ducking) immediately return to good posture. Breath, relax, move! You can also make this a back-and-forth drill, build your grab response out of your escape

movement. For further variations, work eyes closed, or have two or more grabbers!

SITTING PUSH

Let's now take the same principles to the ground. For the first exercise, we will work our basic pushing drill as before, but this time both partners sit or kneel next to each other. The progression / variations are the same is before, though obviously you are unable to step in this version. This means that the upper body must be even more relaxed to deal with the incoming force.

SITTING KICK

For this drill, one partner sits or kneels and the other stands and pushes them with the foot. Once again, use softness to absorb the power of the push.

FLOOR STAMP

Now the receiver lays flat on the floor. The standing partner places a foot somewhere on the receiver's body. It may be on the arm, leg, chest etc. Once the foot is placed, apply a little downward pressure. The receiver must soften the body and move out and away from the pressure. You should work both from a face up and a face down position.

FLOOR GRAB AND ESCAPE

We now work our earlier grab and escape drill on the ground. The first step is to have both partners sitting or kneeling. One initiates a grab, the other moves to escape. As before, we can take turns to grab, or work back-and-forth.

The next stage is to carry that work with both prone on the ground. After that, experiment with positions - one partner kneeling, one prone for example. Build up to slow grappling but do not lose fact of the sight that this is a touch sensitivity exercise.

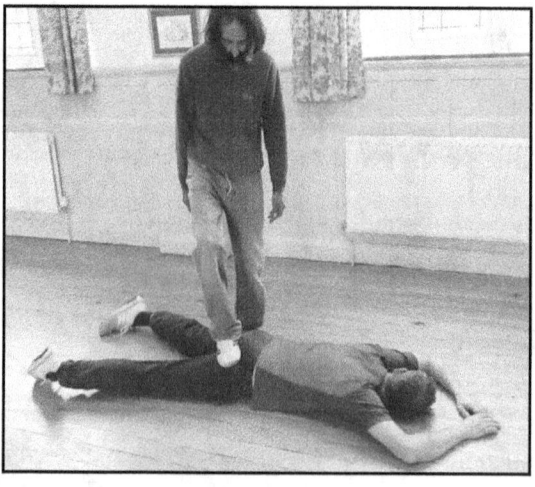

SELECTIVE TENSION

We can also think of tactile sensitivity in terms of our internal state. In other words, awareness of levels of tension within the body. The basic exercise to put us in touch with this is the standard inhale/exhale with tense and relax we described earlier.

Try and be aware in your everyday activities of how unwanted tension creeps in. Check the neck and shoulders if you work sitting at a desk, for example. It is much easier to deal with tension as it arises. Just a few simple movements and some breathing usually suffice.

LETTING GO

Having explored static selective tension and relaxation, let's add in some outside force. To start with, have one or two partners grab an arm. They slowly move and twist your arm around and all you have to do is nothing! Simply relax the muscles totally and allow the arms to be moved in any direction, with no resistance at all. If your partner lets go of the arm, it should flop down, with absolutely no tension. Maintain form but allow the body to be as relaxed as possible, too.

FIXED IN PLACE

The setup is the same as the previous drill, but this time you try and fix the arms in place, do not let them move at all. Keep the arms tense, the fists clenched but do not allow that tension to creep back up into the body. Your partners should work with slow changes, not jerky movement.

HARD AND SOFT

The final version of this exercise is a real test of tension control. Same start position as the last exercise, one partner takes your right arm, one your left. Your task is to keep one arm totally free and relaxed, but the other must not move. It is locked in

place.

Your partners slowly push and pull on your arms. The soft arm has to move to wherever it is taken. The tense arm is fixed in place and should not move at all. You will find either that the tension from the fixed arm creeps into the body and across and vice-versa with the relaxed arm! This can be quite difficult at first, so remember to start slowly with not too sudden changes of movement.

TWO ON ONE GRAB LOCK

An off-shoot of this drill is that now the two partners try to actively lock your arms. You may respond by being soft and wriggling out, or by maintaining the arm structure in order to prevent the lock from biting. Once again, start slow and build up speed. As a variation, the person in the middle can try and tangle the other two partners together and/or add in strikes.

Once you have tried this set of exercises with the arms, lay on the floor and work through the same routine with the legs.

LOOK, NO HANDS

Let's go back to using weapons, the knife in particular. The starting point is the Weapons Push drill. This time, the hands are placed behind the back and we can work only with the body. Our partner pushes with the knife point and we move away as usual. This time, however, our task is to move the body in such a way that we push the knife point back towards our partner. At first, see if you can work to bring the flat of the blade in contact with the body. From there, shift again in order to control the direction of the knife, then thrust out to push it away.

While this may look like a knife

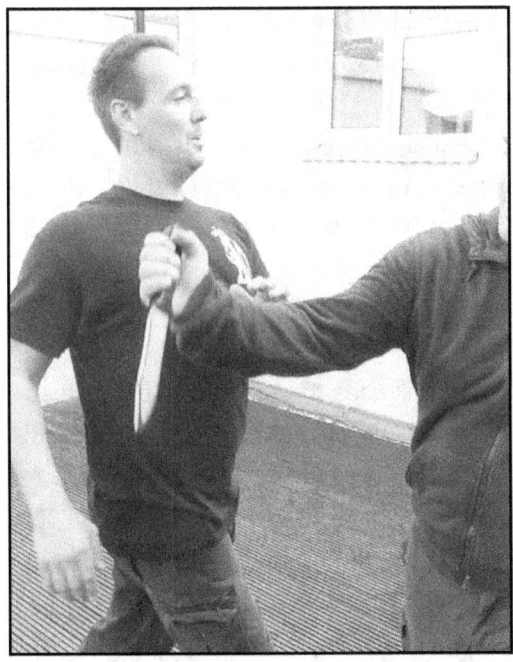

and the knife holder must immediately pull the knife back and try to cut the deflecting arm. The defender can either rotate the arm or pull it away.

THE SCRATCH STICK

There is a more advanced version of the above drill which uses a specialised piece of kit known as a Scratch Stick. The stick is a piece of rod or dowel with a nail pushed into the end. The set up is similar to above, the stick comes into contact with the arm. The stick holder now pulls the stick away, trying to scratch their partner's arm with the head of the nail. Obviously, this drill is a little more "serious" as a good scratch will draw blood. So if you are not prepared for that, please avoid this drill. As the risk is greater, however, we do find that this work really sharpens up sensitivity and movement in the arms.

defence drill (and in an extreme situation it may form part of that!) the primary aim is to develop good mobility in the body, particularly the chest.

FLAT KNIFE

Let's work the same drill but with the arms (a little easier!) The set up is for one person to place the edge of the knife against their partner's arm and slowly try to "cut". The other person must rotate the arm in such a way that they keep the flat of the blade rather than the edge against the skin.

Remember again, this is a sensitivity drill, not a psycho-scenario. Once you have the idea you can increase speed. Another variation is for the knife holder to feed in a stab. The defender deflects it with the arm

DISTANCES

Judging distance is mostly a function of sight but we also use touch to orient ourselves too. This type of skill is especially useful if you are working to protect other people. You may have to move quickly through a crowd with a small child, for example. In this case you have to use your eyes primarily to avoid danger, while using touch to maintain contact with and guide your child.

ARM DISTANCE

Place a hand on your partner's chest or shoulder. Your partner now moves around the training space and you have to maintain contact with them at all times.

At first, your partner moves quite slowly. As you progress, they can speed up, put in more changes of direction and also change levels. You can also vary the start position. Stand behind your partner with hand in small of the back, hand on head, etc.

One thing to bear in mind when working with others, particularly in this type of cooperative drill, is to synchronise your breathing. If you can do this, you will find that the pair or group works much better as a cohesive unit rather than just as individuals.

STICK DISTANCE

This drill uses the same idea but instead of touching with the hand, we use a stick! This is a little more challenging as the stick will drop immediately if contact is broken.

Partners stand opposite each other and place the end of the stick to their chest or shoulder. The aim again is for the pair to move around without losing contact. One person can lead, or both can lead. You can give a set course, eg "walk around the edge of the room", or partners can move in any direction. Next, add in level changes. Go to your knees, seated, floor and back up. You might also add in obstacles, moving through doorways and so on. The next variation is to work in

groups of three. Now the work becomes very interesting! You can add in the level changes as before.

BLINDFOLD WORK

Loss of our sense of sight is a scary prospect, it is probably the sense that we rely on the most. Of course, some people have to live permanently with this condition and it always amazes me how adaptable people become to life's adversities.

It may be a cliché to suggest that if we lose one sight, we increase our "powers" in others. I'm not sure how true that is, but it does feel as though taking away sight causes us to be much more aware of touch, sound and so on. I imagine the brain as a computer, with data constantly being fed into the main processor. At a certain level, the processor becomes overloaded with data and so some information is ignored.

This can be highlighted by a true story. The US Air Force was conducting operations one time to test a new Heads Up Display (HUD). This new piece of kit displayed visually to the pilot a wealth of information: airspeed, heading wind speed and direction, altitude, pitch, radar and so on. The "chiefs" thought it would be great that a pilot could now have all this info flashing before his eyes, no need to check the instrument panel!

The exercise took the form of mock dogfights. The jet fitted with new kit went up and the dogfight began. The pilot was annoyed when he was shot down very quickly by an "enemy" plane that had got onto his tail, followed him and "fired" its missiles. In the de-brief the pilot angrily asked his navigator why he had not warned him they had an enemy on their tail. "I did," said the navigator, "I was screaming it out loud!"

The pilot had been so intent on processing all this wonderful information

in front of him, that the warning from the navigator had gone totally unheard. The HUDs were heavily revised as a result!

Part of our awareness skill, then, is in learning to filter out information as well as take it in. If we work with a blindfold, then a huge amount of information is filtered out for us. This allows us to exclusively focus on touch, sound, etc. But there is also another element to this. Much of the time in Systema, we talk about training the body to respond, or using "body intelligence" or "natural movement". Our bodies are often much smarter than we think- and it is our thinking that often gets in the way of the body process. Left to its own devices, the body can be remarkably fast and agile.

Have you ever opened a cupboard door and had a tin fall out? Imagine that situation and that as it happens you think about how you would catch the can. Chances are, the can has already hit the floor (or your foot, I hope it was not a large can!) Or, without thought, the body reacts all by itself and before you even know it, the can is in your hand.

This level of automatic response shows the tremendous abilities that are innate within us - if we allow them to manifest. Over-thinking often brings fear and tension, or perhaps indecision - do we go left or right? If we allow our sense of touch, for example, to take over, the body will respond naturally and effectively.

People often ask about speed in Systema Some think that we only ever train in slow-motion. Well, speed is a function of relaxation, which is also part of this "letting go" process and allowing our body to work as it will. I often say to people "touch a hot kettle, then tell me how fast you move. I can't teach you to move any faster than that." This is a very deep subject and we shall return to it later on in the book. For now, though, lets explore how using a blindfold can help us to really connect with

our sense of touch

BLINDFOLD BASICS

The first thing to establish with blindfold training is safety. Always work in an area that is suitable for training. Never have absolutely everyone in the room blindfold, there should be at least one "sighted" person over-seeing in case of problems.

Even in an enclosed area you can get a problem! I once ran a blindfold session at our Tempsford venue. At the front of the hall is a car pack, set right on the busy A1 road. At the rear is a nice lawn, fully enclosed by a tall, thick hedge. We ran a simple blindfold drill in the rear area - the group just had to walk around the lawn.

Everyone did fine, except for one special case. He managed to find the hedge and rather than follow it, like everyone else did, instead dropped and squirmed his way under and through it. He then continued on his merry way round to the front of the building. I caught him heading directly for the A1, no doubt he would have climbed the safety barrier too! Point is, you can never take anything for granted, even where you have a very physical, obvious boundary to the training area.

The next thing to establish is a sense of trust. I had one guy who thought that his partner wearing a blindfold was a great opportunity for him to get in some free, way too heavy shots. It was a very unpleasant experience for the partner and the striker was removed from class. So it is very much up to the sighted partner to be responsible for the other person's safety.

Be aware of how you are taking a person down, how you are pushing them, how heavy you are striking and so on. You should be doing all these things as a matter of course anyway, but the blindfold can highlight and bring out extra fears.

For the person wearing the blindfold, try to relax as much as you can. This becomes a good lesson in acceptance. You cannot see the push, so you have to

accept it. Sometimes the anticipation creates tension. This is fear of something that has not happened yet (like so many of our fears!). Learn to let this fear go and purely deal with the event as it happens. This will really help all your other work, sighted or not.

Any and all of the previous drills can be practiced blindfold. So I suggest you go back the Basic Pushing and begin from there. At first, it is best to have just one partner blindfold, then you can try with both. Let's then look at some more specific blindfold drills.

FINDING YOUR WAY

This is a group exercise, though people work as individuals. Have the group walk sighted a few times around the training space. Do not tell them anything else, just yet.

Next, the whole group is blindfolded. They have to make the same journey around the space. If you wish, you can have them work in pairs first, one blindfold and the other as nearby guide to steer only if things go wrong! It is very common when people first do this drill, for them to adopt the "zombie pose", with arms outstretched and lots of tension in the legs. Encourage people to walk with hands down. The smart ones will have counted the steps in the first part of the drill, or touched something here and there to help with orientation!

There are many variations you can add in. People can be spun around a few times before setting off. You can have sighted people running interference, or place obstacles in the way. Going up and down stairs is a good challenge, or perhaps climbing out of a (ground floor!) window. As long as it is safe, you can add in all sorts of challenges.

STEERING

We give out and take in a lot of information purely through touch. This next drill explores that and is also very good for developing team communication, especially if you have a group where people have not worked with each other before.

The basic level is to work in pairs. Partner A stands in front, with blindfold on. Partner B, the "driver" stands behind, with palms

resting on the shoulders. Partner A now begins to walk around the space. This can be a set route as before, or free movement. Partner B steers with light pressure on the shoulders. Press left for left, right for right. Pull back slightly for stop, push forward for go.

The aim is to negotiate the training space without bumping into anything or anyone. Steering instructions should be light but clear. You can, of course, come up with variations in hand position and signals - stand at the side with an arm over the shoulder, work by holding hands and so on - but always work from touch.

THE SNAKE

The basic idea is the same as before. There is a "driver" who is sighted and guiding. This time, though, there are two, three or more people blindfolded. The group stands in a line, hands on the shoulders of the person in front. The driver takes up position at the rear of the group and steers the person in front of him as before. Now, however, the message must be passed along the line to the person at the front.

The interesting thing with this exercise is to see how the communication can change when it is passed through a few people. Even with only a few, quite clear instructions, wires can become crossed and left become right! Once the course is completed, or every few minutes, rotate drivers so that everyone gets a chance to steer the group. The same variations can apply. Have a set route, or free movement. Place obstacles. Have a few teams racing against each other, first to complete the course wins.

FALL DOWN

Our next exercise goes back to working in

pairs. It can be a continuation of the Steering drill, or you can run it as a stand alone exercise. Set up is the same, steerer behind, guiding the blindfoldee (is that a word?). This time, there is an extra signal. If the steerer pushes down on the shoulders, the person must drop to the floor as quickly as possible.

The next stage is for the steerer to more actively take their partner to the ground. This may be by downward pressure, by breaking structure, by throwing and so on, depending on the partner's ability to safely fall. It is up to the steerer to ensure that they guide the faller into a safe space. The faller should really try and get into the habit of going to ground as soon as they feel the pressure from their partner.

The roles in this drill can also be swapped around. This time, the seeker comes in and applies a grab or hold to the blindfold partner, who must then take the steerer to the floor. Use touch to feel the position of the body, arms, head, etc, then use them to break structure, throw, etc.

The aims of this type of drill are to develop sensitivity, of course, but also to work a little on fear control and managing impact. In fact, the same can also be practiced in our next drill!

SUDDEN IMPACT

The blindfold partner will now receive strikes from their sighted partner. We use the usual set up for taking strikes, with the striker standing in front and a little to the side of the receiver. Start lightly, with some fist pushes to begin. Then you can go for punches. How you hit is dependent on the ability of the receiver to take strikes. Watch for tension and fear, always allow the receiver time to recover. Vary the position and intensity of your strikes.

For the receiver, this is an opportunity to really work purely from the body. The first thing you will notice is the fear and anticipation of being hit. The anticipation is often worse than the event. So learn first to deal with this fear. Take note of where in the body that feeling manifests. It may be a tightening of muscles in the solar plex, for example. Use breathing and a little movement to get rid of it.

Next, of course, you must develop the ability to organise the body to deal with incoming force precisely on impact. It is best to have learnt this sighted first, before you try this exercise. The usual Systema methods apply, absorption, deflection, resistance, etc. If it helps, think of it less as managing impact and more as dealing with information!

NAME THE TOUCH

It is interesting to see just how much and what kind of information can be transmitted by touch. This drill explores that concept and works in groups of four.

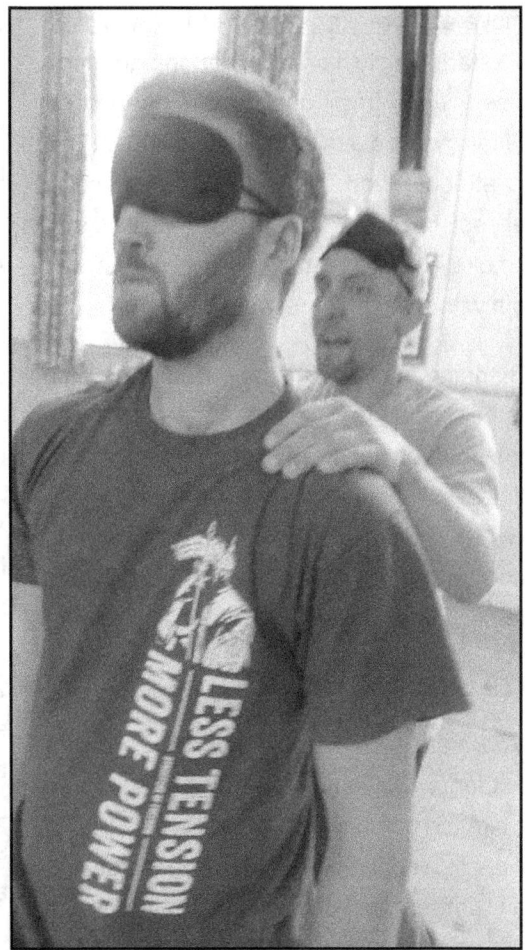

The blindfolded person stands on the spot. In turn, the three other people approach, lay a hand on the shoulder and speak their name to the blindfoldee (I don't care if it's a word or not, I'm using it anyway!). Repeat for five or six times. Now repeat, but in random sequence. This time, though, you do not say your name. The blindfoldee must say who the touch belongs to. So keep the touches the same each time, ie everyone touches the same place and in the same way.

Notice how the touches vary and their different qualities. Heavy or light, gradual, or grab and so on. You will soon find that you will be able to get the right name almost every time.

FIND A FRIEND

Here's another information drill, that works best in a larger group. Half The group are blindfold, half sighted. Each sighted person selects a blindfoldee and allows that person to feel them with the hands. Take a minute or two. Next, all partners separate and the whole group begins to move around the space. Blindfoldees must now find their partner, working only through touch. If you wish, you can add in variations as usual - run interference on the searchers, have the sighted partners more actively "hide," add in obstacles, etc

SOLO BLINDFOLD

It is an interesting exercise to move around your own house blindfolded. Be sure to move any breakables out of the way first! To start, simply navigate around one room. Then work from one room to another. Finally work stairs and all the rooms. This is attribute work but also has a practical aspect. In a fire, a building may be filled with smoke. Would you be able to find your way out without sight to rely on?

Bumping into furniture and obstacles also forces the body to soften more to deal with the impact. Once you've done it a few times, set yourself a task. Can you find your car keys and get to the front door? Can you open a window? Can you find your phone to call the emergency services and so on.

FOLLOW THE PATH

You can take the same drill into the outdoors. Obviously it is advisable to have a sighted person overseeing the drill and to work in a safe environment. But working in an unfamiliar and uneven environment brings fresh challenges.

The first stage is to have a set path for blindfoldees to follow. A simple way to do this is to run a rope or cord through the terrain. The walkers keep contact with the guide rope and move along the set course. It is natural at first for people to grasp the rope tightly. Have them run through the drill a few times, each time making less and less contact with the guide rope. Have it just brushing the leg, for example.

After a few runs, see if the walkers can follow the course without touching the rope at all. From there, you can give them the task of moving from point A to point B without any guide. You may let them do this sighted at first, so they can familiarise their body with the route. Feel for what is underfoot, use a tree as a guide point and so on. This encourages people to be fully aware of their surroundings at all times.

MOVING THROUGH A CROWD

Another good series of drills to run for tactile awareness is moving through a crowd. You will need a larger group of people but you can start with just a few. Have four or five people stand in a line. They should be close to each other but not jammed in tight. Another person has to move through the group causing as little "upset" as possible. At this stage, the group are passive and not resisting the single person. Here's a few tips for moving through a group.

Relax - keep your body soft and pliable so it can adapt and mould to the space available,

Slide and flow - avoid heavy contact, keep any touch light. When you encounter an obstacle, try and slide along it and through

Lead with the hand - use your hand to find spaces and "pull" the body into them. In a large crowd it almost becomes like swimming.

Be vocal - it may do no harm to say "excuse me, sorry, excuse me" as you go through. Manners cost nothing!

See where the gaps are - look how the crowd forms. Is it static or moving? Can you work with the flow of the crowd to carry you where you want to go? Is there a solid point, such as a wall, you can use for support?

Changing level - try working not only upright but in a squat and even on the ground in a crowd.

What is the situation - context is key, again. Are you trying to get through a crowd quickly because of an emergency? Shout and draw attention to that fact. Are you trying to slip through unnoticed? Be quiet and evasive. Is the crowd potentially dangerous? Can you find a safe position or escape route?

Once you can move through a small group, try the same drill with the group tighter together or giving more resistance. From there, if you have a large enough group, you can work to moving in a large crowd. We ran some drills along these lines with a group of around fifty people, which was fun!

To add some focus we added in some simple tasks. Five people have to get through the crowd and touch a particular spot on the wall, for example. If you want to up the intensity, have the crowd "fighting". This can lead us onto all sorts of other drills - breaking up fights and so on - but the first requirement is to be able to move well through a group of people. Needless to say, you can run these drills in a variety of environments, given the usual safety concerns.

USING EQUIPMENT

We have mentioned the use of sticks and knives in our tactile training but there are also other types of equipment we can use too. In fact, we can use almost anything, with a little imagination, both solo and working in drills.

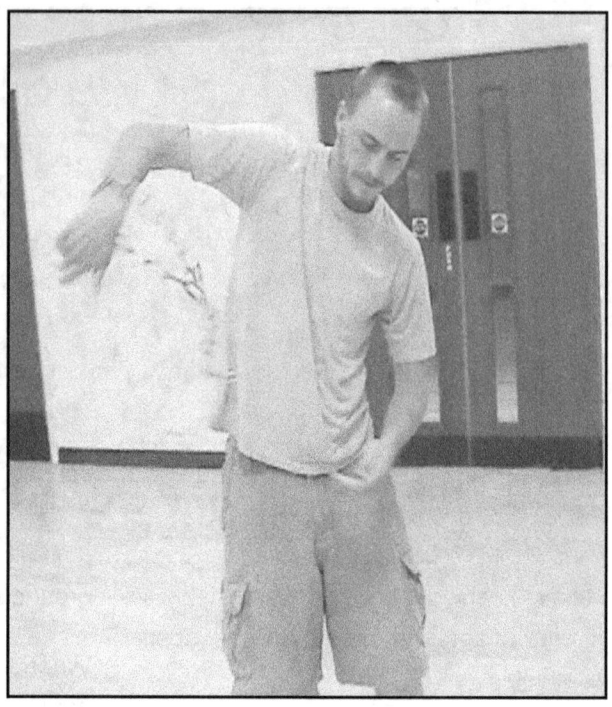

WORKING THE CHAIN

For these exercises you will need a length of chain, around three or four feet in length and medium weight. You can usually find them in most DIY stores. Obviously the chain is flexible and so calls for a higher degree of tactile awareness.

SOLO CHAIN

The first thing to do is to get used to the feel of the chain. Hold one end of the chain and feel the weight of it, move around a little and swing the chain slowly.

Now let the chain hang over your wrists and move your arms around a little. Raise and lower the hands, feeling how the chain slides up and down the arms. Place the chain across the wrists once more, now throw the chain up and catch it across the arms.

Following this, hold the end of the chain in one hand and begin making slow movements to swing it around. Of course, check your surroundings first! Make circles, figure eights or any kind of movement and see how the chain responds. Next, swing the chain from one side to another and "catch it" on the inside of your opposite arm. As the chain hits the arm, bring the elbow in towards the body in order to absorb the force, as we did with the stick earlier, then flick it back out.

Try the same movement against the body. Swing the chain quite hard and as it hits, move the body to absorb the strike, then flick it back out again. You can also do the same against the legs.

Finally, allow the chain to slide around the body. To start, place the chain across your shoulders. Rotate one side in order to get the chain to slide. Follow its movement with your body, moving it to gently guide the chain and stop it dropping to the floor. Try not to use the hands or to grab the chain.

CATCHING THE CHAIN

We can work similar drills with a partner. To start, stand opposite your partner with the chain resting on your forearms. Push out, throwing the chain across to your partner, who catches it on their forearms. Keep the arms and body soft as you catch, in effect you are absorbing the chain rather than "stiffly" catching it. You can experiment with changing level, moving around, etc

ABSORBING THE CHAIN

This exercise develops the absorbing aspect of the previous drill and helps the body become very sensitive to incoming force. The set up is to stand opposite your partner, holding one end of the chain. At first, your partner stands with arms outstretched. Swing the chain, under or overarm, so that it his your partner's arm. Your partner must rotate their arm in order to absorb the impact of the chain.

You will have to gauge that amount of force to put into the strike, especially at first. If you do not swing the chain hard enough, there is not enough energy to absorb. However, until your partner is used to the chain you shouldn't hit super-hard either!

Once happy that the arms are working okay, now have your partner raise their hands above their head and swing the chain to the body. On impact, your partner has to soften and turn the body in such a way to again absorb the impact of the chain. Again, start slow but with enough force in the chain to make your partner move!

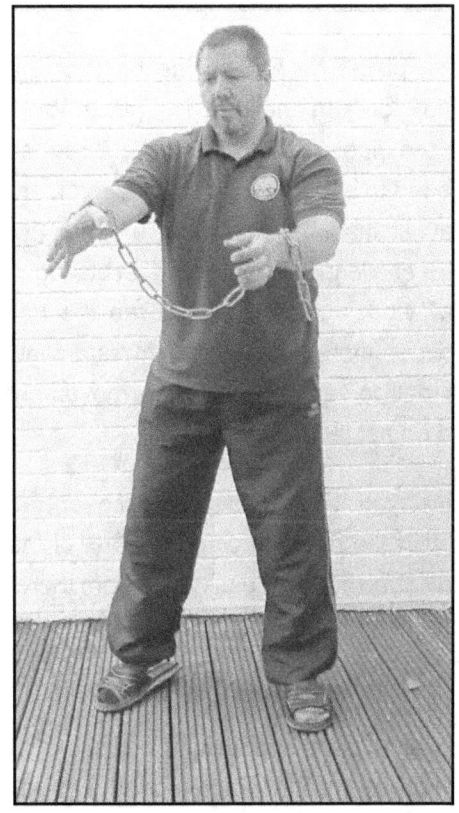

SOLO BALL TRAINING

A ball is another great tool to use for tactile training. Try out these drills with different size balls too- it might be a tennis ball, a football, beach ball or even larger!

To begin with, take the ball in both hands. Stay on the spot and rotate it using your hands and forearms, keeping contact with it at all times. Start walking while doing the same movements. After a while, start level changing, go into a squat, go all the way to the floor and up again, all while rotating the ball in the hands. Don't grab the ball and keep your touch as light as possible. Finally go to the floor and move around in the same way.

Next, place the ball on the back of the hand / forearm and keep it in place. Work on the spot first, moving the body as needed to not drop the ball. Once you are okay at that, begin walking around. For extra challenge, try changing levels too.
Now work against a wall. Trap the ball between the wall and your arm and allow the ball to rotate. Follow the movement and do not let the ball drop.

Once you have this idea, repeat but contact the ball with different parts of the body, the shoulder, back, etc. From there, try transferring the contact point from one part of the body to another, without letting the ball drop.
You should try and keep the touch light with these exercises and allow your body to follow the movement of the ball. You can also work the same method on the ground.

CARRYING THE BABY

This goes back to our earlier drills and simulates carrying a young child safely though a crowd. Repeat the crowd movement drills again, this time carrying a ball under your arm (or similar object, perhaps a doll?)

DON'T SPILL THE DRINKS!

Just as an off-shoot of the above drill and what can be a very useful skill! Repeat the same exercise but carrying drinks - a single cup or a tray of drinks. We advise plastic cups and water only!

PARTNER WORK

The ball drills also work very well in pairs or a larger group. Start with the back of hand contact in pairs. Both partners work to maintain contact with the ball. Static at first, then walking around and level changing again.

From here, try the same drill with different points of contact - shoulder, chest, back, etc. If you want to develop this drill further, try working in larger groups For example, have four people, each with the back of a hand touching a ball. Give the group a simple task to carry out, such as walking to a particular spot, or going to the ground and getting up again. This work is similar to that we previously described with the stick, but the ball gives a different feel.

USING YOUR ENVIRONMENT

As you may know from our other books, we are very keen on the concept of "the world is our gym." With this mindset, we should be able to see the training potential in everything and anything.

If we are talking tactile sensitivity in particular, then check how you interact on a physical level with your day to day environment. Try walking through trees or undergrowth as smoothly as you can, without disturbing any foliage.

If indoors, check how you move through doorways, or around furniture and other obstacles. Outside, in a crowd, check that you can move smoothly through without bumping into people. Try moving around inside your car, work from driver seat, to rear seat to front passenger seat. Experiment with different ways of getting in and out of your vehicle.

Each of these things will help develop your sense of touch. Doing so means that you are directly training and educating your body and nervous system. There is no conscious analysis going on, just pure reaction and response from your body. This helps develop the deep "body intelligence" that we spoke about earlier.

Outside of that, there are many hobbies and activities that will help with your general awareness, reactions and coordination. Horse riding is excellent for tactile sensitivity. We mostly control the horse through touch, a little but of sound and the occasional polo mint!

When riding, you really have to become part of the horse and vice versa. This sets up a lovely two way communication that is hard to replicate in many other situations.

Of course, you will also need to be aware of posture, applied strength and, every now and then, how to fall properly! Working with horses also gets you outdoors and has many other benefits. A veteran friend has been involved in working with horses as part of a program to help people undergoing PTSD, for example. It is entirely possible to build Systema drills around horses. A simple example is the walk and avoid drill. One person walks the horse towards a standing

partner, who simply has to move out of the way. Try the same drill with the target partner standing, kneeling and prone on the floor, the sensations really are quite different!

Further, more interactive drills are best carried out under the supervision of experienced Instructors and riders but I'm sure you can think of many possibilities.

THE POWER OF TOUCH

The use of touch in is the oldest method of healing. In the past, touch, as well as being used to demonstrate care and compassion, has been central to helping others. In the modern technical world of medicine, drugs, computers and machines, however, what place does touch have in health and healing? T h e skin is the largest organ of the body yet one we frequently taken for granted. Our first experiences in life are of touch, for most of us the nurturing touch of a mother.

That means that as humans we have a very deep seated response to touch.

Modern times has seen a movement away from direct contact with patients. Over time, this raised concerns. Research was carried out and it was found that hospital patients actually had improved recovery times when an element of direct personal contact was brought back into the nursing process. In that situation, touch can be categorised into four main areas, instrumental, protective, expressive and therapeutic.

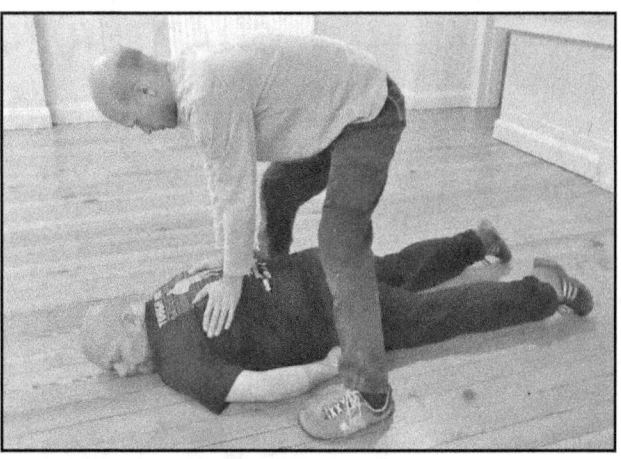

Instrumental touch is a result of performing procedures or direct care. For example, washing and dressing.

Protective touch is when a care giver touches a patient to prevent them from endangering themselves. For example preventing a patient from pulling out a nasogastric tube.

Expressive touch is that which conveys support and compassion. For example holding a patient's hand or placing a reassuring hand on someone's shoulder.

Therapeutic touch is specific work in order to facilitate relaxation and healing.

I just want to add in one more category to the above list and that is general human contact. This doesn't have to be physical, it might be someone asking "How are you?" In other words, the simple fact of being seen and noticed by another human being. We should not downplay the adverse effects of social isolation in the field of healing and overall health, physical and mental.

Systema encompasses many healing practices. Even just the solo training on breathing, movement, etc can have powerful healing effects as well as being preventative to future problems. Massage is one of the most important aspects of Systema health work. That can take many forms, from simply rubbing someone's shoulders to full massage routines, which can take up to an hour. This is something we will cover in more detail elsewhere, but for now I would just like you to consider the role of appropriate healing touch not only in Systema training but in everyday life.

CHAPTER FOUR
HEARING & SMELL

Both of these senses have played a vital role in earlier times, but also apply very much to modern self defence. Can you smell burning? The first indication of a fire, perhaps. Did you hear that shouting from up ahead? A sign of trouble round the corner of the street. These are quite obvious examples, there are many more. The point is that our senses act as a cohesive whole, each feeding information into the nervous system. To ignore or downplay any single one is a potentially dangerous error.

HOW WE HEAR

Hearing is a complex process of picking up sound and attaching meaning to it. The human ear is fully developed at birth, in fact even before birth infants respond to sound. The ear is divided into three parts, outer, middle and inner.

The outer ear comprises the ear canal and eardrum. Sound travels down the ear canal, striking the eardrum which causes it to vibrate.

The middle ear is behind the eardrum, and contains three small bones (ossicles). This chain of bones is connected to the eardrum at one end and to the opening to the inner ear at the other end.

Vibrations from the eardrum move the ossicles which, in turn, creates movement of the fluid within the inner ear, or cochlea. Movement of the fluid in the cochlea creates changes in tiny structures called hair cells. This movement of the hair cells sends electric signals from the inner ear up the auditory nerve to the brain. The brain then interprets these electrical signals as sound.

MY DOG HAS NO NOSE

Smell is a very direct sense. In order for us to smell something, molecules from that thing have to make it to our nose. Everything you smell, therefore, is giving off molecules, bread in the bakery, perfume, a piece of fruit for example. These molecules are generally light, volatile (easy to evaporate) chemicals that float through the air into

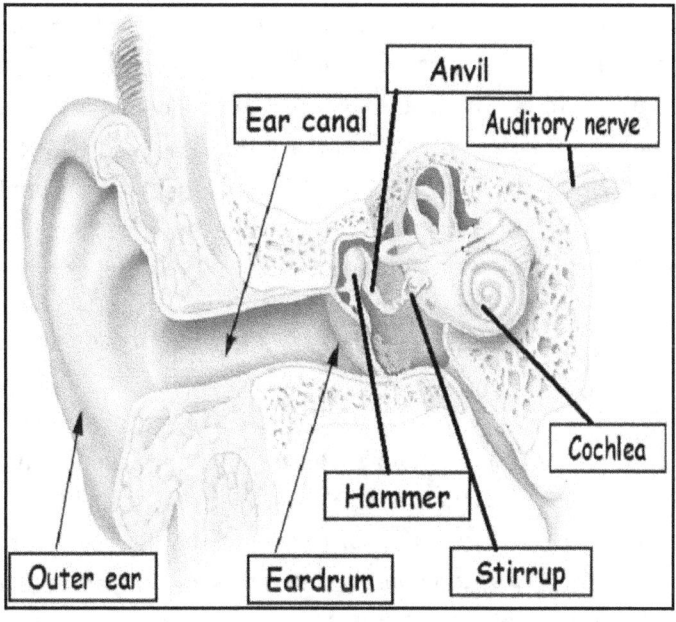

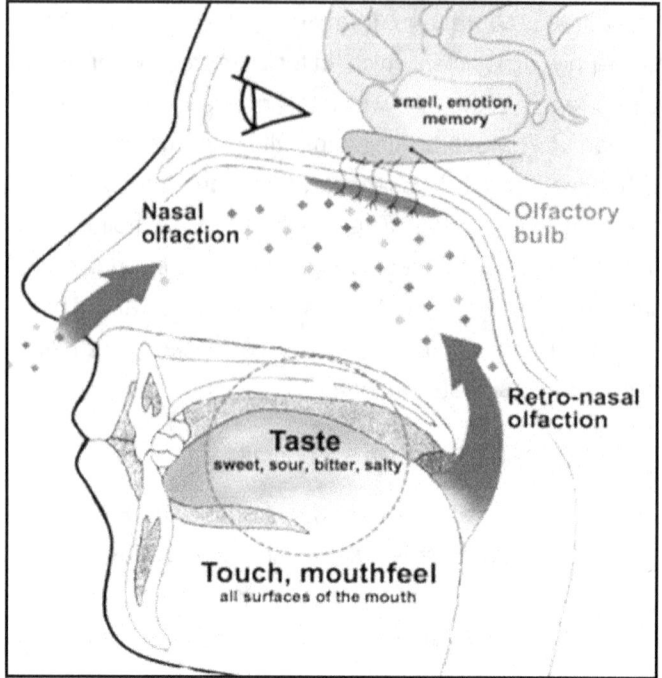

your nose. A piece of steel has no smell because nothing evaporates from it - steel is a non-volatile solid.

At the top of the nasal passages behind your nose is a small patch of special neurons about the size of a postage stamp. These neurons are unique in that they are out in the open where they can come into contact with the air. They have hair-like projections called cilia that increase their surface area. An odour molecule binds to these cilia to trigger the neuron and cause you to perceive a smell.

Humans can distinguish more than 10,000 different smells (odourants) detected by our olfactory receptor neurons. Each of these is encoded by a different gene and so recognises different odourants.

If your DNA is missing a gene or if the gene is damaged, it can cause you to be unable to detect a certain smell. For example, some people have no sense for the smell of camphor.

THE AMYGDALA

Before starting our drills, let's also take a look at the role of the amygdala. These are two clusters of nuclei that lie deep within the temporal lobe of each brain hemisphere. The term *amygdala* comes from Latin for almond because of the shape of the nuclei.

The amygdala is one of the most important components of the limbic system and has roles in emotion and behaviour, fear behaviour in particular. When we are exposed to a fearful stimulus, information is immediately sent to the amygdala, which then send signals to areas of the brain such as the hypothalamus to trigger a fight, flight or freeze response.

Information about fearful stimuli can reach the amygdala before we are even consciously aware of it. There is a pathway that runs from the thalamus to the amygdala, and sensory information about fearful stimuli is sent along this pathway to the amygdala before it is processed by the cortex. This means we can have a fear reaction before we even have time to think about it. A good example of this is a loud bang! Without thinking, we flinch and turn towards the sound.

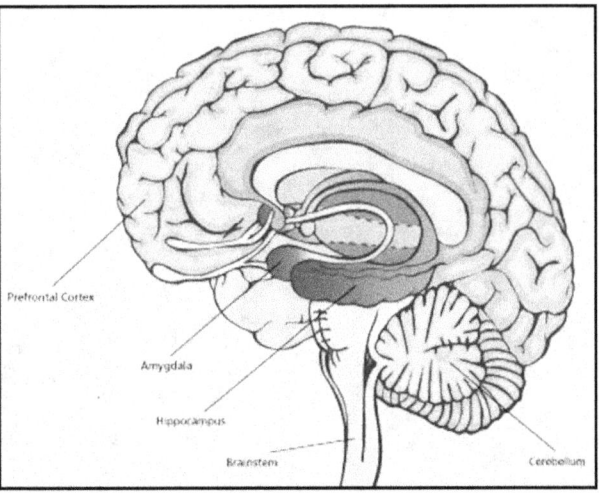

In addition to fear response, the amygdala is also involved in forming memories associated with fearful, or strongly emotional, events. It is also thought to play a role in anxiety. While fear is a response to a threat that is actually present, anxiety is the dread that comes from thinking about a potential threat, one that may not even materialise. Some studies suggest that the amygdala may be overactive in people with anxiety disorders. Recent research has also found that the amygdala is active not only when one is experiencing something threatening, but also during positive experiences. This has led researchers to review the role of the amygdala to also assigning positive value to stimuli as well as aiding in the formation of memories that have a strong emotional component, whether positive or negative.

SOUND DRILLS - NAMING THE STICK

Our first drills work on testing our response to sound. We begin with something easy - our own name! This drill calls on what is known as the "cocktail party effect" where, despite background noise, we have the capability to pick up the mention of our own name from across a crowded room.

The set up for the drill is the earlier Moving Circle stick exercise. The group of people begin moving randomly and throwing and catching the stick as before. However this time, before we throw the stick, we call the person's name that we are throwing it to. You can, of course, add in another stick or two in order to increase the intensity of the drill.

So the aim is to be not only visually, but also aurally aware. You may even find that you can focus less on vision, to some extent, as the primary stimulus for your action is now hearing. This is also a great "icebreaker" drill for groups, as everyone gets to know everyone else' name!

CLAP AND DROP

The next exercise works more on a specific reaction to a trigger sound and there are two basic versions. The first is to

have people walking or running around the training area. At a given sound signal, such as a clap, everyone has to go to the ground as quickly as they can. At the next signal, they get up quickly and resume their movement.

There are several variations to this drill. You can have people work in pairs, moving and staying in contact. At the signal, you must take your partner quickly but safely to the floor. This is a useful close protection drill and I'm sure you can see how other factors could be added in - drop your partner and draw a weapon, for example. But the primary issue is that as soon we hear that trigger sound, we respond in the appropriate way. We cannot, and should not, seek to override out natural "startle" reaction but what we are learning is to modulate a reaction as quickly as possible and not get stuck in that startle/freeze mode.

CLAP AND HIDE

The second version works best outdoors, particularly in a wooded or forest area. The leader walks through the terrain - along a path is ideal. The group follows, about ten paces behind. When the Instructor makes the signal (outdoors we use a whistle), the group has to conceal themselves as quickly as possible. The leader gives a second or so then turns. Any students visible can face some kind of penalty as an added incentive (a crack with the whip works well!)

KNIFE PUSH UPS

Here's another reaction drill that uses sound as the trigger. Partners face each other in push up position. They should be a few feet apart to begin with. Place a knife in-between. We recommend a training knife, for reasons which will become clear!

At the signal, a clap or shout "Go!", Each person has to grab the knife and make a single slash or stab at their partner. Whoever fails to get the knife must evade the attack. After that one attack, the knife is replaced and the drill repeated. Variations can include start distance, change of position, more people (try four people and two knives, for example).

SOUND INSTRUCTIONS

Another nice outdoor drill (or inside in a large area) is to have people guided by sound. Students are paired up and one of the pair is blindfolded. The sighted person leads their partner to a spot in the training area, then moves away and stands still nearby. They then must guide their partner to them by giving directions - "three steps forward, two left" - and so on. For an extra challenge, add obstacles into the mix, or work amongst trees and vegetation. As a variation the guider can be close by the walker and guide them verbally through a specific route, much as we did with the blindfold touch drill.

SOUND GUIDE

For a variation on the above, the guider now makes a noise rather than give instructions. It can be a clicking of fingers, a whistle, or similar. The blindfolded person has to find their partner guided purely by the sound. You can also decrease or increase the starting distance. The sound can be more or less regular. The guide can be static or moving.

If you have less space, or want another variant, then give each pair a specific sound which the seeker must distinguish from all the others.

SOUND AND POINT

Another close protection drill, or at least one more related to pistol work, is to have the person or group stand with eyes closed. The "sounder" moves some distance away and makes a loud noise. The group must immediately point to where they think the noise is coming from. They then open their eyes to see how close they are to the target.

Of course it is easy to substitute training guns / airsoft for pointing. Once you have the basic idea, you can also add in the Clap and Drop drill. So the group is moving around slowly, eyes closed. At the clap,

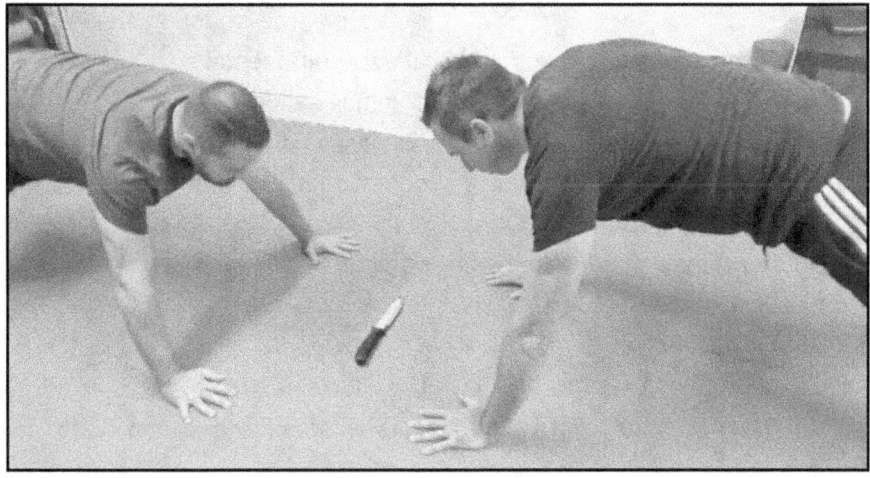

the must drop, draw, and point their gun towards the sounder.

Hopefully you can see through this how it is easy to begin "stacking" these drills to add in further levels of complexity or intensity.

IGNORING SOUND

All the previous exercises have used sound as our stimulus. But what if we have to ignore or blank out the sound? We can work on this in a few different ways.

One method is to train to loud music. This is quite common in modern gyms, where the music is usually loud and pumping. For me, this is counter-productive to our general Systema training. But it is good to experience it sometimes, in order to learn how to disassociate ourselves from what may be either a distraction or an over-stimulation to our nervous system. So train to loud music but try not to let it affect you. It is very easy to see how people start working to the rhythm of the music, or become a little agitated by it.

By contrast, you can try also working to some softer music, to see how that impacts the training. Best of all, buy my CDs and train to them all the time!

In this case, the sound is quite passive, it forms a background to our activities. This environment will be very familiar if you work security in a club, for example. The music may be so loud, that it not only affects your mental state but also hinders communication. So something else you can work on in training is non-verbal communication with a colleague (hand signals and gestures, perhaps) and communication with customers (gesture, touch, expression.)

Let's look next at more directed sound. This is something aimed specifically at you, and is usually a person shouting. Martial arts often train people for a fight - an attacker punches, so I do this or that movement. However, most fights start way before the first punch is thrown.

One component of this is verbal abuse, or just pure verbal aggression. If you have never experienced this, it can be overwhelming. As we have spoken about with the amygdala, that loud sound can cause a totally automatic reaction, usually a freeze. This is perhaps a hangover from the days of predator and prey. When you hear the lion roar, you freeze, hoping the lion doesn't see you and eats someone else instead! Most predators work off of movement (there's that peripheral vision again!) so freezing makes sense in that situation.

Where our predator is a loud, aggressive drunk, freezing makes less sense. In fact, it is usually seen as invitation to escalate. Aggression thrives on fear and the enemy of fear is movement. So we learn to react with positive movement to an aggressive sound, to break the freeze reaction.

One way to set this up is to give one person a simple task - move from A to B, make a text on their phone etc - while another screams, shouts and gives verbal abuse, up close and "in their face."

The first time you do this, you will likely get a "spike" in your nervous system. Overcome it with breathing and complete your task. If it helps, think of the unkind words as slaps or hits. You can tense against them, or you just relax and let them slip off. For the shouter/s it is also interesting to see how being aggressive affects your nervous system. See how your vision and breathing changes, and how much effort it takes to sustain a high level of aggression beyond a few minutes.

It is also fun to see how creative you can be with your insults! It is good beforehand if you decide which boundaries to set. There are all sorts of social and cultural

sensitivities at play when it comes to insulting language, and the aim is not to upset or offend. For those reasons this is also a drill best trained in private and not out where others may see or hear and get the wrong impression. Feel free to set whatever boundaries you feel appropriate, but also be aware that we must also live and work in the real world,and face the prospect of having to face such behaviour head on.

It is also easy to add a tactile aspect in to this type of drill, with the use of slaps to the body and face. You can use focus pads for this, or slap with the bare hand. For the full experience, have three people slap and shout as you maintain your cool!

MOVING QUIETLY

Another aspect of sound is those that we may make during our activities. In general, become aware of the type and volume of sounds you are putting out. Do you know one of those people who is constantly talking at twice the volume of everyone else? Perhaps they have a hearing issue. Perhaps they lack a little self awareness and are not aware they are bellowing!

So modulating the level of our voice is one thing but how do we learn to move quietly, particularly in conjunction with our earlier work on camouflage and "sneaking about." The first consideration is what is underfoot? Dry twigs, leaves, gravel are all difficult to move across quietly. The next thing to consider is footwear. Are you wearing something with a thick sole and not much bend, such as heavy boots? Or something that gives your foot more "feel" with the ground? The third thing is purpose. The usual reason for moving quietly is to sneak up or to hide, but there are other reasons for developing a quiet walk.

I illustrated this at a recent event, where the training space had a large sprung, wooden floor that gave a nice bounce beneath the feet. I noticed that when some people walked around, they made a loud thump-thump-thump sound. This is an indicator of tension in the lower body. I had the group stop and explained how this type of walk was the equivalent of "punching" the ground with every step. Imagine the shock going back up the legs and into your knees and hips! I next demonstrated how, despite being a lot heavier than many people there, I could walk quite normally across the floor with very little, if any, sound. I showed how this noise was largely due to tension in the hips and we ran through the following drills in order to fix the problem.

As tension is an issue here, the first thing is to practice some joint rotation and perhaps some stretching to get the lower body relaxed. Now think of the mechanics of how you walk. People often push up from the floor to raise the foot and reverse the process to roll the foot back down onto the floor. Instead, rotate the hip to lift the foot. If you do this correctly, the whole sole of the foot will leave the ground in one go. Now rotate the hip again to bring the foot back to the floor, the whole sole at once.

It is a good idea to exaggerate this

movement at first. You can practice stepping over a low obstacle, such as a box or low fence, backwards and forwards. Then move around your training space for bit, with a big hip rotation - what we call the Charlie Chaplin walk! Over time, refine the movement down until it becomes your standard method of walking. You will find that not only do you move more quietly, but you will experience far less impact on your joints.

NINJA WALK

I've seen and experienced a few different methods of "quiet stepping." Some of them were extremely elaborate, involving rather theatrical high knee movements and lots of crouching and tension in the upper body. Instead, we should be able to walk in a reasonably normal and natural way, if we are using our legs correctly. Now, context is key of course, but assuming we are in some kind of creeping up to or away from situation let's look at a few useful tips for walking quietly.

If you want to experience real foot sensitivity, then walk around in different environments barefoot. Obviously, exercise caution, but if you practice this regularly, indoors and outdoors, you will certainly increase feeling in your step. The next thing is to experiment working with placing different areas of the foot down first - the heel, toes, outside edges. From that initial contact point roll down/across into full contact with the ground.

Also, think about your weighting. To get maximum sensitivity, though it is a slower walk, try a 100% weight shift. In other words, place all the weight in the supporting leg, lift the other and closely place the foot down without any weight shift. Only when the moving foot is full down does the weight shift - 100% again.

Another method to try is the "gliding" step. For this, the foot remains in contact with the ground and slides across it to move around. This works best on smooth surfaces, of course and does cut down on the potential heavy weight shift of a conventional step.

Generally speaking you want to make sure you keep your steps quite short. Overextending the stepping leg may lead to loss of balance. The upper body should be relaxed, try and avoid hunching over. Height of your stance can vary according to the situation. This is where your previous training in duck walks will pay off!

Another low stealth option is the Knee Walk that forms part of Systema ground movement. Although there is an element of dragging the leg involved, this method keeps your profile low, your hands free and your speed under control. From here you can also transition very quickly to standing or fully prone.

CREEPING AND CRAWLING

Another option for stealth is to drop down on all fours, or even go full body crawl. This may be useful where there is little or no high cover and you want to keep a low profile. The downside is that crawling can be a lot slower than walking and also more demanding on the body.

In a way, we can think oft this as going back to the very roots of our movement - crawling around on the floor! At its most basic level, lay flat on the ground and propel yourself forward by moving your arms and legs. You can work off of your front, back, or sides. To keep the body off the ground, get into plank position and move by bringing the knee up the elbow and walking forwards. The key here is to use minimal tension, move the leg from the hip and to keep the body level to the floor in order to keep the profile low

Of course, this type of work is the staple of much Systema ground movement, so I won't go into any more detail here. Simply to add, from a stealth point of view, to be aware of what lays ahead and underneath.

Practicing on a nice wooden floor is one thing, crawling across a muddy (or worse!) field is something else.

In short, there is no one "quiet" method of moving because the activity is context sensitive. Stick to the major principles of control, breathing and relaxation, then adapt other factors as necessary. Just one other point to make, which we touched on earlier - check your kit! Having equipment that jangles is not good. Ditto trousers that swish as they rub together. And it should be obvious, but you'd be surprised....switch off your mobile phone!

STEALTH DRILLS

Many of the previous hiding type drills are easily adapted to help us train moving quietly. For example, one partner is blindfold and another has to creep up on them. If the blindfoldee hears a noise, they call "stop" and point to where they think the stalker is.

Of course, terrain is the main variation here. It's good to practice this on a range different surfaces - grass, gravel, twigs and leaves and so on. Also consider background noise. Is there heavy traffic, a rainstorm and so on.

WORKING WITH SMELL

Let's now take a look at using our sense of smell in training. Smell is often overlooked as a useful sense yet we use it far more often than we may think. Smell is very closely tied in to our memory. I'm sure you have all experienced a smell that took you suddenly back to childhood. It may have been cut grass, or wood smoke, or a particular perfume. Immediately, we are transported back in time. This is because incoming smells are processed by the olfactory bulb, which has direct connections to both the amygdala and the hippocampus, two brain areas strongly implicated in emotion and memory. Interestingly, visual, and tactile information does not pass through these brain areas. This may be why smell, more than any other sense, is so successful at triggering memories.

A downside of that is that smells may also trigger negative thoughts and emotions, if they are tied in to a previous stressful or traumatic situation. This has particularly been shown to be the case with PTSD sufferers. One other interesting fact is that our perception of what we are smelling can be altered by what we *think* we are smelling! A study carried out in 2001 found that participants rated an identical odour as more pleasant when it was presented with a positive label (*parmesan cheese*) rather than a negative label (*vomit*).

WHAT'S THAT SMELL?

Our first drill is very simple. Have a person close their eyes. Present a variety of things for them to smell and they have to say what each one is. Some will be obvious, a flower, an onion. Other things may be less obvious. Experiment with distance and different positions. Given the study above, also try telling the smeller that the item is something different before they have to guess. Incidentally, when trying to identify a particular smell, you may find it useful work with a shallow sniff rather than a long deep inhalation.

THE SMELL LINE

Participants are blindfolded and take up position in a row at one end of the training space. You need a large area for this. At a point along the length of the space, say about halfway, we set up a "smell line."

We do this by burning a bundle or two of incense sticks and walking in a straight line across the width of the space. Now have the participants walk the length of the space. They must try and detect where the "smell line" is. Once they think they are there, they can stop and remove the blindfold to see how close they are.

FOLLOW /TRACK THE SMELL

Once again, participants are blindfolded. This time, their sighted partner leads, holding incense sticks or anything that gives off a clear odour. The blindfoldee has to remain close and follow the smell. Again, you can work in obstacles if required. You can also have people track a smell, in the same way as our earlier tracking drills, but using a smell. Use incense or similar to create a smell. The seeker must find and follow it to the source. You can complicate this by having several pairs or groups working in the same space, each with a different smell!

Of course, working any of the above drills outdoors is somewhat dependent on the weather. A strong wind and rain make the drill somewhat challenging!

IMPROVING YOUR SENSE OF SMELL

In general, be more attentive to the smells you encounter in everyday life. In the same way as our visual observations, be aware of things that seem out of place or are absent. You can go further and adopt a specific training regime. Start by choosing four smells that you are fond of, say, fresh coffee, bread, shampoo, a scented oil. Take a minute to smell each one individually to stimulate the receptors inside your nose. Repeat this four to six times every day.

Evidence suggests that even visualising smells can help to improve your sense of smell. So take some time each day to imagine your favourite scents. There is also evidence to suggest that prolonged exposure to bad odour can numb our ability to smell so try to avoid prolonged exposure to strong smells. If you do have to be around them, consider wearing a mask to help filter them out.

Our sense of smell and taste are very closely linked. We can stimulate our taste buds by mixing up our diet. Try new recipes, foods you don't normally eat. Eat only fresh ingredients as much as possible and avoid processed foods. These usually contain a lot of sugar, salt, chemicals and artificial ingredients, which can negatively affect our sense of taste.

CHAPTER FIVE
THE SIXTH SENSES

We have covered four of the main five senses but there are more - some say seven, some nine, some count up to twelve or even more. The traditional model of five senses, sight, hearing, taste, smell, and touch, dates back more than 2000 years. This model is so ingrained in our culture that any additional method of perception is usually called "a sixth sense".

However, by any objective measure, humans actually possess more than five senses. The five senses model can serve as a helpful framework for early learning, but beyond that is somewhat limited. Unfortunately, there is no universal agreement as to how many senses humans actually have. The count can vary depending upon how you define the word *sense*. Another problem is that as you add more senses to the list, the boundaries between them blurs, and therefore the count depends upon where you decide to draw those boundaries.

Added to that is the fact that some animals possess senses that humans do not. For all of these reasons, experts disagree as to how many senses there actually are. So without a general consensus as to what model should replace the five senses, it retains its popularity. A key characteristic of this model is that all the senses are related to interacting with external phenomena. We see, hear, smell, taste, and touch the things around us. But if we limit our count to senses that detect external phenomena only, our list is quite limited, though it will still be more than five. One approach is to itemize the categories of detectable phenomena that originate outside the body

LIGHT (EM RADIATION)

Our eyes detect light, or more precisely, they detect a limited range of frequencies in the spectrum of electromagnetic radiation. Several species of animal have the ability to see frequencies of light into the ultraviolet, which humans cannot see. Some types of snake can detect infrared light using "pit organs" in their heads, allowing them to detect the body heat of their prey. Of course, as already discussed, detecting something with the sense organs is only the first step. The information is then relayed to the brain via neural pathways, and the brain assembles and interprets that information. It is our brain that sees patterns, colours, and movement in the data sent from the eyes.

SOUND (VIBRATION)

Our ears detect sound waves in the air, within a certain range of frequencies. As we have two ears, we have a sense of what direction a sound is coming from.

Some animals are skilled at detecting vibrations in other media besides air. Animals that live in water will, of course, detect sounds waves in water. Other animals can detect vibrations in more solid objects, a spider in its web, for example. Elephants are able to detect and interpret vibrations coming through the ground. We all know that bats have the ability to "see" their surroundings through echo-location. They can determine the location and shape of nearby objects by detecting sounds waves bouncing off of them.

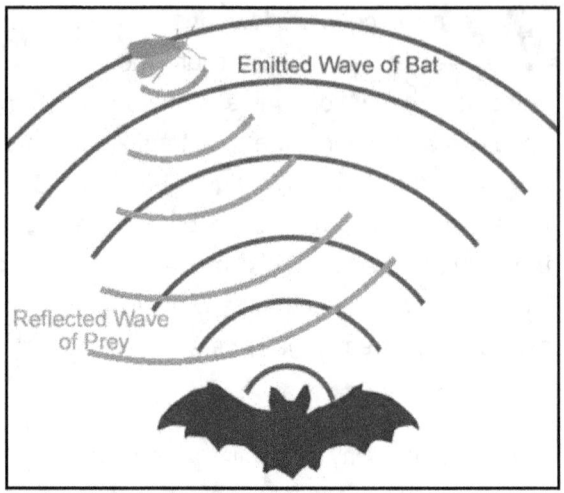

Some claim that humans can actually develop a similar capability, using mouth clicks. The organization *World Access for the Blind*, under the guidance of Daniel Kish, leads blind teenagers hiking through the wilderness, with a technique that he calls Flash Sonar. Kish has been blind since he was a baby and learned to make palatal clicks with his tongue when he was still a child. This is a method you may wish to explore further as part of the blindfold training we covered eariler.

ODOURS (MOLECULES)

Our senses of smell and taste are both based on detecting molecules of various substances that come in contact with our bodies via nose and mouth. There are five distinct types of taste buds, while the nose includes around 400 distinct olfactory receptors. This results in a huge amount of possible combinations, allowing us to detect millions of distinct odors.

We know that there are many animals that smell with their noses and taste with their mouths. The surprise is that certain creatures can taste or smell with other sense organs. Some insects can detect airborne molecules with their antennae, in effect using them to smell. Some insects can detect molecules in materials that they touch with their feet, meaning that they have a sense of taste in their feet.

TOUCH (DIRECT CONTACT)

Receptors in our skin allow us to determine when our body comes into contact with an external object. The sense of touch can be extended over some distance by the use of a long, slender appendage, such as a cat's whiskers. In many cases, the same antennae contain other kinds of sense receptors, allowing for smell, taste, hearing or other capabilities.

TEMPERATURE (HEAT AND COLD)

Another type of receptor detects changes in skin temperature. Our skin is heated or cooled by contact with the air or other objects, and also by exchange of radiant energy (primarily infrared radiation). Receptors detect the change and feed the information back to the brain. So when we feel the heat of a fire, it is not by directly detecting the radiant energy contacting the skin, but by detecting the resulting change in skin temperature. Of course, when it comes to temperature, cold water dousing and similar are very much a part of Systema training and great health practices!

GRAVITY & ACCELERATION

Our ability to detect gravity and acceleration is commonly described as our sense of balance. For this we rely upon the semi-circular canals in our inner ears. Gravity is a phenomenon that originates outside of our bodies, though only thing we learn from detecting it is which way is *up*. This allows us to maintain our bodies in an upright position, even when our eyes are closed.

This is a very real sense, with an easily identified sense organ and yet the sense of balance is not included in our traditional FS model - partly because the model predates our understanding of the role of the semi-circular canals.

MAGNETIC FIELDS

A recent study suggests that humans can subconsciously sense the Earth's magnetic field, a capability, called *magnetoreception*. Regardless, we know that many kinds of animals are able to detect magnetic fields. This results in a powerful sense of direction (especially north and south). The best-known examples of this phenomenon are migrating birds.

ELECTRICAL FIELDS (STATIC)

Many sea animals have the ability to sense changes in the electric field in their immediate vicinity. Sharks, dolphins and rays, for example. This sense is used to identify prey and other nearby objects.

For animals that live in air, the direct sensing of electric fields is not possible. However, some animals, including humans, can detect static charges through indirect means. I'm sure we've all experienced the hair on our arms standing up, for example. This ability could be categorized as an extension to our sense of touch.

So far we have identified eight detectable external phenomena - nine if you separate airborne molecules (smell) from non-airborne (taste). Each of these phenomena corresponds to a specific sense in various animals. Humans have seven of these nine senses, therefore, any model of the senses should list at least those seven. But this is only complete if we define the word *sense* to mean purely the detection of external phenomena, In fact, our bodies have additional sense receptors beyond the ones we have catalogued so far that provide information about our own bodies. The most obvious example is our sense of pain, triggered by pain receptors located not just in our skin, but also deeper within our bodies.

Think how we are also aware of other internal phenomena, such as being hungry or needing to go to the bathroom. All of these require some sort of sensor within the body in order to detect the issue. The sensors, in turn, send messages to the brain via the nervous system.

Therefore, we could legitimately refer to a sense of hunger, a sense of thirst, or a sense of being full. In fact, scientists have catalogued a long list of such internal senses. If we were to include all of these in our list, then we could easily reach twenty or more distinct human senses.

An important sense only recently been explored in the mainstream is proprioception. This is the sense of knowing how the various parts of your body are positioned, without relying on sight or touch. A demonstration of this is to close your eyes, then reach up and touch your nose. However, to just explain proprioception as a sense of location would be misleading, as the receptors in our muscles, tendons, and joints do not actually sense the location of our limbs in space. Instead, they detect the degree of muscle flexion and the angles of the joints. This allows the brain to deduce the position of the body and each of the limbs. So a better term may be *a sense of position*. We can now expand our list of human senses to:

Sight
Hearing
Smell
Taste
Touch
Balance
Temperature
Pain
Proprioception

We should always remember that while the science models we use are helpful tools for learning, they are usually a simplified approximation of reality, rather than a perfect reflection. Therefore we should not confuse our models with absolute truth. And that brings me on to the last of the "Sixth Senses", a controversial topic in mainstream circles - intuition.

HUMAN INTUITION

Intuition is defined as *the ability to understand something instinctively, without the need for conscious reasoning.*

It is quite often referred to as gut instinct, working on a hunch, survival instinct, premonition or perhaps the subconcsious. I doubt there are any of us that have not experienced this at some time - that tingling in the neck when someone is looking at you from behind. The feeling that something is "not quite right". Or a sponataneous action that seems to come out of nowhere but is exactly the right thing to do in a situation.

So intuition actually becomes something of an umbrella term for a wide range of actions and situations. In some cases, it will be our senses working in such away that we are not really aware of. It may also be a combination of that and previous experience, skill and so on. It might just be good or bad luck! As far as the latter goes, I'm with the old saying *"the more I train, the luckier I get!"* Given, of course, the right type of training.

Anyone who has been training in Systema for a while will be aware of the emphasis placed on natural movement and instinctive reactions in the work.

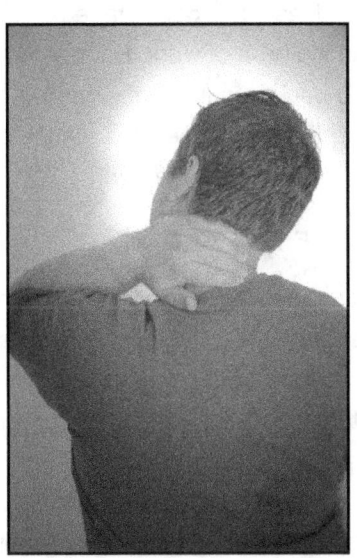

Detractors may denigrate this as "magic" or fantasy. In fact, many new scientific studies are confirming that the ability to understand something instinctively can not only inform but actually improve our decision making.

Of course, everyone who goes through the training, soon realises how real and un-mystical this type of work is. It is simply another layer of awareness, one that runs the risk of being lost or subsumed in the digital age, where we interact more and more with machines rather than humans.

Again, we could go off on several different tangents on this subject and I encourage you to research, test and train as much as you can. But for the purposes of this book, I'll keep our work on intuition to a fairly narrow band. This will give you some good ideas to get started in this fascinating area of work. But prior to that, let's go back to our list of nine and begin working through those other sense areas we have not yet touched on.

BALANCE TRAINING

Gravity is acting upon us permanenty (unless you are reading this in space!). Even while standing still, our body is contstantly re-adjusting in order to maintain our upright position. Apparently simple things, such as standing and walking well are vital aspects of training. They can be overlooked by people wanting to get quickly onto the "good stuff" but anything you do is only as strong as your foundation. If your basic posture and locomotion are lacking, progress will be limited.

In traditional Eastern martial arts, this work takes the form of stance training. Long minutes endured in set positions that teach the body optimum structure, position and relaxation. Systema is more about movement so, while we may occasionally use a static posture, we tend to focus on movement. To this end, we tend to use walking as our "stance work." In some classes we may practice walking for up to thrity minutes.It may sound odd or dull, but the results are profound and feed into all the other work. The same goes for rolling and ground movement, or course, both other ways of working with gravity.

I've spoken a little about a walking method already, so won't go any more into that

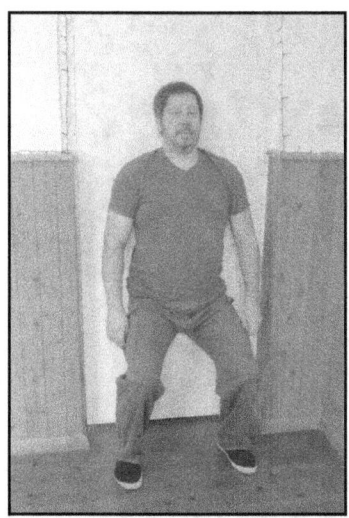

here. Suffice to say, for now, that when standing still or walking, maintain a good overall awareness of posture and tension. In theory, we should be able to hold any "normal" position cofortably for a period of time.However, this is very much dependent on our freedom of movement, core strength and relaxation. In some parts of the world it is normal for people to sit in a low squat for hours at atime. In other places, people can barely manage to get into that position, let alone stay there. But let's start with something very simple - standing still!

STAND STRAIGHT

Stand with feet shoulder width, spine straight. First thing, check yourself for excess tension. Shrug and release the shoulders a few times, shake the limbs, rotate the hips a little. Check in a mirror if you can, to make sure that shoulders and hips are level and your back is upright and not leaning.

You can also use a wall to check your posture, place your back against it and squat a little. You should have good contact between your wall and your back all the way down. Check for any large gaps and correct.

Try and be aware in your daily life, when standing, sitting or walking, of your posture. Pay special attention if you regularly carry something such as a bag or case, seehow it can distort your posture. Every now and then, go into a squat, either against the wall or unsupported. You can try a full squat or the heel raised version. Get used to resting in thsi position in class, between exercises.

RAISE A LEG

From a normal standing position, simply lift one knee. It doesn't have to be high at first, just whatever you are comfortable with. Check again for posture and tension. Balance is easier if you are relaxed. Just

a little tension in the supporting leg, where neccesary, but especially work to relax the upper body. If everything is okay, raise the knee higher, move your arms around or, for a further challenge, close your eyes.

ROUND THE CLOCK

Once comfortable in the above position, start moving the lifted leg around. Imagine you are standing at the centre of a clock. Slowly push the lifted foot out to 12, 3, 6 and 9 o clock. Again, you can adjust the height and extension of the leg as required, plus close the eyes as before.

FOUR KICKS

You can try the above exercise in a group. Four partners stand around you and you have to extend and push each with your kicking leg. Don't put the foot down until you have touched each person. You can work to just touch or, if you also want to start developing kicks, push them away with your foot.

BALANCE PUSH

While standing with one leg raised, have your partner give you a push to the body. It shouldn't be too hard at first but should be firm. Relax the body to absorb the push without losing your balance! If at first you need it, it's okay to hold onto to your partner or something else for a little support.

BALANCE PAIRS

This time, we are both working. Make contact at the forearms. Each person raises one leg. You now try and unbalance your partner while maintaining your own balance. To start, you can keep this drill fairly sedate. As you progress, become more active with the leg. Use it to try and hook your partner's leg, for example, or to work (with care) against the supporting leg.

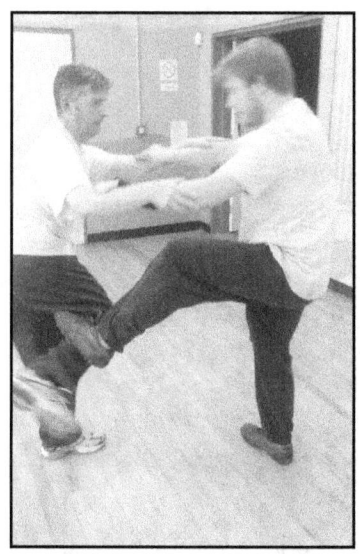

SQUAT PUSH

For this one, both partners get into a squat position, you can experiemnt working with heels down or heels up. Make contact with the palms at first and see if you can unbalance your partner. Then you can work with forearm contact, similar to the sticky hands type exercises we did earlier. Remember, the goal is to take your partner's balance while maintaining your own.

BALANCE GROUPS

Both the above exercises can also be worked in groups of three or four. Maintain contact at some point, usually the hands and arms, and work the same way. Now you have to learn with more than one incoming force. One key to doing this is relaxation, so if you are finding these drill difficult, then here's a simple partner drill to try.

PULL AND SINK

Stand in a normal position, with your feet around shoulder width. Your partner takes your wrist and pulls it out straight. Your aim is to sink, keeping the back straight and so maintain your balance. The key really is learn how to relax down into the pull. Check that you are not leaning back by having your partner suddenly let go of your wrist. If you fall, you were leaning!

WOBBLE BOARD

A good solo piece of balance training kit is a wobble board. You can buy these ready made, or improvise with items you may have around the house, such as a large ball. Be aware of safety, make sure you have a nice space to fall into!

At first simply stand upright and get a feel for the board. Then you can start doing things like moving your arms,

riasing afoot and so on. For more of a challenge, try doing squats or even pistol squats on the board (providing you can first do them normally!)

STAND ON A FRIEND

An alernative to a board is to stand on a friend! This is one part of our standard massage routine, the back walk and so on and so is also good preparation for that. Again, start with normal position, then raise a leg, squat, etc. Work both back and front and be mindful of where you place your feet and your partner's reactions. For the person being stood upon, try using selective tension under your parnter's feet to give them some support.

WALK THE LINE

A tightrope or similar is another great bit of kit for training balance. You can buy low training ropes that have a guide rope, or again, safely improvise with items available. The important thing is not to go high at first! You will also find how you step and place the feet is very important in this drill, as well as having to deal with the movement of the rope. Again, the key to balance here is relaxing and lowering the centre of gravity, without leaning!

WALK THE PLANK

In the absence of boards or lines, you can test balance by walking along a narrow plank or piece of wood. You can turn a gym bench upside down, for example, and use that. See if you can get access to an assault course, or even some types of playground equipment. Remember, the wold is your gym!

In all the above cases, if safe, you can also work with a partner applying pushes or pulls as you are on the equipment, or blend in our earlier drills of dodging or catching TBs.

BEYOND BALANCE

A big part of understanding balance is also knowing when it is gone. Trying to fight gravity is a futile exercise, at least without mechanical assistance! This leads us into falling and rolling work, another topic in itself, but I just wanted to explain this following drill as it demonstrates a very important aspect of Systema training - acceptance.

A common injury resulting from falls is a broken wrist /forearm. This is due to people outstretching the arm in order to prevent the fall. Unfortunately, the fall is already happening! This is where the concept of acceptance comes into play. By all means, struggle to maintain your balance but once it's gone, accept that it has gone. It is time, then, to go into falling mode. Allow the body to relax and organise itself to ensure a soft as possible landing.

There are many ways to practice this, leading all the way up to the more tactical "throwing from the throw" drills. For now, however, we will stick with something simple. You stand on one leg, your partner takes your wrist as before. This time, rather than pull in a staight line, your parnter is more actively trying to takeyour balance.

Maintain form as much as possible but once it is broken, accept and go into a fall - your partner should release your wrist at this point. As skills improve, add more movement into the drill. Walk, while your partner holds your wrist and again tries to throw you. Your partner can also work to make the falls more challenging, adding in trips and more spiral movements.

This is a simple exercise but contains so many important lessons. I advise you give it serious attention as the skills absorbed here will serve you very well in all other aspects of your work.

EXTERNAL BALANCE

Another aspect of balance is to work with objects. The simplest is to get a stick and balance it, end first, in the hand. Stay still

at first, then start moving around, change level, work in pairs, passing the stick back and forth etc.

PAIN CONTROL

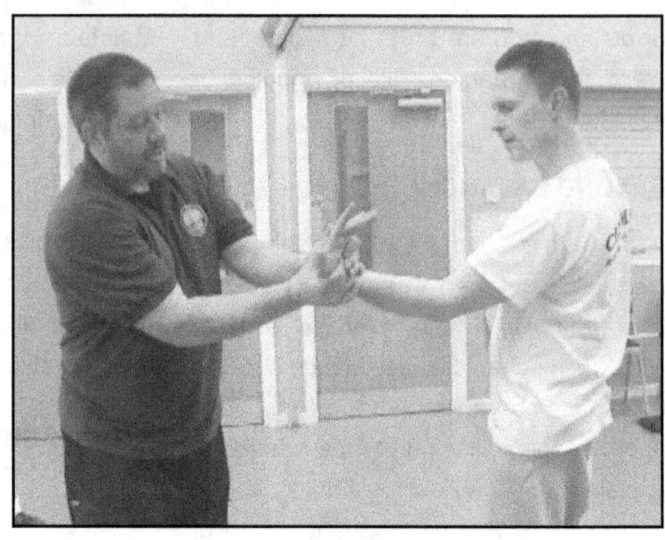

This is another big subject, relating to fear and tension especially. There is also an element of the idea of acceptance that we previously mentioned. Pain is there for a reason, it informs us that something is wrong. People sometimes assume that pain control is about denying the pain, but that is not the point. The point of our training is to accept the pain, understand it, but not let it control us. This does not mean that we willingly go along with the situation that is causing the pain - though in some cases we may have no choice. What it does mean that we are able to regulate how we deal with the pain, away from a purely fear based reaction to a controlled response.

There are many levels and layers to this work, again I will give you a good base level set of drills that you can develop further, should you wish. We will be working with locks as our primary "instruments of pain", as these are easily applied and controlled.

All pain work should be applied slowly and incrementally. The aim is to cause pain, not to damage or injure. If the person undergoing the drill says stop, then everyone stops immediately. There should be no judgement involved, no macho posturing, no negativity. This should be a positive experience for all concerned, especially at the deeper, more intense levels of this type of work.

You may find that this type of work, particularly when it moves to the striking methods, can evoke a strong emotional response in people. This may manifest in several ways, it is often tears, sometime laughing, or maybe even aggression. This is nothing to be concerned about, generally it's just a release of emotions that have been locked into the muscles. Now, that may be an indication of deeper issues which should be addressed in the appropriate way. It may also just be symptom of the fear leaving the body. Don't go looking for a response, there's nothing worse than an over-zealous

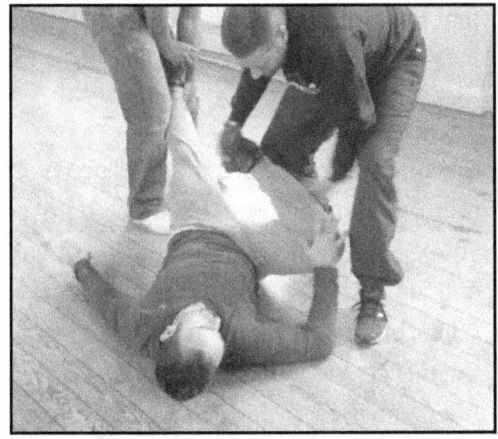

eagerness to heal everyone with your punches!

By the same token, be prepared for this possiblity. Be supportive, give the person space if they need it or resassurance if that helps. This is something that develops with experience and perhaps the most important experience is going through that process yourself. This is one reason why it is so important to get regular training with the top teachers, Mikahil and Vladimir are masters of giving you just what you need to help you address your issues.

So, back to our ground level drill. We will start in pairs. One person stands, sits or lays on the floor. Their partner takes an arm and starts applying a lock. We might start with the wrist. Slowly bend the fingers towards the inner forearm in order to apply pressure to the wrist.

The person receiving the lock must relax and allow it to come on. When the pain becomes more intense, relax even further and begin to burst breath. This is your partner's cue to hold the lock where it is, maintain the pressure and do not apply any more. Listen to the breathing. If it regulates back to normal, you can continue with a little more pressure, until you hit the burst breathing stage again. Hold for a while, then slowly release.

Work with the arms and legs. You might also like to work on nerve points, or apply a pinch or two, anything that will cause discomfort. In all cases, be aware of your partner's condition, listen epsecially to the breathing. If they say stop, you stop!

From this, you can move onto working with two, four, even five partners. Each takes a limb or works on some other part of the body. Once again, the recipient must realx, accept the pain and relax against it using the breathing. This all sounds quite simple but can be far from

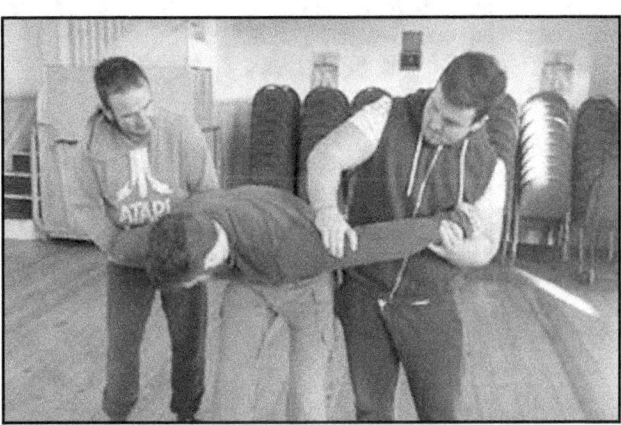

easy. First of all, how does doing a bit of breathing take away the pain? Well, it doesn't. The pain is information from our nervous system. I've been involved in other methods of pain control that work from the opposite perspective. They seek to deaden or de-sensitize the pain receptors at the surface. This type of work usually involves repetitive striking of the relevant body part in order to "deaden the nerves". I'll leave you to draw your own conculsions on the health implications of that approach.

Instead, we are accepting the information. Then, what to do with it? There is an old saying *pain is compulsory, suffering is optional*. In other words, we can allow the incoming information to give us an emotional spike, flood the system with fear and so tense up against the incoming force. But the force is already there, the lock is already on. This is analagous to putting your arm out to stop the fall mentioned earlier. I never had a lock yet that felt better if I applied tension against it. Quite the reverse in fact, it increases the pain.

So, breathe, relax, accept the discomfort, it is only temporay and will not damage you. Focus your mind on your breathing, nothing else. Don't feel that you have to burst breath, only do so if neccesary. Scientific studies show that correct breathing has a profound effect on our pain threshold. They also show that swearing helps with pain relief. Well, it's a type of breathing! Theories as to why this occurs vary but the practical effect is easy to test with the above drills.

In terms of awareness, this type of work gives us a very good tool for monitoring our internal emotional state, levels of tension and so on. Of course, this also sets the groundwork for later drills on escaping and countering locks and so on, all of which work better from a response rather than a reaction.

PROPRIOCEPTION DRILLS

As we have already mentioned, proprioception, or kinesthesia, is the sense that lets us perceive the location, movement, and action of parts of the body. It enables us to judge limb movement and position, force, heaviness, and so on. It combines with other senses to locate external objects relative to the body and contributes to body image.

The word *proprioception* comes from the Latin, meaning unconscious perception of movement. It is carried out by internal sensors, such as the muscle spindle stretch receptor and Golgi tendon organ. The vestibular system in the brain is a key component in proprioception and also in maintaining static, mixed, or dynamic balance.

Proprioception is occasionally impaired, especially when one is tired or, perhaps "under the influence". This is why drunk people bump into things! Similar effects can sometimes occur during epilepsy or migraine attacks. These effects are thought to arise from abnormal stimulation of the part of the parietal cortex of the brain involved with integrating information from different parts of the body.

The proprioceptive sense is often unnoticed, because we constantly adapt to a present stimulus; this is known as habituation, desensitization, or adaptation. It means that proprioceptive sensory impressions disappear, just as a scent can disappear over time. One practical advantage of this is that unnoticed sensations can continue in the background while our attention can move to something else.

In many ways, our Systema training addresses these unconscious elements by bringing attention to them, usually by practicing a new movement with a focus on how it feels to move in the new way. It should be obvious that high level movement requires a high level of body sense. For example, there is no way to perfrom a backflip onto a narrow balance beam without knowing exactly what your body is doing at all times! That accurate body sense is also essential for feeling good in your body and being free of pain. The key to this are the body maps we discussed earlier, in our section on the

Homonculus. Another interesting thing is that the brain will even devote space to representing inanimate objects which we need to sense and control, such as a cricket bat, tool or a hat.

Confused body maps can cause pain. Researchers have found that they can cause pain in subjects by creating unusual sensory illusions using mirrors or other perceptual tricks. These illusions effectively create a "sensory motor mismatch", a conflict in the information represented by the brain maps. The result is often pain. On the basis of these and other experiments, many experts believe that gaps, smudges, or other inaccuracies in the body maps can be a significant contributing factor in many chronic pain conditions, and that fixing these problems is a potential way to cure pain.

Our body maps are built by movement and are constantly being updated to reflect the current situation. In order to make long term or permanent changes in your maps, you need to place demands on them consistently over a period of time. When a certain body part or movement is used repeatedly in a coordinated and mindful fashion, there are actual physical and observable changes in the part of the brain that controls that body part or movement. This is part of the reason why you get better at what you practice!

Movements that are most likely to lead to changes in the quality of the maps are those that are curious, exploratory, novel, interesting, rich in sensory input, slow, mindful, playful. Sound familiar?

Lack of movement will reverse this process. If you fail to move in a certain way for a period of time, you lose the ability to accurately sense and control that movement. This is called *sensory motor amnesia*. The brain's body maps get less clear. Imagine if the pelvis or spine is never moved through its full range of options. After years of neglect, the whole midsection will move as one big block. In other words, move it or lose it!

Pain is another way to lose the quality of your body maps. Pain reduces the brain's ability to process proprioceptive information, as it is busy listening to high priority pain signals. The pain signals effectively crowd out the proprioceptive signals, making the signal to noise ratio poor. If a part of the body hurts, you can block processing of the pain signals by rubbing the area and so sending a pain free signal to the brain. This is why we rub ourselves when we hurt.

Pain also tends to lessen movement in an injured joint, which further reduces the proprioceptive information. So injury can cause a potential viscious cycle - pain reduces movement, which reduces coordination, which reduces movement further and causes further pain, and so on. This is one of the reasons a person might repeatedly sprain the same ankle.

Proprioception is present in every muscle movement, so the term "proprioception training" is a little misleading, as almost everything could be viewed as PT. However one form of specific PT that has become popular is unstable surface training. This usually takes the form of

working on a wobble board, or an unstable push up surface for the shoulders. Both will help improve stability in the relevant joints. We have already discussed wobble board work, so let's look at the equivalent for push ups.

HANDLE PUSH UPS

You can quite easily buy a pair of handles, either the normal ones, or ones that also rotate. They are designed to give you a less stable surface to work on when doing your push ups. This develops the small stabiliser muscles in the joints. In the absence of handles, you can try other things. We used to use bricks, for example. Once used to them, you can vary hand positions for an extra challenge.

BODY PUSH UPS

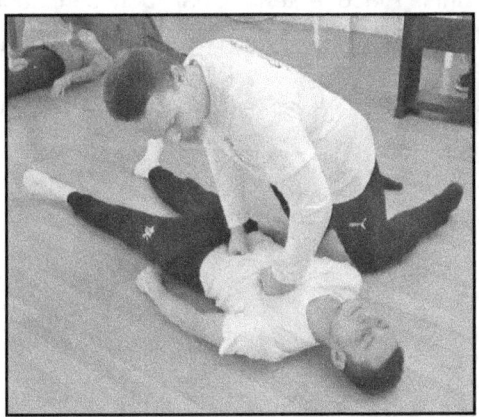

Another great source of an unstable surface is the human body! For this drill, your partner lays on the floor and you do your push ups on them. Place the fists on their body, it is best to place onto

muscles. Do a couple of press ups, then change position. Your partner can tense at the point of contact, to provide support, or relax as much as possible, which gives you a different feel. You can work from front, back and sides. This is also a very good drill for developing strikes, but that is another topic!

GROUP PUSH UPS

If training in a group, you can also use your partners to provide a great unstable surface. Have a partner hold each ankle for support, then lift. The other two partners stand so that you can place a hand on each shoulder. Now work your press ups. At first, this is static, later your partners can slowly move your hands / feet around as you go. There are many variations on this idea, you can use sticks as support, for example.

THE PILATES BALL

A pilates ball, or similar, makes another great unstable surface. Rest the feet on it for press ups, try doing a squat on one, body surf on it and so on. Sitting on one rather than a regular chair means you can work out as you sit at your computer!

From stability, let's move back to our concept of awareness. Many of the drills we have shown connect us to our senses, let's now look at how we connect our system more directly to that of another person. Doing this works not only our propiroecption, but also often our tactical sensitivy, awareness of another persons' breathing and so on.

PARTNER EXERCISES

Carry out the core exercises in pairs. Side to side, back to back or whatever other variation you can think of. The aim is for both partners to carry out the movements smoothly and in a coordinated fashion. Vary speed, position, etc as required. From pairs, move into threes, fours, or even larger groups. You can also add in the ball training we mentioned earlier for this. Place a tennis ball between each

person, for example.

MIRROR IMAGE

Of course, all of our previous tactile training will help develop our proprioception but now we can start to work a little deeper. Once you are aware of your partner's position, try and tap into their breathing. One way to do this is through mirroring drills.

Stand opposite your partner. Your goal is simply to mirror their posture at first. They raise their right hand, then so do you. The next stage is to detect tension. Your partner tense a muscle group - the left thigh, for example. You have to copy the movement again. The next stage is to mimic your partner's breathing. They can make their inhale/exhale quite obvious at first, then become more subtle.

Once you can do all this from visual contact, run the same drill but working in contact with your partner. You can close the eyes if necessary. To start, the work can be fairly static. Add more movement in as you gain experience. This can become very challenging as your partner walks, changes direction, holds their breath, does a roll, etc. But this drill progression will really sharpen your awareness skills, both internal and external.

CROSS BODY COMMUNICATION

If we are in good health we should be able

to carry out simple movements with no problem. Sit down, pick up a pen, stand, squat, roll, etc. With practice, we carry out more involved movements - play the piano, type on a keyboard, play tennis and so on.

As mentioned, if we wish to continue to improve our self awareness, we need to find new movement patterns to challenge us. This may be something as straightforward as learning a new sport or activity. However, there are also some Systema drills that are specifically designed to help sharpen our proprioecption and so our general coordination and cross-lateral connectivity (CLC).

If you've ever tried patting your head with one hand, whilst rubbing circles on your belly with the other, you'll have experienced CLC. The nervous communication in play for you to create

these asymmetrical movements simultaneously is termed *left-right brain integration*. In other words, both hemispheres of the brain are working as a partnership. In this example, the CL movement is a limb from one side of the body doing something different to that on the other side, but it can include any movement that crosses over the body's midline. The following exercises will help develop your CLC.

THE BIRD DOG

Get onto all fours, wrists under shoulders, knees under hips. Fix your gaze on a spot ahead and slightly down so your neck is elongated a little Next, reach your right leg out behind you, toes pointing to the ground, hips stay level. Now stretch the left arm forward, palm in, drawing the belly up a little for support. Hold for a while, keeping the breathing steady. This allows the combination of CL activity and balance to register in a calm nervous system.

STANDING CROSS CRAWL

In this exercise, it is important to find your full range of motion. This really helps with brain development as it creates more challenge and the storing of new movement modes.

Stand with feet shoulder width apart. Simultaneously lift the right knee and the left arm, then bring both down to the starting position. Next, lift the left knee and right arm and lower. Alternate this movement, focussing on keeping

synchronised movement of limbs. Return to the start position. Now take the movement across the mid-line. As you lift one knee, bring the elbow of the opposite arm to it as close as you can. Repeat on each side as before, focussing on quality of movement.

HEEL TOUCH

Stand with hands raised. Slowly raise one leg and take your foot backward. Now reach back with the opposite hand and touch the raised heel.

THUMBS

Here's a fun little exercise that is harder than it looks. Place both hands out in "pointing" position, finger out, thumb up. Retract the thumb on one hand, the finger on the other. The drill is to switch - so if it is left thumb up, right finger out, you have to switch to right thumb up, left finger out. You have to do both simultaneously. Give it a try!

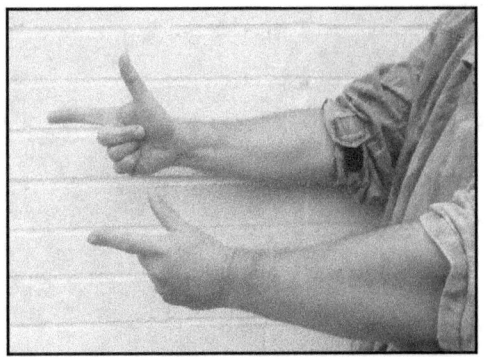

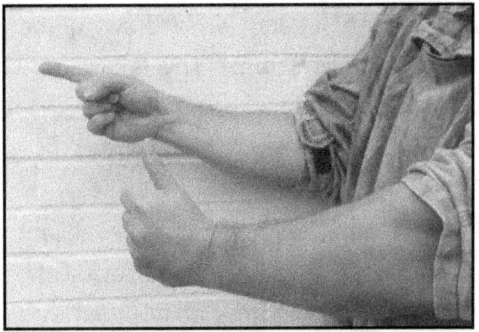

NUMBERS & LETTERS

Using one arm, draw out the numbers one to nine in the air in front of you. Repeat with the other arm. Finally, do the same with both arms.

Next, follow the same procedure with the feet (also a good balance exercise.) For both feet you are allowed to sit or lie on the floor! The next stage is to "walk" the numbers. Imagine a large number on the floor, you have to walk its shape. The final step is to combine both the arm movements and the walking. So as you walk the number three, you are also drawing it in the air.

Now go back to the start. This time, you are drawing letters with hands, feet and then walking. You can try writing out your name, for example. Follow the same procedure as with the numbers. The final

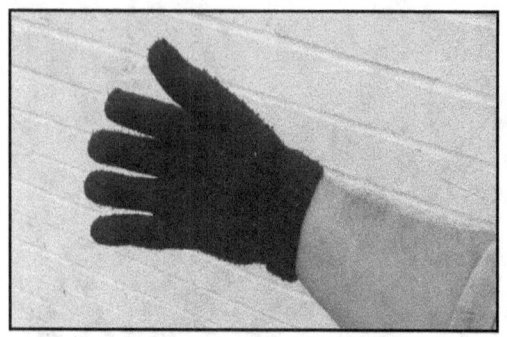 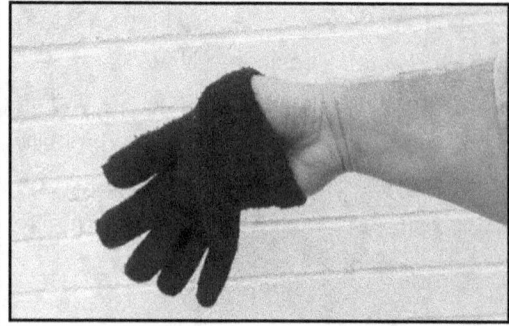

stage is to combine both drills. Walk out your chosen letters, while drawing the numbers with your arms. This takes some getting used to, so take your time!

GLOVE REMOVAL

This is another very simple but excellent drill that works awareness and sensitivity. It's taken directly from Vladimir Vasiliev's *Strikes*, just one of the many great exercises in that book.

All you need is a glove, some time and lots of patience! Place the glove on your hand. It can be any type of glove, but best to start with a slightly loose one at first. The aim of the drill is simply to take off the glove, but without touching it with your other hand - or teeth, come to that! In other words you have to kind of wriggle your hand out of the glove.

This drill works on a physical level, in terms of developing fine movement but this is also a great psychological drill. If you are anything like me, at some point you will want to just rip the glove off with your free hand! Persevere, breathe, monitor your internal tension levels!

MULTI-TASKING

All our earlier catching drills, with stick or ball, will assist with body awareness and coordination. To more specifically target proprioception, add a catch and throw component into other movements. Have one person perform push ups while a catching and returning a tennis ball to a partner. This multi-tasking element adds in extra layers of challenge. You could easily switch catch and throw for carrying something.

Whilst walking, pass a cup of water to a partner without spilling any, for example. Next pass the cup from person to person while both doing exercises.

STICK FALL

Another aspect of multi-tasking and body awareness that you can practice solo, is to move with a stick. At first, simply hold it in your hands. Later on you can place the stick in different positions, across your shoulders, above your head, even down your trouser leg! The drill is to keep contact with the stick and move from standing to the floor and back up again.

Different positions call for different types of movement. Holding in the hands is the easiest but even then, you have to learn how to get back up off the floor without using your hands.

INTUITION DRILLS

To some extent a number of the drills we have already covered involve an element of inututition, particularly the blindfold ones. Similar to prioperception, intuition is a sense that is constantly running "under the radar". However, we can work some drills that more specifically target this "sixth sense."

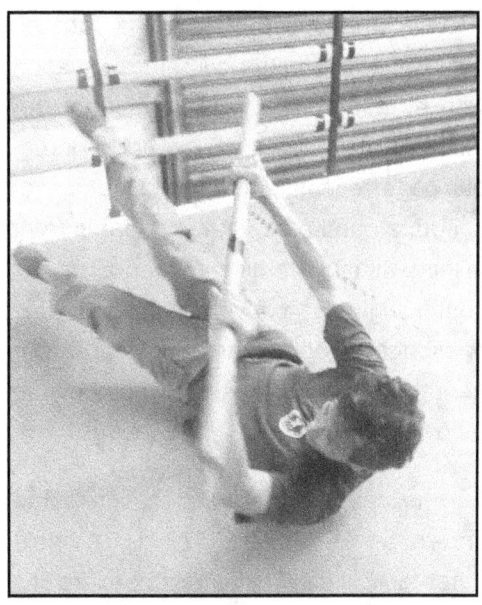

One issue we have to consider when it comes to training intuition is that we are trying to train something that is natural in an artificial way. In a drill, we are fully aware that this is not a real situation, it is a setup. So already our conscious mind can be overlaying the instinctive one. This means we have to sometimes try and trick the brain into thinking that this actually could be a real situation. Taking away the sense of sight is one very good way to do this, as it seems to help us connect very quickly with our sub-conscious. Likewise, working any of the Hide and Seek type exercises we've discussed also helps us tap into our more primal state.

This could perhaps explain why people are so attracted to some sports - paintballing, bungee jumping, etc. They help us reconnect to that "simpler" self and so bring us very much into the present. Being in the present is something I will talk about more in a later chapter. It is a vital compononet of all types of awarenss training, even more so when working instinct.

Before we get onto the drills, let's clarify a couple of points so we are clear on what we are trying to acheive with this type of training. First of all, the training presented here is psychologcial and physical. It does not involve any mystical energy or "supernatural agencies." To me, at least at this stage, our instinct is a kind of extended sense of touch. We "feel" that someone is looking at us. There is a definite physical sensation. How often do you hear someone say "that made my skin crawl"? Or did you ever shiver for some reason a few seconds before something happened?

The second aspect of instinct is carrying out exactly the right action in a situation with no apparent conscious thought. An example may be, as happened to one of our guys recently, smoothly steering, at speed, around a car that shot out in front of him without warning. All while calmly continuing his conversation with his passenger (who screamed in fear at the near miss and took some moments to recover!).

This is one facet of what has become known as *Flow State*. This is a whole other topic in itself but, in short, exercises like the Circle Stick Catches help get our minds into that Flow State, where even fast actions are carried out with no stress or panic. In terms of drills, let's begin then, with that idea of extending our sense of touch.

SENSING THE KNIFE

Bearing in mind what we said about fooling the brain into thinking we are in real danger, it is good to use a metal knife for this practice (assuming you are aware of all the safety issues.) The setup is the basic knife push. One partner stands, the other prods them with the knife.

The person being pushed can close their eyes, or be blindfold. This gets us used to working from a purely touch rather than sight reaction. Allow the body to relax as much as possible, and simply move away from the point of contact. It doesn't have

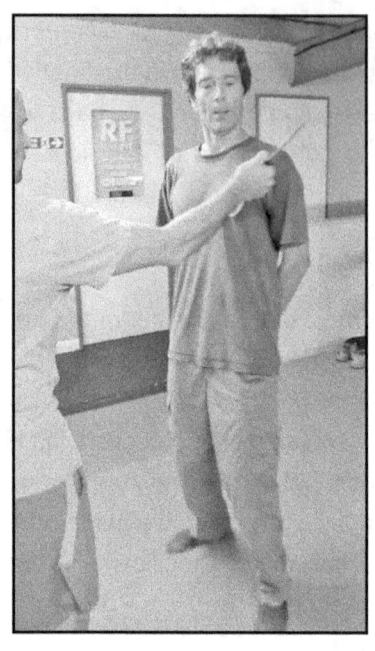

to be a big movement. Try to become very aware of the sensation in the body as the knifepoint touches.

With this work, it is important that the knife holder really pushes you with the knife, not just touches. The body needs to feel that it is under threat, not just doing a drill! It is also interesting to work on touching different parts of the body with the knife. I can guarantee the feeling and reaction will be different when the knife touchs, say the upper arm than when it touches the throat. Explore this and discover whih parts of your body are more sensitive to this feeling. Now, open the eyes and work the same procedure. See if you get that same body feeling as the knife approaches. If you do, act upon it, moving the body away as though it had been touched, but now just prior to contact.

If you are not getting that feeling, have your partner be more threatening with the knife. Again, we want to scare the body into feeling it really has to move. Beware, though, that we don't slip into making the body freeze on the flinch. This is more about feeling the beginnings of that flinch and responding rather than reacting.

Now the fun begins. Have your parnter take up position behind you, about six feet away. They slowly push the knife, with intent, towards a particular area of your body. It might be right between the shoulder blades, for example. Your job is to feel for that body sensation again, that warning that something is approaching. When you feel it, act upon it. That sensation will give you a direction, allow yourself to be moved by it.

If you feel nothing, go back the original pushing drill, with particular emphasis on the back. We work from the back first as this area seems to be more senstivie to incoming information. When you do drills like this, it is very important that you work from sensation and not from imagination. Because we know we are in a training drill, it is easy to guess or to imagine that we feel the knife. Try to put this to one side and work purely from body sensation. Your partner can tell you each time if you are right or not.

They can also watch for a tell-tale muscle twitch as they approach. Sometimes the twitch happens but the person ignores it and does not move. The knife holder can mention if this is happening.

If you are getting a good success rate with this stage, try working at the next level. Now we extend the range a little and the knife holder stays in place. They make a repeated movement with the knife, aimed towards a specific part of the other person's body. For example, you may make a cutting motion aimed behind the knee. Keep working the motion for a few minutes. It may take longer for the sensation to build in the "target", but again we are feeling for that particular sensation to trigger our movement.

BLINDFOLD DRILLS

Let's return to some blindfold drills to further work this sense of extended touch. If we want to really focus on a single sense, we can also block hearing as well

as sight, as depending on the surface underfoot, it may be difficult to approach without making any sound. A simple set of headphones or similar should suffice. You may play music, personally I find that more distracting but give it a try.

To start, work fully sighted. One partner stands and the other partner walks towards them. Not just towards them, if the target person does not move, you should walk through them. Obviously the stander will pick up the approaching walker visually. But I want you to ignore that as much as you can. Instead, focus on the feelings in your body. At some point, as in the previous knife drill, you may feel a kind of twitch or involuntary muscle movement. You may feel a slight sensation of discomfort, or similar. As soon as you feel that, move out of the path of the walker.

Once you have that basic idea, experiment with some variations. Have the walker come in from different angles and at different speeds. Also change your own position. Work standing, sitting and laying on the floor. Note how your body feels each time. The next stage is to run through the same procedure but now the stander is deprived of sight / sound. This time, the walker approaches and as and when the stander "feels" that sensation, they call "stop!" and point to where they think the walker is. Remove the blindfold to check and reset.

Once again, try this in all the different positions and speeds. Don't rush the drill and also try and work in a good amount of space. If there are several pairs working, you don't want them interfering with each other. This is usually one of our outdoor camp drills, where we have the use of a large field but it's good to experiment in different environments, too.

Having got the idea, you can then carry this method over into many other drills. Think back on our Hide and Seek drills, for example. Revisit them but think about working more with your "extended touch" rather than relying purely on visual information. Because, remember, our sense of touch is the quickest! Everything we see has to be interpreted by the brain. Anything we touch, especially if dangerous, is instantly felt and can trigger an immediate response.

As an example of this, let's imagine you are scanning a treeline, trying to spot a person hiding there, as in one of the previous camouflage drills. You visually scan, noticing shapes or colours. Perhaps you think you can spot an arm, so you peer a little closer. Your brain is working to make sense of the information coming in. If we add in our sense of "feel", we may get a different result. Walk along the treeline until you get that tingle. Now bring the eyes into play to zoom in on the area in question.

Once you get this feeling, bring it over into your daily life. Take more notice of your body feelings, particualrly in stressful or potentially dangerous situations. Studies have shown how in cases of sexual assault in particular, the person attacked oftensaid "something didn't feel right," but went along with the situation in any case. Social pressures, not wanting to make a fuss, putting it down to "imagination" are all blockers of our deep seated intuition, our gut instinct.

Remember, too, that science now tells us we have a "second brain" in our gut! The stomach is under the control of what's sometimes called *the little brain*, a network of neurons that line our stomach and gut. There are over 100 million of these cells, all overseeing the daily grind involved in digesting food, all the mixing, contracting and absorbing that goes on to help break down our food and begin extracting the nutrients and vitamins we need.

These neurons lining our digestive system keep it in close contact with the brain via the vagus nerves, which often influence our emotional state. For instance, when we experience "butterflies in the stomach", this is really the brain in the stomach talking to the brain in your head. As we get nervous or fearful, blood gets diverted from our gut to our muscles and this is the stomach's way of protesting.

There are, of course, further drills and exercises that we can work in this area, but it is best to begin wth those detailed here and establish a good foundation before going on to the deeper levels. In short, pay attention to your body and all its ticks and twitches. And most of all, listen to your gut instinct. You will be surpised how often it is right!

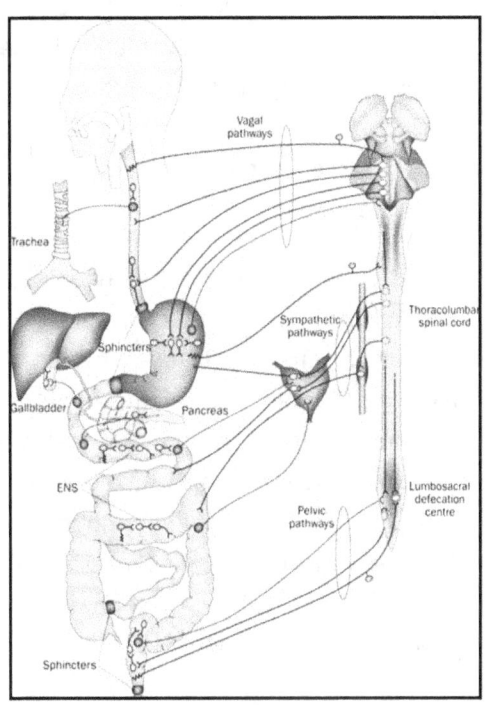

NO CHOICE

The next set of drills are designed to work on our instinctive response. Again, we have already worked this in some ways with our earlier catch drills. I want to briefly revisit those, this time through the lens of working "in the moment." Let's go back to a simple catch and throw with the tennis balls. This time, we want to work more on an instinct level, so we will begin with eyes closed!

One person stands with eyes closed. Their partner calls "go" and throws the ball to them. The partner opens their eyes and catches the ball as quickly as possible. That is the basic set up. Of course, you can adapt to hitting pads, as we did earliler, catching something or carrying out any acitivty that requires some specific type of movement. The key is that we trying to cut down to a bare minimum any "thinking time." The body simply has to respond to the situation in the correct way.

If you run this drill and find people are struggling, drop it back to simple throw and catch. Then go to eyes closed but allow a short gap between the signal and the throw. Once people are catching the ball everytime, start to make it more difficult. Make the signal call a lot quieter. Or even try giving no signal at all, let the person "feel" when to go for the catch - now there's a challenge!

SPOT THE KNIFE

Let's now move to a exercise that has an element of choice in it. In short, we have to decide who is carrying a knife. Here's the set up. The observer turns their back on a group of three people. One of the three conceals the knife somewhere. They may tuck it into their belt, put it down their sock, etc. When ready, the group gives the signal for the observer to turn. On turning, the observer must point to the person they think is carrying the knife.

We can run this drill in two ways. It can be an observation drill similar to what we did before, or a body language drill, something we will talk about in the next chapter. For now, however, I present it as an intuition drill. Make an instant decision on turning. Don't over-analyze. What's your gut instinct? We are training to make a quick decision based on that certain feeling which, hopefully having run the previous exercises, we are now fully in touch with. You can, of course, combine this with the earlier knife sensing drill. Rather than just hold the knife, the wielder moves in with a slow attack which you have to sense and evade.

FRIEND OR FOE?

This drill is along similar lines, in that we are working on a quick response based on feel. Again, this can work as a body language exercise but I want you to feel rather than look at first. Your partner approaches from a distance. They have two options when they get close - hit you or shake your hand. Your job is to detect their intention as soon as you can and move accordingly. It is important that your partner is honest and does not try and trick you, so don't think "shake" and then punch!

INCREASING PRESSURE

One way to increase the intensity of the drills, to enhance that feeling of real danger. With our experienced people we have worked in water, used moving cars and explored other ways to "enhance" the drill. However, these should always be carried out under suitable spervision and only whenall particiapnts are ready. Fear is a doulbe-edge sword in our training. It can build or it can destroy. If the fear is too

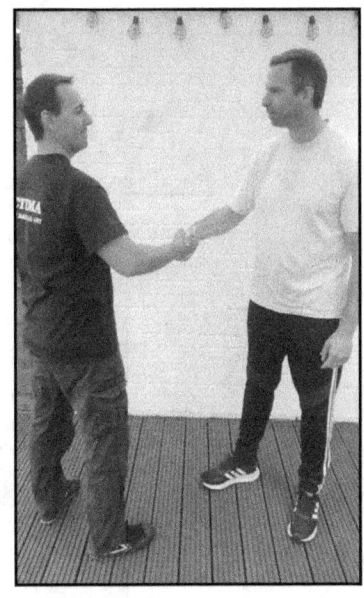

great, the over-rding instinct can be one of blind panic. If that happens we are actually reinfcorcing the fear and encouraging a poor type of reaction. Used correctly and in increments, we can use their fear to help people develop a healthy and useful response to a dangerous situation. Because whatever the situation, the effects and feeling of fear are generally very similar.

When given the tools to manage fear, we find that people's instinctive response natrually flourishes and their overall awarenss, both internal and external, imporves greatly as a result. So take this training step by step, never rush, be patient. And, above all, make it part of your daily activities. I really can't stress enough how useful that is!

CHAPTER SIX
PERSON TO PERSON

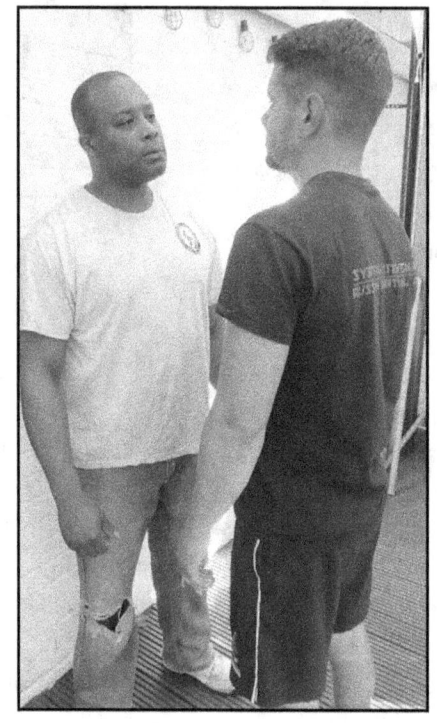

So far our work has been largely mechanical in nature, in terms of working with direct information gathered through our senses. But even in what we might call a neutral situation, where we are looking at, say, a tree, there is an element of interpretation involved. Information is received and analysed, in terms of shape, colour, sound but there is also an emotional response as well. We enjoy the shape of the tree, we think about sitting in its cool shade and so on.

How much more so is this true when we come to the area of interpersonal communication. It's a commonly held view that that communication is 7% verbal and 93% non-verbal. The non-verbal component is made up of 55% body language and 38% tone of voice. The accuracy of those figures might be open to debate, but I feel the general principle holds true.

We take in far more information visually as a rule, even to the extent that it takes just one-tenth of a second for someone to judge us and form a first impression. As the saying goes, *you never get a second chance to make a first impression!* That impression can be positive or negative. Factors involved in that might include body language, clothing, grooming, perceived status, personal prejudice and so on. There may also be an element of that "gut instinct" involved too.

To start with, we are going to cover largely the visual aspects of interpersonal interaction, what is generally known as body language.

BODY LANGUAGE

It is virtually impossible for humans to not display something of our internal or psychological state in our physical being. Body language is the study and understanding of what these physical signs indicate. This is a deep and wide field of study and here I'll discuss some of the basic principles and methods. Once again, I would encourage you to research and study further as this is such a rich and rewarding area and one that, as I hope to illustrate, ties in on so many levels with our Systema training.

THE LIMBIC RESPONSE

The limbic system is a network of structures located beneath the cerebral cortex. This system controls behaviours essential to life, such as finding food, as well as emotion. The amygdala, already discussed, is part of the system, along with the thalamus, hypothalamus and hippocampus. The limbic system works constantly, instantly and reflexively, without conscious thought. It sends signals to other parts of the brain which then often manifest in our faces, hands and so on.

As these reactions occur without conscious though, they are often called

"honest" reactions, so giving a true insight as to a person's true thoughts or intent.

In this context, we might think of the neo cortex (the area of the brain responsible for intellect and higher functions) as the creator of "dishonest" reactions as it is capable of creativity and deception! On a practical level, this means that a sudden and direct response is more likely to give a truer indication than a more studied or formulated response. Or that people in an aroused emotional state are more likely to be clear in the body language than a person who is calm and collected.

Already we can see a strong connection to Systema training, where a calm mental approach can help mask our physical intentions. Likewise, good observation depends on a calm mindset, as discussed in our earlier work on peripheral vision.

THE TEN COMMANDMENTS OF BODY LANGUAGE

Before we get onto specifics, let's take an over-view of some general principles. There are various versions of this list around, I have drawn this one from the works of Joe Navarro, an FBI agent, whose books I highly recommend.

1. Competent Observation

The fundamental requirement, as without observation there can be no information! Get into the habit of observing, of seeing rather than just looking. This is a developed skill and any skill takes practice to master. We already mentioned the ball passing test, and will speak more on situational awareness later on. In short, switch on!

2. Context is Key

When reading body language, you have to relate everything to the context in which

it occurs. Is a person nervous? Well, yes, but they are about to give an important lecture at work. Is someone incoherent? Yes, but they could be drunk or perhaps in shock following an unpleasant event.

3. Recognise Universal Behaviours

There are some indicators that are universal, regardless of culture. For example, lip compression is a universal sign of being troubled.

4. Recognise Personal Behaviours

While some behaviours are universal, others are relatively unique to individuals. In the case of people you interact with often, friends, family, workmates, watch out for movement habits particular to that person. In poker these are usually known as tells. Watch out for your own, too!

5. Establish Baseline Behaviours

Observe a person's "normal" posture, facial expressions and so on. This will make it much easier to spot any changes due to stress, etc. Even when meeting someone for the first time, try and get a feel for their "neutral" state.

6. Watch for Clusters

A cluster is a group of multiple body signals. A person may cough, touch their neck and cross their legs all at the same time, for example. Look out for patterns, too.

7. Watch for Changes in Behaviour

Sudden differences in posture, expression and so on are good indicators of an emotional change in a person. That might indicate a sudden interest, or fear, or many other things. If you can pick this up you can often be

predictive as to a person's actions and so act accordingly.

8. Detect False Signs

Surprisingly enough, when people lie, they might try and disguise the fact! They may even know some things about body language and use that knowledge to mislead with false indicators. This is where the real skill begins to develop, as the work becomes very subtle.

9. Distinguish Between Comfort and Discomfort

Probably the biggest single indicator when observing behaviour is to determine whether a person is stressed or at ease. We may think of stress as anger, fear, lust, anxiety. A person at ease, is happy, confident, relaxed. In general we can broadly divide every emotional state into comfort or discomfort and both will exhibit their own particular physical manifestations.

10. Be Subtle!

There is a principle in scientific experiments about how the presence of the scientist may influence the outcome of the experiment. How much more so with personal observation! You may deduce that your fellow passenger on the train looks somewhat nervous and stressed. Perhaps that is because you have been staring intently at them for the last half hour!

So our vision exercises from earlier become useful. We can learn to observe indirectly, to take in general information, such as posture or shape, with a wide glance, zooming in on detail as we need to. This, again, comes down to practice and I suggest you get into general habit of being more aware on all levels in your daily activities.

THE THREE F's

Something unchanged in our behaviour over thousands of years is our response to immediate danger. It is as true in a road rage incident today as it was when our ancestors were confronted by a dangerous predator. In each case, our limbic brain response falls into one of three categories: fight, flight, freeze. We see much the same response in the animal world, it is an ingrained survival response in many species. In humans it can also be triggered by an event that doesn't even approaching a pure survival situation. Your boss shouting at you, for example. There may be no real actual physical threat but the limbic system is spiked and puts us in

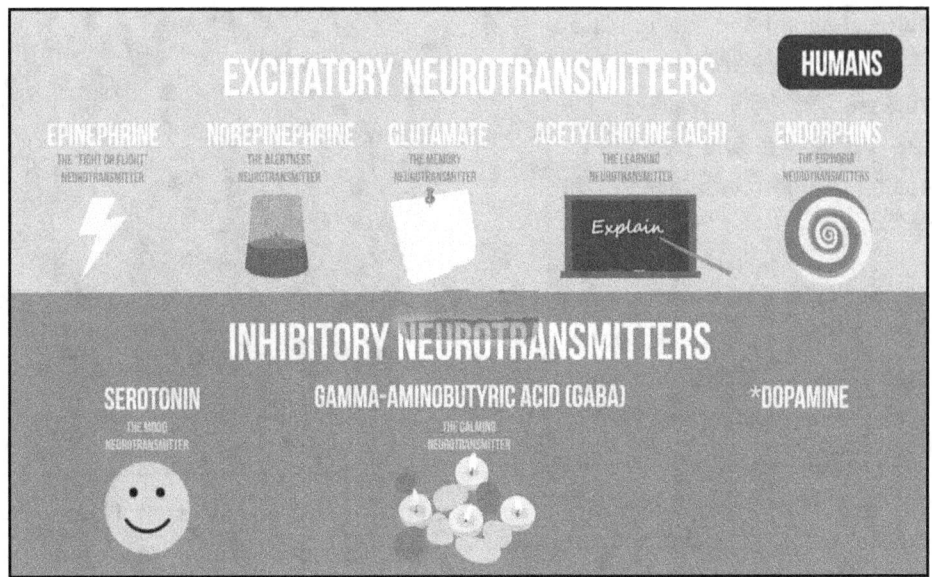

"survival mode". Understanding how each of these works is important not only for our own behaviour, but in predicting that of others.

In common use, freeze is often left out of the equation and people talk of fight or flight. This term was first used by M.D. Walter B. Cannon in 1915. He taught psychology at Harvard University and specialised in the research of physical reactions of laboratory animals under pressure. Cannon observed noticeable physical changes in the digestive systems of animals experiencing fear. He subsequently spent some 20 years studying the relationship of psychological and physical effects of stress on animals.

Cannon also redefined the biological term *homeostasis* to signify the internal balance of the body. According to Cannon, our bodies continuously seek to maintain a predefined state of equilibrium by regulating the complex interdependent system of organs. Changes in variables such as body temperature and fluid balance set off a series of processes aimed at returning the body to its original balance.

The homeostatic definition of stress is: "A condition where expectations, whether genetically programmed, established by prior learning, or deduced from circumstances, do not match the perception of the environment. This discrepancy between what is observed or sensed and what is expected or programmed elicits patterned responses."

Our sympathetic nervous system triggers the fight/flight response before we consciously make any decision on how to act. Several things happen very fast. The hormones epinephrine (adrenaline) and norepinephrine (noradrenaline) are released into our system. This causes rapid pulse and respiration, increasing oxygen intake for fast action.

Blood pressure rises and extra oxygen is sent to the brain, increasing alertness. Sight, hearing, and other senses become sharper. Blood sugar (glucose) and fats from energy stores are released into the bloodstream to give us the extra energy we need. Skin temperature rises and the increased sweat on the palms of our hands improves our grip. Digestion is slowed, as all our energy is now conserved for staying alive. Physical indicators of fight flight response include:

Rapid heart beat and breathing
Pale or flushed skin
Dilated pupils
Trembling

FIGHT

This response aims to turn the fear we experience into anger or rage. In the case of fighting for survival, this may have some merit. If you're involved in a an argument at work, it is a less useful option! Having said that, it is easy to be aggressive without physical contact. This usually takes the form of puffing out the chest, throwing the arms wide, being verbally aggressive and so on. These are all gross indicators, very easy to spot. However, if we are not used to such behaviour it is easy to become overwhelmed by it and have our own fear response triggered.

FLIGHT

One way to survive an attack is to escape, to flee. This may be an obvious action, such as someone running away. It may also be more subtle, such as someone backing off in an argument, or even just leaning away from someone. It may also manifest in "blocking" behaviours. Remember we spoke earlier about people putting their arm out to prevent a fall that is already happening?

Watch and see how often people try to block out an unpleasant situation by covering their eyes or ears. It's as though the body is trying to protect us from the event by not allowing us to see or hear it.

FREEZE

The third response to danger is to freeze.

This probably developed from the desire not to be seen by a predator. As we mentioned in the section on peripheral (hunter's) vision, movement attracts attention! Some animals even play dead when in danger, an extreme freeze response that is also mirrored in human behaviour (one example was in recent school shootings in the USA).

Again, this reaction can be seen in less dangerous situations, in various degrees of "freeze." A person may stop talking, become rooted to the spot, stutter and so on. If you've ever seen someone dry up mid-speech you'll know what I mean. We sometimes call it the "deer in the headlights" moment.

Another version is the mini-freeze, where we may stop mid-activity, remember we left the oven on, and turn around to rush back home. In that case, the freeze is there to give us the space to recall something.

The breath hold is another major indicator of the freeze. This may be a sharp intake and hold, if surprised, or the breath become very shallow, as if we don't wish to make any noise at all.

MANAGING THE 3 F's

So these responses are very useful in our work of observing others, but how can we manage our own reactions when put in this state? The first step is to be put into that state. Some of the drills we cover will achieve this (taking slaps, for example). But there are many other ways. Here's one, perhaps not available to all, but an event that was quite "primal" for me.

A few months back, my wife and I visited a local zoo. It is a conservation zoo, doing a lot of good work and one of the main attractions are their rare tigers. We had the opportunity to get very close to one of them, a huge white male Bengal (pictured above). He had come in to his indoor enclosure and was lying sound asleep on the floor, just the other side of the viewing window. If the glass had not been there, you could have reached out and stroked him. To be honest, that was the first instinct, being a person who is owned by two cats. He looked so peaceful and furry, you just wanted to chuck him under the chin. Then the tiger woke up.

In one swift move, he turned over, was up on four feet and made his displeasure at having his nap interrupted very clear. We and the other people behind us, jolted back as one, I'm not kidding the hairs on my arms stood up. It was a very strong and strange reaction, we were perfectly safe after all.

Yet that primeval instinct kicked in, you had no doubt that this magnificent creature could kill you in an instant. My feet felt glued to the floor, my back was locked straight. It took a serious breath to unlock, then we all laughed, of course, to release the tension. The cat, as they usually do, turned his back on us in contempt and calmly commenced to wash himself.

This also reminded me of a recent story on the internet (so it must be true!). Apparently an MMA fighter claimed he would be able to "take on" a wolf in a bare hand fight. Now, on paper, perhaps he thinks he has a good chance. The reality is, that when you come face to face with such a powerful predator, particularly for the first time, something happens that you have very little control over. The space that your freeze reaction creates is all that a predator needs to finish you off. One or two bites, that's it, there's no "sparring" involved.

Now, of course, people can and do get used to that situation – we've all seen the crocodile hunter types, for example. We've also run some great training days with the assistance of my friend Danny and his highly trained security dogs. But to suggest your ring skills, however finely crafted, can standup against a feral animal is something else entirely, both on a physical and psychological level.

So, having been triggered into that state, how do we manage it? I already mentioned the main method, the good old burst breathing. This is very good at breaking us out of the freeze response, especially if we have been doing our "breath and move" type drills. Movement is next. Remember the F's are a result of fear, and movement is the enemy of fear.

For less physical threats, learning to be in the moment is important and I will talk more on that later on. If the state is triggered by a phobia or similar, we can use progressive methods of exposure to the trigger to learn to inoculate against the fear. In short, a good awareness of why, how and what is happening to us gives us the major tools to manage our "adrenal" response.

Neocortex: Rational or Thinking Brain

Limbic Brain: Emotional or Feeling Brain

Reptilian Brain: Instinctual or Dinosaur Brain

Some approaches, particularly in the combatives world, call for us to fully immerse ourselves in the fight state, driving ourselves in to a rage or fury (or a pretend one in training). In the past I have gone deep into this approach, though more through the prism of "animal mindset" from other arts and it is not an approach I recommend, for several reasons. Far better to step out of it and have a response rather than a reaction to a situation, which is, of course, the Systema or "professional" approach.

REPTILE BRAIN?

Speaking of animal mindset, I'd just like to mention the Reptile Brain or Triune Brain theory. This was very popular a while back and formed part of my training at that time, as mentioned. The theory was developed by Paul MacLean, an American neuroscientist in the 1960s. It was later picked up and applied to martial arts, particularly the Chinese internal systems.

In brief, the theory is this. Our brain has three main components, each laid atop the other. They are reptile, paleomammalian and neomammalian brain. The reptile brain equates to the brain stem and is the oldest part of the brain, according to the theory. This part is is responsible for pure survival instinct. That is food, fight and…reproduction. As we developed, the paleo brain came next and overlays the reptile. This corresponds to the limbic system and so includes memory and emotion, care for our young and so on. The last to develop was the neomammalian, corresponding to the cerebral neo cortex. This is responsible for higher functions, abstract thought, planning, creativity, language and so in.

That's the theory, in a nutshell. It provides a very neat model and was and still is popular in some martial art circles, particularly those that style themselves on "predator" animals such as snakes and dragons. The idea being that through adopting certain postures and behaviour patterns, we can switch at will into "reptile mode" and become savage fighting machines. However, modern research has shown the theory to be lacking in several areas. For example, the brain stem is also involved in emotional functions, such as self control.

Also, our brains aren't fundamentally different from those of reptiles, or even those of fish. Every mammal has a neo cortex (not just the really intelligent ones), and all vertebrates, including reptiles, birds, amphibians, and fish, have a type of cortex. In fact, the very idea that new brain structures emerge on top of old ones is fundamentally at odds with biology: new structures are typically just modified versions of older structures. The mammalian neo cortex isn't a completely new structure like MacLean thought it was, but is instead a modification of the cortex. Neuroscientist Terrence Deacon explains: "Adding on is almost certainly not the way the brain has evolved. Instead, the same structures have become modified in different ways in different lineages."

For this reason, I don't consider the Triune Brain theory as a viable one to base all aspects of our training on. Having said that, it can serve as simple model to get some principles across, as long as you make it clear that it is just a model. As for "turning into a snake", or similar, as mentioned already I do not feel that is a healthy approach for us. We should be striving to be more human, not less.

PACIFIERS

One of the Commandments mentioned earlier was the ability to recognise stress and comfort. So let's look now at some signs that a person may be under stress. These are known as *pacifiers*, actions that people take in order to help calm themselves. Some are quite obvious and some more subtle. This is a quick overview of behaviours to watch for.

Touching and stroking are one of the main types. People will often stroke their neck or face when under stress. Any such movement of a person being questioned may indicate a less than truthful answer. Some speculate that touching the neck, particularly just under the chin (the carotid sinus area) is an unconscious response to increased blood pressure. The person is trying to calm themselves back down. A similar move may be to adjust the tie knot or to tug on the collar. Men tend to do this more than women, who tend to cover the neck rather than stroke it. As far as the face goes, people may rub their forehead, massage an earlobe or lick the lips.

Breathing and sound are another good indicator of pacifying behaviour. People may puff out their cheeks, then exhale loudly. Whistling is another calming activity. Stress can even cause excessive yawning, a response to the mouth becoming dry. Of course, shortness and shallowness of breath will often indicate nervousness, so listen to how a person breathes, or works to adjust their breathing.

Arms and legs are another area to watch. Crossed arms can be an indicator of the "self hug", particularly if the hands rub the arms. The "leg cleanse" is a common movement, too. People place palms on their upper thigh and rub down towards the knee.

Let's now take a run through the main body areas and discuss the signals that each may give away. Again, this is quite a brief overview of this topic, but is enough to give you some good tips and a starting point for further study. Remember to apply the commandments in all cases, particularly the one on context!

FEET & LEGS

We will start with the feet as, surprisingly perhaps, they are known as the most "honest" part of the body! The zoologist Desmond Morris observed that the feet reveal our feelings more honestly than any other part of the body. Perhaps this harkens back to days of survival, the F's again, where our feet are the most hardwired part of the body to the limbic system. In any event, watch the feet.

People in a good mood may jiggle or bounce their feet. Lifting the toes or rocking up and down is also the sign of a good mood. We are so happy, gravity can't affect us! Jittery feet, or foot tapping, may indicate impatience. Foot direction is important, too. When you see a pair talking, observe which direction the feet point in. We tend to turn towards something we like and away from something we don't. If one foot keeps turning away, then back again, it may be a sign that person wants to exit the conversation. This applies even when seated. It can also be accompanied by a forward lean and a knee clasp.

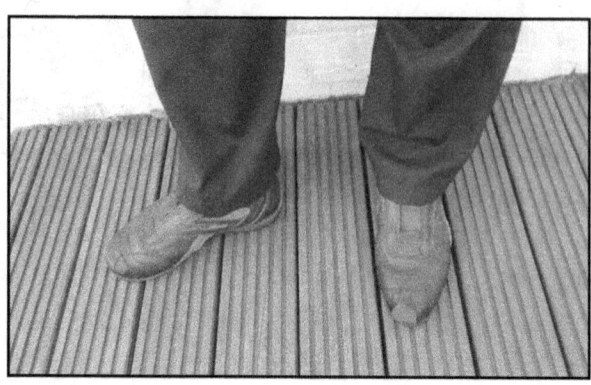

Legs are a great indicator of mood, they are often used in territorial displays. Feet and legs splay out in confrontational situations, perhaps an attempt to increase "size" or space occupied. Standing with feet together tends to give a more passive signal.

Crossing legs when standing is often a sign of comfort (or needing the loo!). It compromises our balance, so is not a stance usually seen in a stressful situation. Done in a pair, it shows that the people are at ease with each other. If a stranger enters the situation, the legs will probably uncross.

The seated cross leg position is a little different. Direction becomes important again. A thigh can be used as a barrier. However if the knee faces the other way, this shows a person at ease with the other party.

Our legs are primarily used for walking and there are a whole host of indicators in the way a person walks. Watch for any obvious tension to start and observe the general posture. Hunched or straight? Speed of walk is important too, nervous people tend to speed up. Someone carefree may breeze along, taking in their surroundings as they go. Watch someone on their phone having a happy chat to a friend. They will saunter. If that phone call brings bad news, the person may suddenly begin to hurry, hunch the shoulder and so on.

Walking can also be a good measure of intention. You should be able to spot the

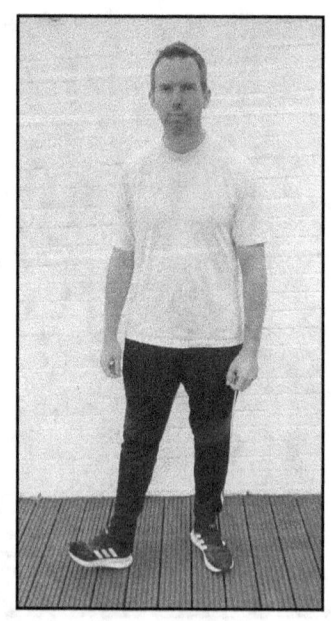

person from across a room who comes barrelling over to punch you in the face! On the other hand (or foot) watch how friends approach and greet each other – sometimes there is a little dance, followed by a handshake or hug. A walk may also be an indicator of concealed weapons. Years back I used to do a trick at workshops, asking "how many knives am I carrying." Most people guessed between one and five. I actually had about eight knives, a machete, a gun and a hand-axe, all concealed while wearing just a t shirt and joggers. However, if you asked me to run or walk carrying that, my gait would certainly not be my normal one. So watch to see if the walker is tense in one spot, almost as though trying to conceal something with the posture.

TORSO

Let's move up to the torso. If you think about out, the torso contains most of our vital organs – heart, lungs, kidneys, etc. Perhaps for this reason the usual behaviour of a stressed torso is to create distance.

Have you ever seen someone in a social situation being "chatted up" by a person they don't like? This is a prime place to observe the "torso lean." The person feels they cannot get up and walk away, but the body will lean away from the offending party. Another version of this is blading. This is where the torso is turned at a slight angle from the perceived threat.

Fronting is a more aggressive action. We actually used to call it "fronting someone up." The chest is puffed out, the arms splayed. A classic territorial display, like the legs mentioned earlier. It may even lead to chest bumping and what has become known as the "monkey dance," where two people want to show they are willing to fight but might not really actually want to yet! It's also not uncommon to see the torso bared in these situations, men ripping off their shirts as part of the display.

Covering the torso with the arms may be pacifying behaviour, it can also be a method of shielding or blocking. Chest shielding is generally more prominent in women, for obvious reasons, perhaps, but men will exhibit the same. Crossing an arm

over the body to fiddle with a cufflink, for example.

By contrast, an open torso reveals confidence. Look at how the Royal Family walk around. Hands behind the back, torso open. This is telling us "I am in charge, I am in no danger." It may also be a posture designed to keep the hands out of sight and so not give anything away!

Bowing is a sign of respect or deference. While it is more obviously prevalent in some cultures, all cultures have their own form of it. Even a brief head nod can be considered a bow. Watching a group of people meeting, bowing can be an indicator of the relative perceived status of each person. It can also be used as a gesture of "thanks."

Our shoulders are quite expressive. Think how often you use them in communication. A shrug that says "I don't know," or perhaps even "I don't care!" Sometimes the shoulders rise slowly. This is known as "turtling" almost as though the person is trying to withdraw into their shell. It's usually a sign of discomfort or of not wanting to be associated with whatever is going on.

ARMS

The shoulder is the most mobile joint in the body. Correspondingly, our arms tend to be very expressive. We use our arms as barriers, we use them to welcome, we use them to occupy space.

Shielding by crossing the arms is usually an indicator of dislike or discomfort. Buttoning up a jacket may show a similar thing. We have already mentioned the other version of crossing arms, the self hug, as a pacifying gesture. By contrast, when happy or joyful we tend to raise our arms, as though defying gravity. As a rough guide, think hands up happy, hands down, sad.

Hands behind the back can show confidence, as in the "Royal stance". They may also be saying "don't come close." You can think of it as a reverse hug. Of course, in a self defence context, concealed hands may also indicate potential weapon threat.

Arms are also used in territorial displays. We have mentioned the "chest puffed, arms wide" stance but there are more subtle actions too. Ever jostled for the arm rest on a flight? Have you seen how some people spread themselves across a train seat, or spread their arms across the chairs on each side of them?

Another variation is the "hands on hips" stance, with elbows pushed out to the side, usually a display of authority. One last arm position is where the hands are held behind the head. People often do this while leaning back in their chair. It is called "hooding" and can be a display of authority. It is interesting to note that if someone with greater authority enters the space, the hands are immediately removed back down to normal position!

FACE

The most expressive part of our body and the one we observe the most in order to gauge another person's thought or emotions. The number of human facial expressions is estimated as over ten thousand. For the most part, they are universal across all cultures. Sad people look the same sad all around the world!

However, we can, to a degree, control our facial muscles, so the face may not always be the best indicator. Having said that, there is something called *micro-expressions* that we can watch out for.

Micro-expressions are very brief, involuntary expressions that appear on a person's face according to the emotions being experienced. They usually occur as fast as 1/15 to 1/25 of a second. Unlike regular expressions, they are difficult to fake.

There are seven universal micro-expressions: disgust, anger, fear, sadness, happiness, surprise and contempt. I'm sure you are able to recognise each of those - the brows knit for anger, the lips turn up for a smile for happiness, down for sadness and so on.

The trick is to catch these expressions as they occur. On a person attempting to mask their emotions, they will quickly regain control of the facial muscles to

present whatever it is they wish to project. However, that little flash of honesty may give the game away, so watch out for them!

If we go back to our idea of comfort and stress, it is generally true that negative emotions bring tension with them. Brows furrow, jaws clench, nostrils flare, lips press together. When happy, our faces tend to "open" more. We smile, our eyes widen, the eyebrows raise and so on. These are all very obvious indicators of state of mind.

However, as we mentioned, we do have some degree of control over our facial muscles and can use this to mask our true feelings. The most common example of this is the false smile. We all have a real smile and a fake one! The interesting thing is that we use different muscles for each, perhaps because the fake smile is a conscious movement.

With a real smile, the lips spread out and up. The muscles used in the fake smile only move the lip corners to the sides. The eyes are another giveaway. A real smile is expressed with the eyes as well, they express emotion and crinkle slightly at the edges. Watch any politician and see if you can spot the difference!

Incidentally, politicians and others trained in public speaking make good test subjects for observation. Watch how they stand, what they do with their hands and listen to their speech patterns. Of course, it's easy to tell when they are lying... their lips are moving...

EYE ACCESS CUES

Speaking of lies, let's move onto the eyes, the windows of the soul! Many people say that the eyes are one of the best indicators of truth or fib telling. In fact, some people

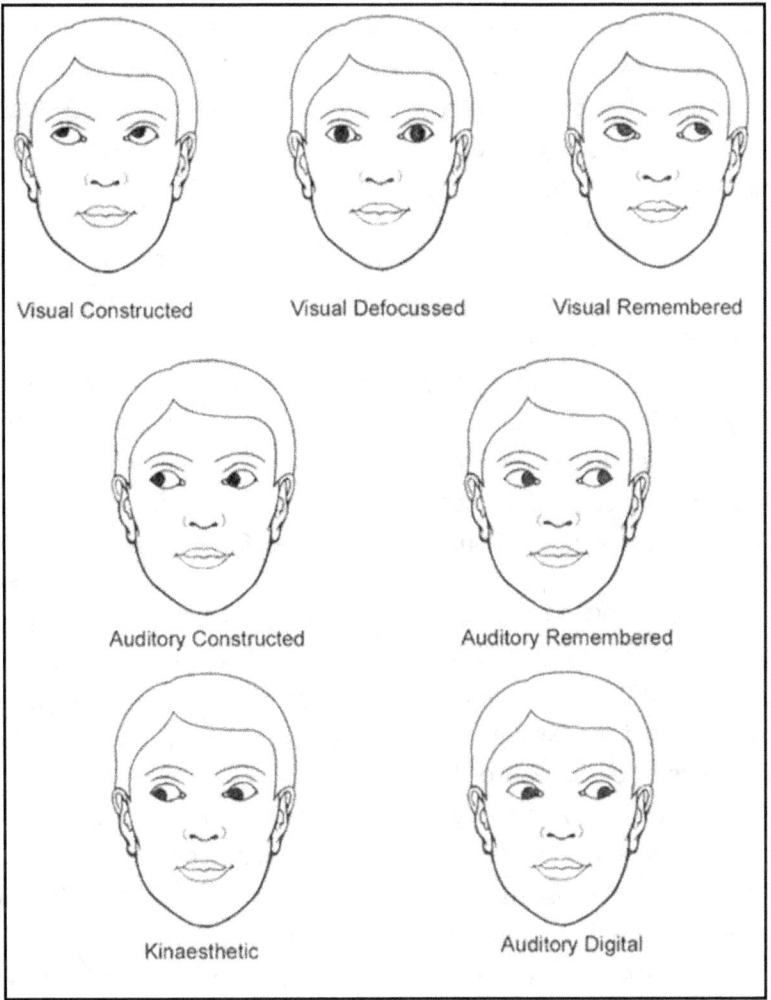

developed a whole method out of this, known as Eye Access Cues (EAC).

EAC grew out of Neuro-linguistic Programming. I'm sure you've heard of NLP, an approach to communication, created by Richard Bandler and John Grinder in 70s. Now, NLP has attracted its fair share of supporters and detractors and exactly how scientific it is seems to be a matter of debate. However, much like the Reptile Brain theory earlier, I think there are some interesting methods within the NLP approach and some things that certainly mirror Systema methods and other schools of psychological training.

The basic idea of EAC is that we move our eyes in certain directions according to the type of thought or memory we are accessing. The standard NLP movement directions are illustrated in the diagram above Just imagine this diagram is superimposed on the person's face to get the correct directions. However, we should be aware that not everyone follows these "rules". Many do, but some do not! In fact, when people are thinking about recent events or information with which they are very familiar they may not move their eyes at all.

This means that the EAC rules simply offer a starting point. If that's the case, why should we pay attention to them? Well, being able to notice a person's eye movements still provides some useful information about how they are thinking.

Let's say you are explaining to a colleague how to do something and they tell you they are struggling to follow your description. You may notice that as they say this, they are looking up, either to the left or the right, indicating that they may be trying to visualise. This can indicate that you would be better to explain the task visually rather than verbally, so they can *see* how to do it. Treat the EAC as a general indicator, or as just one part of the overall picture.

The distinction between a person looking up to the left or to the right has given rise to the "Lie Detector" test. The theory goes that you can tell if a person is lying merely by watching their eyes. How true this claim is has been the subject of some debate. At best, we can say that EAC may give some hints as to veracity but is not totally reliable.

One difficulty is in not having a baseline behaviour pattern to work from. With people we know, that may not be so much of an issue. Much like our earlier body language work, we can observe and become familiar with a person's idiosyncratic actions and tells. T h e same goes for the eyes. When meeting a person for the first time, while we can use general EAC indicators, they may not be so specific to the person in question. Some also say, that the directions are reversed if a person is left handed.

Interrogators get round this by asking a series of apparently innocuous questions during an interview. This helps give them baseline indicators and they can fine tune their observations from there. How can we work this in practice? Let's look at a drill.

TRUE OR FALSE

A simple set up. You ask a person three questions. The person responds with two true answers and one lie. You have to spot which one is the lie.

From the chart opposite you will note that there are three categories: visual, audio and kinaesthetic. This refers to the type of memory being accessed. If you ask someone what colour their front door is, they will access a visual memory. So we need construct our questions accordingly. Here's three examples:

What colour was your first car?
What does your doorbell sound like?
Did your father have a deep voice?

The second variant is in the direction of eye movement. According to the theory, an upward to the right movement (from the questioned person's perspective) indicates a visually constructed memory. An upward left indicates a visual remembered memory. In other words, if the car is red but the answer is green, the memory is false / constructed, so the corresponding eye movement is up and right. If the car is red and the answer is red, the eyes access an actual memory, and so move up and left.

The same applies to auditory memories, right constructed, left remembered. Eyes moving down to the left indicate that a person is accessing a feeling, either a tactile sensation or an emotion. Down and to the right indicates an internal dialogue - the person is "talking to themselves."

If the eyes are unfocussed and staring straight forward, this may indicate accessing a visual memory that is very close to the surface, such as "what's your name?" The file is to hand, the brain doesn't need to dig to the back of the filing cabinet to get the answer!

Now, when both people know the drill, it is tempting for the person being questioned to really try and control their eye movement. So, at first at least, try and give a quick answer without too much thought. After a while, you can flip the drill into more trying to conceal your untruth!

Give this drill a try, if nothing else it can be good fun. The last time I played it was a long train journey with some Norwegian friends. Two of them got very good at concealing the false answer but the third lady burst into uncontrollable giggles every time she lied! That leads us to another body language topic, the fact that EAC are just one part of the overall picture. So what are the other indicators that a person may not be being totally honest?

LIE INDICATORS

We have already spoken about the use of pacifiers when people feel stressed. So this is one indicator to look out for that a person is not being honest. Of course the more experienced a person is in telling fibs, the more comfortable they will be in a lying situation.

We also have to consider the effects of mental state, drugs and, to some extent, cultural issues. Without wishing to stereotype, people from different backgrounds may express themselves in different ways. English people are typically supposed to be quite reserved. Italian people use a lot of hand gestures and so on. These are generalisations but are worth considering as part of the overall picture.

Let's go back to comfort - it is much easier to spot stress due to lying if a person is reasonably comfortable. This is another reason professional interrogators work to put their subjects at ease. It is difficult to spot "lying stress" in a person who is already stressed out by the situation, or by having you shouting at them. Of course, the reverse of that is to put deliberately put a person under duress, using quick fire, repetitive questions to try and catch them out . This is less about body language, though, and more about psychological pressure.

Returning to the eyes, darting eye movements may indicate stress. The person is looking for a way to escape the situation. On the other hand a person who fixes and hold your gaze for what feels like a little too long may be trying to convince you of their sincerity. This may be accompanied by open hand gestures of the "hey, you can trust me!" type.

Breathing is an obvious indicator of stress. Shallow breathing, a dry throat, wavery voice, shaky hands. As mentioned, these are all part of our limbic response to stress. The trick is to distinguish the falsehood indicators from the general stress ones. Some people fidget when under pressure. The face may twitch the lips quiver. Though also watch for those who remain too still. This may well indicate a very conscious attempt going on to control body language. The best liars do so completely naturally, at ease with the situation and, presumably, the consequences!

Distance is another good indicator. People who lie often seem to want to avoid proximity and physical contact. That's probably why, as a kid, my mum always used to hold my hand when asking "Did you break the window?" Mum's make the best interrogators! Another indicator of distance is the person making a barrier, perhaps using a desk or bag to create a "wall."

Something else I often notice is head movement. I've been in social situations where a person answers a question, usually an invitation, in the affirmative, but their head is shaking "no"! The other similar response is the "we'd love to!" response with the fixed, fake smile.

These are some of the major indicators that a person is not being honest. There are others, of course, but the key is to get a good overall feel for a person's base behaviours and work from the there. Watch out for stress, watch out for sudden, uncommon movements. Be prepared for anger too. Many times I've seen people accused of something - theft in particular - act in an indignant or even emotionally

aggressive way, as though "how dare you accuse me of that"!". The standard response back in day was "It weren't me, mister!"

That also brings in the question of social status as well as the earlier mentioned cultural factors. A person of "higher" status may feel they can brush aside any accusations, almost act with disdain towards the questioner.

As with most things, context is key. While there are broad, general truisms, a kid being questioned about eating the cake is a world away from a serial killer being questioned about murders. Also consider this. Some people tell you what you think you want to hear.

I had a friend involved in large business contracts overseas. He was constantly frustrated by what he saw as misleading information. The issue was that, in that particular culture, people don't like saying "No". So, when he asked "will the product definitely be ready by February?" then the answer would always be "yes, yes!" even if it wouldn't be ready until March. Once he realised this, he learned to frame his questions in a different way.

We all lie at some time, even to ourselves! It may be you have to lie in a professional capacity, or to protect someone. In those cases, the above information may be useful in terms of what not to do. Another friend of mine worked undercover in potentially highly dangerous situations. That calls for a whole new level of skill, not to mention extreme nerve and calmness. For most of us, fibs are confined to "yes, of course I fixed the tap" or "no , I didn't forget our anniversary." Though that can lead to danger too!

I SECOND THAT EMOTION

Let's start looking at some drill s that will help with personal observations skills and communication. The first is very straightforward. Your partner exhibits an emotion through their body language and you have to say what it is. Anger, sadness, joy and so on. This should be very easy at

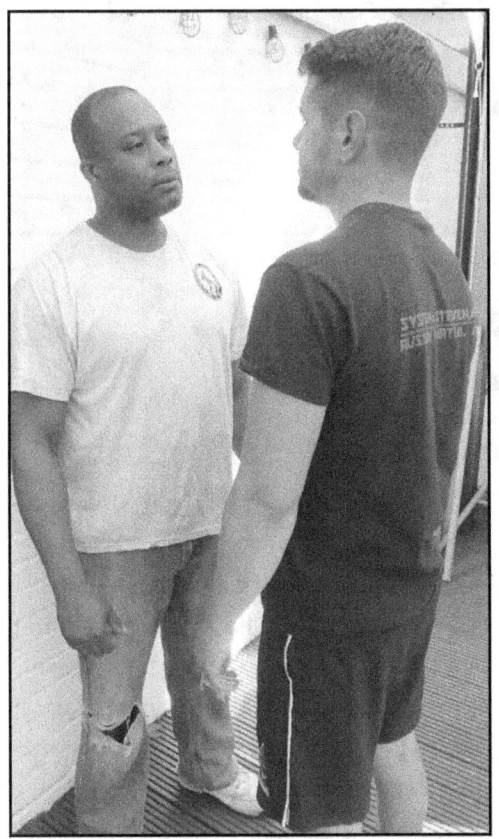

- though in some drills there is the capacity to release anger, or any other emotion. But don't feel you have to keep everything locked in like some kind of robot.

Just to digress slightly, this has been one of the greatest uses of our end of class "circle up." I've written on this before, suffice to say that some of the things shared in those circles have been truly humbling. Another aspect of that is to keep emotion out of our work - but more on that later!

SPOT THE TENSION

This drill is to help you spot tension in a person. You stand opposite your partner and they make a movement towards you. As soon as you see the movement, you point to that part of their body and say "ah!" Reset and repeat.

first. To take the drill further, have your partner try and conceal the motion a little. Even better, as there is no acting involved, try and spot your partners' emotional states during training.

A short while back, one of our students was training fine but was very quiet. Subdued but in an angry way. When I spoke to him about it, it turns out he had been to the funeral of a friend earlier that day. Never be concerned about expressing emotion during your Systema training. After all, it is an art based on feeling and personal dynamics. That doesn't mean taking anger out on partners

Once you have that down, rather than move, your partner tenses a muscle group - calf, shoulder, etc. Again, you point and call. From there, work down to smaller movements of tension. A cheek, your foot, your hand and so on. So the spotting must become progressively more focused without, where possible, going into tunnel vision.

Why do we point and make a noise? For two reasons. One, the point is a "forward" type movement. This starts to build a habit of moving forward into an attacker's space. Two, the noise "ah" makes us exhale, so helping unlock the breath and overcome any potential freeze reaction.

You can run this drill with watching two or three people and add in any further responses you want, a move in and takedown, for example, or perhaps create space and escape. However you do it, the key is to remain relaxed and not become twitchy in your response.

GRAB THE CUP

Another good drill for spotting tension is for two people to sit each side of a table. Between them is a plastic cup or similar object. The goal is simple - grab the cup before the other person does. If you wish, you can at first have a third person give a trigger - "go!".

After that, work from no trigger. Watch your partner's body language to see when the intention to grab the cup forms, then beat them to it! Once again, it is easy to add variations to this drill, positioning, objects, numbers of people and so on.

MIRRORING

So how about if we want to gain what is called rapport with a person? We want to make them feel at ease, or to approach them in some way without causing them stress? One approach is by mirroring, again a popular concept in NLP. The basic idea is that two people in synch usually mirror each other's body language. This is the opposite of the shielding or foot direction work we discussed earlier. People who are in synch typically face each other, draw close, leave their torso uncovered and so on.

So try this. Talk to your partner and as you chat, slowly adopt the same posture as them. Add in an open expression, a smile, tilt your head slightly. Maintain eye contact, nod, raise your eyebrows. These are all signs that you agree with and are comfortable with this person. By the same token, do the reverse. Close off, cross your arms, look away frequently, angle your body. Ask your partner how each feels to them. Always be aware that mirroring, like observation, should be a subtle process. Too overt and it just looks weird, so causing stress! Once you have the idea, work it with your boss when asking for a raise next time!

PERSONAL SPACE

We have quite distinct zones of comfort around us. The study of these spaces is called Proxemics. The term was coined in 1963 by cultural anthropologist Edward T. Hall. He defined proxemics as "the interrelated observations and theories of humans use of space as a specialized elaboration of culture." There are four zones within this model.

- public space is categorised as being at least 12 feet away

- social space is within the range of 4-12 feet

- personal space is defined as a range of 1.5-4 feet

- intimate space is from touch to 1.5 feet.

The distinctions are fairly obvious. Around friends and family, we feel no discomfort at being at intimate distance. In another situation, a stranger moving even to within personal space, may trigger stress or alarm. There are other factors to take into account, most notably the concept of territories. These are defined as:

- public territory, not under the control of a particular person, which anyone may freely enter

- interactional territory, where people congregate informally

- home territory, where people continuously have control over their individual territory

- body territory, the space immediately surrounding us

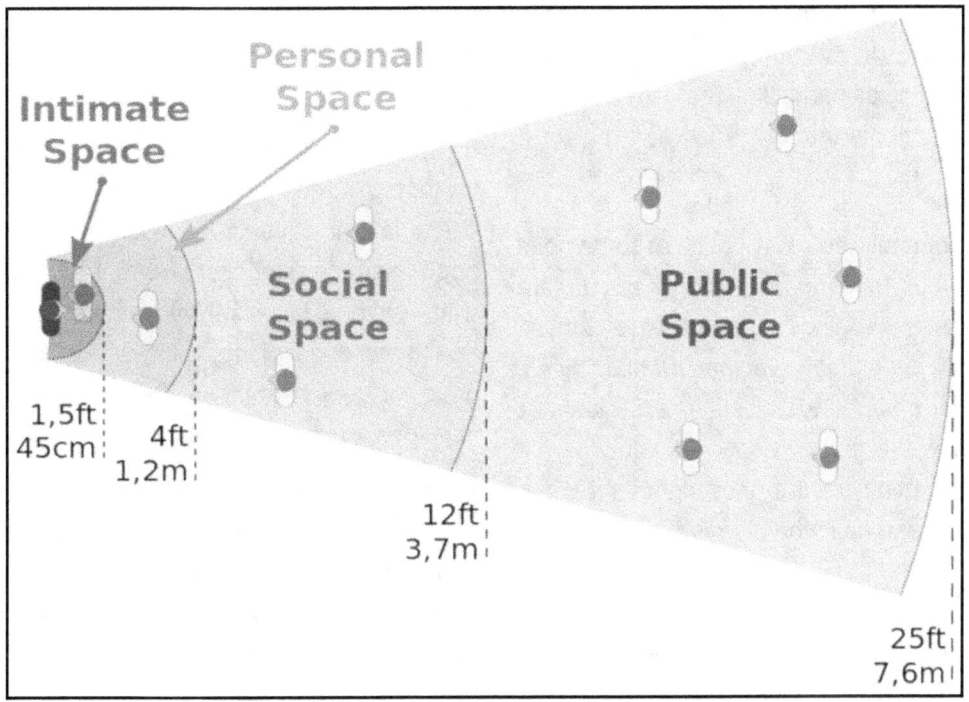

The situation is further influenced by culture and environment. People living in a large city versus those who live in a rural area, for example. Or people who typically greet with a hug as opposed to a formal handshake. As an illustration, consider the following situations.

You are standing in your large admiring the roses. A stranger approaches and stands six inches behind you.

You are on the morning commute to work and are on the train reading your paper. A stranger approaches and stands six inches behind you.

The same range but your reaction and your internal state will likely be very different. In the public space, we accept proximity as part of the deal. The same for interactional territory, such as a bar or a concert.

Incidentally, you may notice at some point in your training, as I did, that you are constantly being "triggered" by proximity. For a short time I even had it while driving, other cars felt too close! That's okay, it's a new skill that will soon "calm down" a bit like getting used to the bright light when you wake up in the morning!

FEEL AND MOVE

How do we build this into drills? The first step is that earlier drill we did, where someone approaches and, when your body feels like it should, you move out of the way. To add more layers, have your partner approach exhibiting different intentions. Anger, open arms, even ignoring you and so on., Try to gauge your body feeling each time.

UNDER THE RADAR

The reverse of this drill is gaining the ability to move into a person's space without triggering stress or discomfort. This is useful in many situations. Door work is a good example. The best people I worked with were able to smoothly lead a potential troublemaker out of the vicinity without any need for unpleasantness. Let's look at a few tips for achieving that.

Approach from the side - going straight towards someone can appear confrontational and trigger a response. Sidling up is much less noticeable. Suddenly appearing from behind can also

trigger a response, though you may be in a good position to work!

Common point of view - as you reach the person, adjust so that your direction of vision is the same as theirs. In other words, you are both looking at the same thing. This establishes a stronger feeling that you are "together" rather than opposing.

Facial expression - want to scare someone Snarl, grimace, shout. Want to get compliance? Smile and nod.

Understand motivation - why is a person acting the way they are? Perhaps they have a genuine grievance. It could be they are under the influence of alcohol or drugs. Peer pressure is something else to consider. A person may act quite differently alone than with a group of friends or in front of their partner.

Establish contact - continuing from above, build a connection. "Hi, what's your name?" Talking calmly, especially asking questions allows us to move closer.

Build empathy - understand the person's point of view. If possible, get them to understand yours, or extend you some sympathy. "If I don't ask you to do this my boss may fire me!"

Give direction - if you want someone to move, show them where you would like them to go. Pointing is good, the eyes naturally follow a pointing finger. Use your other arm as a soft barrier to emphasise the direction. It is better if the person feels it is their choice to move.

Explain yourself - make it clear why you are asking the person to move. Don't just bark orders at people.

It's for your benefit - explain the advantage to the person for doing what you ask them to do. "If you stay here, you may get bumped into, there's a crowd of people coming through. I wouldn't want you to spill your drink."

Be firm but fair - be open and confident, do not show fear or aggression. Be clear in your aims but not totally inflexible.

Be prepared! - should it go wrong, always be ready to take action. We will discuss this later on! Also bear in mind what we said earlier about tone of voice. How you say is as important as what you say.

ZONES OF AWARENESS

I once had an experience with Vladimir where he popped up behind us at the airport. I wont' repeat it as I have written about it elsewhere. Suffice to say that he managed to get within touching distance of both of us, despite the fact we were looking out for him and the environment was closed in with few hiding places! He explained this to me as people having *zones of awareness*.

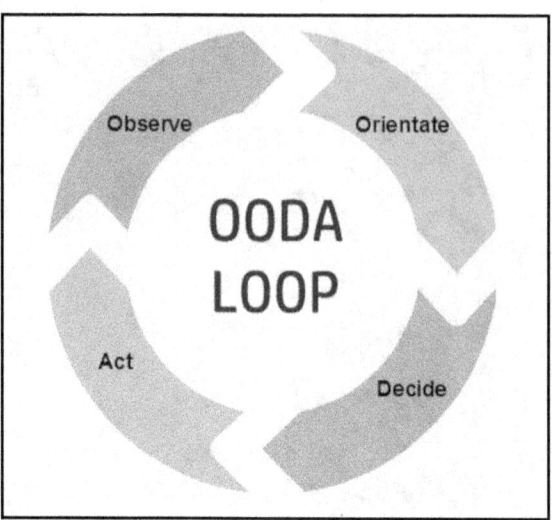

When you observe people, see if you can determine where their awareness is focused. An obvious example is a person looking at their phone. Perhaps they also have earbuds in. How wide is that persons's zone of awareness? Can you approach close to them without triggering a reaction? Think of their awareness as a spotlight or torch beam. Visualise where their attention is focused and see the "dark spots."

We already covered some drills for this type of work but make it an observational habit to pick out peoples' zones of awareness in your daily activities. If they notice you doing so, you are doing something wrong!

THE OODA LOOP

Our earlier drill on spotting tension as it develops leads us into another interesting area - that of predicting movement and cutting into what is known as the OODA Loop. This concept was developed by John Boyd, based on his experiences as a fighter pilot during the Korean War and later as an instructor.

In short, it breaks the decision making process down into a cycle of four stages - Observe, Orient, Decide and Act. It came about through Boyd's experiences and observations in aerial combat, where split-second decisions are crucial. When implemented during that conflict and beyond, it led to an increase in success for pilots. Since then it has been used in military settings as well as beyond.

There are many aspects to the OODA Loop, again I am presenting the basic version here, particularly how it relates to and can be incorporated into our Systema training. Let's first look at those four stages.

Observe - being aware of what is going on around you. Observe implies visual but of course our other senses are also fully

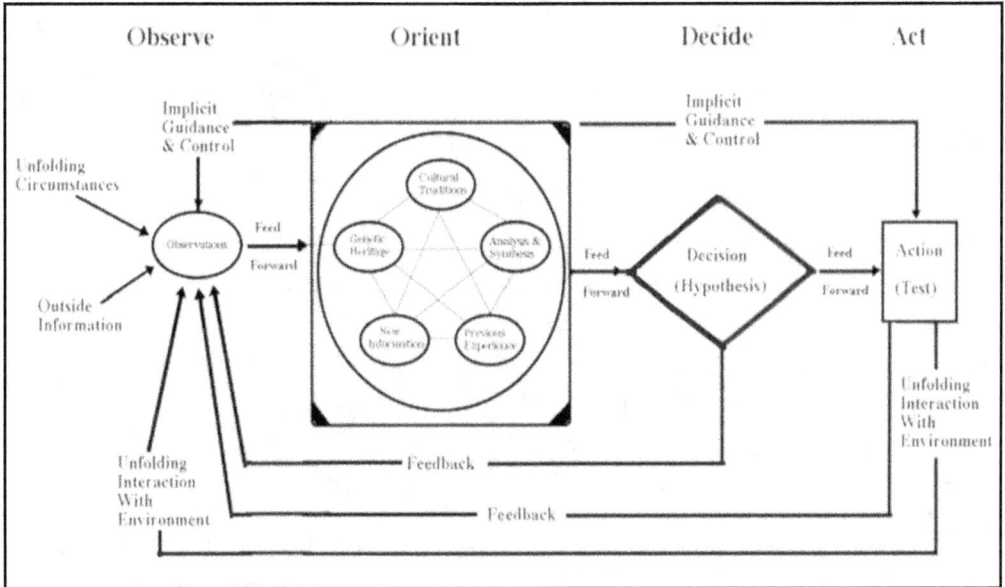

involved in that process.

Orient - assessing the incoming information from the first stage. This assessment may be influenced by a number of factors, including cultural traditions, previous experience, physical make up, world-view and so on.

Decide - we make a decision based on the above

Act - once the decision is made, it is acted upon.

This series of steps may take place very quickly and, it is important to note, is a loop. By that we mean that it plays continuously, each step always feeding into the next. A simple example - you are walking along the street and see a bakers. You catch the smell of fresh bread and feel hungry, turning to face the shop. You decide to buy a cake, so go into the shop and do so.

Now, let's say that as you walk towards the shop door, someone walks in front of you. This begins a new OODA Loop, where you take evasive action to avoid bumping into the person. For that second, you are not thinking about the cake. Once that situation is dealt with, you re-orient and go into the bakers, hopefully enjoying your tasty treat. This interaction with environment is going on constantly. In some situations, responding quickly to situations and taking appropriate decisions, gets us ahead of our opponents.

On a wider level, John Boyd applied this concept to organizations. According to him, when managers and employees become prisoners of their own views it can stifle creativity and cause unnecessary complexity. An organization can only thrive if it breaks through this impasse by adapting itself to changing external conditions.

Going back to working person to person, how can we implement the OODA Loop in terms of self defence? The first step is to be observant, in other words implement the awareness ideas we have been describing. From there, we assess and carry out the appropriate action. Let's start with some basic drills.

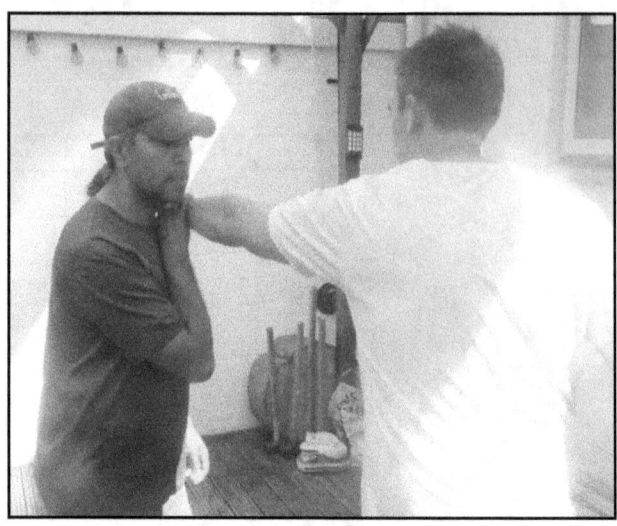

COUNTING THE PUNCH

Two partners stand opposite each other, in touching range. One person slowly pushes out a punch, counting 1-2-3-4-5. So 1 is the start of the punch, 5 is contact.

At first, allow the punch to contact and let it push you a little. Keep the body relaxed. From there, begin to work a little earlier. Move to avoid the punch on the 3 or 4. At slow speed, you should find this easy. When things speed up it becomes a little more challenging.

Next, as you evade on the 4 count, give the attacker a punch or push. In other words, you hit them just as their own hit misses. The important thing here is that you are creating a small gap by evading the punch. When a person throws a punch, they expect it to land. Physically and psychologically, they expect to receive the support of the strike landing.

Removing that support means the OODA Loop has to be reset. In a person who is fast or trained, that takes an instant. In a person less capable that may take a little longer. The extreme example is a person who takes a wild swing that misses and they actually lose balance as a result.

So we have that small gap. If we do nothing, the striker will likely throw another punch. This is where we start cutting more actively into the Loop. We fill that gap with our own response, be it a push, punch, or other movement. In other words, before their OODA Loop has a chance to reset, we have countered them. Once our own OODA Loop is dominant, so to speak, we have to keep it that way until the situation is resolved.

Having got that idea, next start working to evade on the 1. Don't move too far or too fast, just reposition yourself so the punch will miss and you are in a position to place your own strike Following that, think back to our earlier Spot the Tension drill. Watch now for the pre-1 movement. You are looking for the point where the intention forms; watch for when the shoulder tenses, when the hand begins to clench. Move at that point, apply your own punch or push.

So we are creating that gap again, just earlier in the process. Once you have this basic concept working, you can start to speed up and also begin to explore different ways to reset the Loop. A physical touch is the most obvious, As the person starts to punch you, you punch them. Of course, this needs good observation skills and awareness, not only of your attacker but also of your own movement, tension levels and structure. Once moving, you continue until the situation reaches a logical conclusion.

Incidentally, this is an important aspect of training. People often talk about sparring as a means to gain skills in martial arts. It is certainly one aspect of training that can help develop movement, positioning and son on. However, a flaw with most types of conventional sparring is that they seek to prolong an encounter. Extending the spar allows both people to "have a go.", That can build a tendency to wait for your partner to feed in an attack, then respond with your own, a bit like a tennis match.

In actual dangerous situations, we want to resolve the issue as quickly as possible, whether it be by removing ourselves form the situation or acting directly, verbally or physically. Think of cutting into the OODA Loop as off-balancing a person both, psychologically and physically. Once there, you want to keep the person unbalanced and not allow them to regain their equilibrium.

So, to return to our drill, experiment with different ways of interrupting the Loop. It doesn't even have to involve contact, just the threat of contact. As the person approaches, a sudden movement to the knees or groin may cause a flinch. Slightly repositioning yourself also gives out subtle signals that can also interrupt the Loop. Mikhail, of course, is a master at this type of work. I've seen him work

with an experienced boxer, who circled Mikhail for several minutes before giving up in confusion. "I couldn't see any place to go in." was his explanation. Every time he intended to move in to attack, Mikhail slightly shifted his position.

You might think this work is beyond you but almost all of us have done it at some time with the "pavement dance." You know, you are walking along and are on a collision course with someone coming the other way, You both move left, then right, then left again before finally getting it right and moving around each other. The process can be as simple as that. This sets the scene for further no contact methods, which works into many different layers and levels of psychology.

THE HANDSHAKE SNUB

This work need not be on the physical level either, the same principles can be applied to conversations. Sales, business meetings, hostage negotiations are all areas where this concept can be applied. If you want to train some of this, ask a person to shake your hand. Smile and come forward to meet it, then at the last minute withdraw your hand. See what effect this has on the other person.

You can try the same concept verbally. Ask one person to tell the group a joke. Prime the others before hand not to

respond at all to the punchline. Or have one of them interrupt just before the punchline is given with a totally irrelevant question. Or perhaps, they could turn away at the same point. Once again, observe and ask what effect this has on the joke teller. Now think how that could work in another setting. If you want to keep someone off balance, you interrupt at a key point in their speech. You drop in a strange question, or perhaps throw a glance over their shoulder. Each will force a reset of the OODA Loop.

Don't think this has to be confrontational either. One of the best examples I saw was with a very aggressive guy confronting a doorman. Just as the man launched into his tirade of abuse, the doorman shifted his position a little, looked concerned and asked "Are you alright, mate, you look a bit unwell? Have you been feeling okay lately?" He reinforced

the questions with a reassuring touch on the arm. At that, the aggressor stuttered to a stop, looked confused, then burst into tears. As we said before, aggression is often a mask for fear.

DODGE THE FIST

Let's also look at the OODA Loop from the other perspective - developing our own ability to assess and respond quickly. We have already covered some reaction drills but here's another one you might like to try. We need three people. One stands with fist outstretched at face height. The second person (the dodger) faces them about five feet away. The third person stands behind the second. The job of person three is to push the dodger quickly and suddenly towards the outstretched fist. The dodger, naturally, must dodge! Gradually shorten the distance until the dodger is inches from the fist. Even this close, with good relaxation and response, it is possible to dodge. So far, so good, but this is primarily a touch and respond drill. Let's add in an orient aspect. Now, the dodger works with eyes closed. At the push they have to open their eyes and dodge as before. To make things more interesting, the "puncher" can place fist or foot in different positions. To add in further pressure, have the puncher make an actual punch/kick (slow to start) to add to the decision making process.

Once you have the concept of hits drill down, I'm sure you can think of many variations and other possibilities. The key is giving participants the opportunity to work on quick decision making skills and also to encourage them to be creative in their responses. With the push drill, you can add in an extra task such as a counter-strike or takedown, for example.

HEAR THE PUNCH

Vladimir recently posted this to Youtube, it's an audio drill. This time, we work in pairs. One person holds up a hand or focus pad. Their partner stands in striking range and counts slowly out loud from one to ten. At some point during that count, they throw a punch at the hand or pad. The task is to move the hand or pad and avoid the punch/

Now, there can be a visual element to his, in that we see the tension as before. That's okay but I also want you to listen to the count. Maybe even close your eyes. See if you can pick up the change in tone and breath just before the punch. Before people strike, especially in an argument type situation, they need to prepare themselves. This may be by adjusting the breath, as in the above drill but there are other indicators too.

FIGHT INDICATORS

We have already spoken about the gross indicators, the chest puffing out, arms being flung wide and so on. But here are some other things to look for.

The Look Away - a person sometimes has a quick look around before launching an attack. This may also take the form of a look down or a sudden break in eye contact. One is perhaps to see who is watching, the other may be an internal dialogue issue.

Lining up - watch a person's stance and body position. Are they just posturing or lining you up for a shot?

Hands vanish - hands dropping to the belt or similar may indicate a weapon is about to be deployed.

Quickened breath - following along from the previous drill, listen for changes in the breathing pattern, sudden panting and so on.

Eyeing the target - people sometimes glance at what they are about to hit.

Pushing or jabbing - this serves two purposes. The person pushes or jabs with the finger when they are not quite ready to fully commit. It's a way of building themselves up. The other purpose is to measure range for a punch.

Tension - the shoulder tensing may indicate a punch is coming.

Asking a question - one tactic is to ask a question to engage the other person's brain just before launching an attack. "What's your mum's name?" used to be a common one, it's personal and enough out of place in an aggressive confrontation to cause a "What??" Reaction.

Intuition - your own internal indicator, based on all the above, plus previous experiences and "feel." Listen to it!

WHERE SHOULD I LOOK?

Given all the above possible indicators - which come with the usual caveat of context, culture, etc, - where should we be looking to observe our opponent? While we have spoken about eye cues, once at this stage it is best not to get drawn into involuntary direct eye contact. It narrows our focus and can increase fear if someone has a "hard stare."

Instead, think about softening vision a little and looking just over the shoulder. Vladimir advises looking just above the head, something else to experiment with. Again, context sensitive, especially in a crowd situation. There may be cases where a hard stare is part of your response, particularly if bolstered with positive verbal instructions! However this should always be a response and not a reaction. Above all, don't get drawn in to the "monkey dance."

EYE TO EYE CONTACT

Should you wish to use eye contact, be sure you are good at it! Fixing a strong gaze then breaking contact will be seen as a sign of weakness. Here's one method that works very well, in that it saves the eye contact until the last moment. You can practice it easily with a partner.

As you approach, keep your gaze down. You are still using peripheral vision but keep your eyes "hidden". At the last moment, suddenly switch your gaze up directly into your partner's eyes. The psychological effect is quite interesting. You can experiment with other positions, of course.

Something else to consider is drawing a

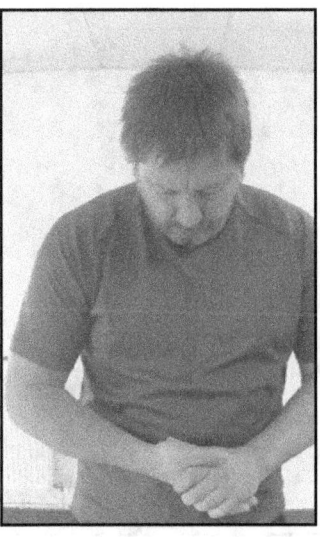 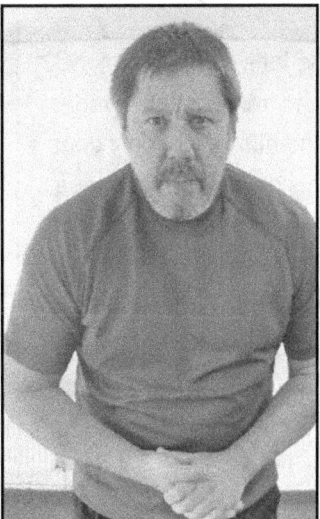

person's gaze, or even their movement, with your eyes. Some time back a person asked me, "Does all that no contact stuff really work, isn't it all nonsense?" Just as he finished his question, I glanced over his shoulder and nodded as though at someone behind him. He caught my eye movement and half turned to look himself. Then he turned back to me as I said, "No, not really, it doesn't work." He went away happy.

Try adding this into some of the previous drills, or just try it out in every day conversation

MOVE AND HIT

Here's a good drill to develop response. A and B face off to person C. At some point, one of the pair launches an attack towards C, whose job is to pick up on the attacking move, evade it, move through and strike the other person.

So let's say A attacks C, who immediately evades and hits B. Not only does this build good response, it's a useful tactic if faced by two attackers. The response doesn't have to be a strike, you might grab person B and use them as a shield, for example.

IT'S ALL IN THE PATTER!

Of course there are less physical interactions that we can consider as well! Two things that have always fascinated me are what we might professional "operators" of various types and magicians. The former includes street sellers, dippers, con men and the like. Morally reprehensible but, let's be honest, we can all admire the artistry of a good "sting".

The latter includes any of the above performed purely for entertainment - I always particularly enjoy good pick pocket and tie removal routines - as well as the more conventional magic tricks, especially what are known as mentalism or "mind reading" routines.

I grew up in an area with a vibrant street

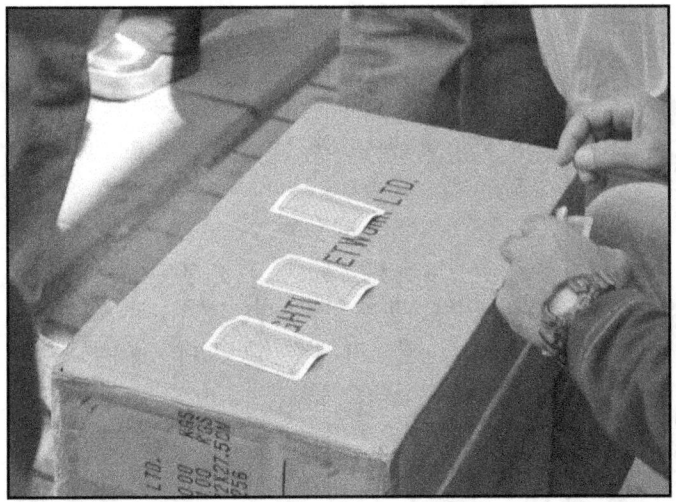

life, so street trading was very common. Most of that was from costers on the market stalls or people selling out of "pop up " shops. As well as that there were those guys who would open a briefcase on a busy street and start selling dodgy perfume, knocked off cigarettes and the like. Their patter always fascinated me, how they could draw in a crowd, control it and even persuade people to hand over five pound notes for what was, usually, cheap tat.

An off-shoot of street traders were the people who ran "chase the lady" or "three card monte" games and similar. The sleight of hand and accompanying patter again led to money being handed over, though sometimes there would be aggro from aggrieved punters. That's why those guys usually had a "hulk" lurking nearby!

When I was still at school I got a Saturday job working in a local store. I was on the till one time when a guy came in and paid for a newspaper with a large note. I took the note, opened the till and was sorting his change when he said something like "Hang on, give me that back, I've got the right money here."

The resulting back and forth exchange - I think he changed his mind again - left me bewildered. Of course, at the end of the day the till was £20 short, I'd been had.

To this day I can't say how he did it and luckily my boss was understanding. But I thought how cleverly I'd been caught out and what a marvellous skill that man had shown. Not that we condone fraud, of course!

Later on, that led me to an interest in mentalism, coinciding with the rise of people like Derren Brown and others. The interesting thing with these guys was their new approach. Less of the "Amazing Marvo", complete with glamorous assistant and more working close up and on the street, citing being able to read body language as the basis for their mind reading capabilities. I was familiar with sleight of hand with cards and coin, but this was a different level altogether. On investigating and learning some of these routines, I found that far from being pure body language skills, these routines also

Marvelous feats in Mind Reading

often relied on trickery but they were very well crafted, nonetheless.

On workshops or camps I've occasionally demonstrated my "mind reading" capabilities - telling you your PIN number, for example, or the name of a long lost school friend. It's a bit of fun but does have a serious point. It shows how well our attention can be directed, how we can be easily deceived and how we can so readily ascribe mysterious "powers" to a person.

I always take pains to reveal how the routine is done and have found, on a couple of occasions, that people were quite disappointed that I didn't actually have the power to read minds! Interesting!

I'll leave it to you as to whether you wish to research this area further but I think you will find it a fruitful area of research. Once you know a few decent bar tricks you might never have to buy a drink again - now that's a very useful skill to have!

MUSCLE READING

Having said that there is trickery involved in mentalism routines, that's not to say there aren't genuine perception skills going on too. One of those skills is the ability to recognise a person's intentions through their physical movements, or what is known as the *ideomotor response.* These are the slight, unconscious movements in a person's muscles that indicate their conscious intentions.

To get a feel for this, stand in the centre of the room and have a partner stand on your right side (if you're right handed). Ask them to extend their left arm out from the elbow, palm up and open. Take hold of the of the open hand with your left hand. With your right hand support your partner's forearm and ask them to totally relax that arm.

Now have your partner think of one of the four corners of the room. Tell them to focus on that corner and to guide you with their thoughts alone. For instance, if you go to the right and the corner is to the left, they are to instruct you mentally to go left and vice versa. They should not physically push or pull but just keep the arm relaxed and let you carry the weight of it.

As you move forward, slightly move your partner's hand to your right and left in small motions. You will feel a slight resistance in one direction and not in the other. The lack of resistance indicates the direction to go in. Once you can work this with a

reasonable level of success, try the next level.

This time, ask your partner to hide a small object somewhere in the room. The object must be hidden somewhere within reach and must not be on the person. Leave the room while the object is hidden. When you go back in the room take one of the subject's hands as before. Again, tell the person not to lead you but to repeat over and over in their mind where the object is. Start in the middle of the room and tell them to now begin repeating in their mind which direction the object is in. Move their hand as before, feeling for the direction with least or no resistance. Once you think you know which general direction the object is in begin to pull the subject towards it, still being aware of resistance.

When you get to the general location of the object ask the person to repeat in their mind the direction. Is it up or down? A little more to the left or right? You might feel the arm move. Move the hand, again feeling for resistance. You should now know where the object is. You can work this as a training drill or, once skilled at it, present it as mind reading!

COLD READING

This is a method of convincing a person that you know more about them than you actually do! It is most often used by fake mediums, psychics and the like, but may also have other applications in a situation where you are trying to gain congruence with a person. It also makes a neat party game!

There are two components to cold reading. The first is in observing the characteristics of your subject and making deductions from them. The second is the questions you ask and how they are framed. We are also watching for those micro-expressions and other body language indicators we covered earlier.

Characteristics

We can think of obvious visual clues: gender, age, ethnicity, weight, apparent health, personal hygiene. Also any noticeable disabilities, scars or bruises, evidence of smoking, drug taking, alcohol use, etc. Clothing, hairstyle, jewellery and badges, body decorations are other things to note,

Look for any marks on the clothes such as mud, oil, or stains. As well as looking, listen to voice quality, noting regional accent, pitch, pace and modulation. Consider also the person's vocabulary.

Deductions

From observing the above, we may be able to draw conclusions. The person may be wearing an engagement ring, for example, indicating a forthcoming wedding. Clothing may give an indication of likely occupation and social status.

Pigeon-hole

All of the above helps the reader place the subject into more specific categories. They may then make certain assumptions from there. An elderly person is more likely to have suffered loss or illness, for example.

An experienced people reader can already draw up a list of likely facts purely from the above. In the cold reading situation, they also get to ask questions and make statements! There are a few different types used, along with some other techniques. They are:

Shotgun Statements - these rely on general information, what you might call a scatter-shot approach. Something is bound to hit! The purpose of these questions is to be vague, but specific enough to convince. For example,
"You have been on a journey," or "Something in your life has recently changed."

Barnum statements - named after the American showman who claimed "we've got something for everyone!" These seem to relate to a particular individual but

actually apply to almost everyone. Examples are:

"You have much unused potential."

"You have sometimes told white lies to save another person's feelings."

"You have a strong need for approval and recognition."

Statements like this are often used to encourage trust and confidence in the reader.

Fishing statements - these are what seem to be very specific statements that may or may not be true. If the statement turns out to be true, the strength of the "hit" will greatly impress the subject, and the statement will be clearly remembered. If wrong, the reader can simply move on to something else and the 'miss' will very likely be forgotten. Alternatively the reader may prefer to use an 'out' to excuse the failure (see below). Examples are:

"The name Simon is significant in some way."

"You used to own a black cat."

Note that, when fishing, you should generally use statements rather than questions.

A variation is to go fishing with several baits in one sentence. For example: "I am hearing the name Jane, or perhaps it is Joan, or June, or John.". This obviously increases the chances of a hit.

Fishing is especially effective when cold reading with a large group. You might call it collective bait! You will sometimes hear readers say something like, "There is someone named Bill who has a message for a woman". It is very likely that at least one woman in the audience will know a Bill who has died.

Verbal ambiguities - some words have more than one meaning. For example, "The word 'book' is somehow relevant". This could refer, for example, to an ordinary book, or "the Book" (Bible), the phone book, a reservation for a flight, a police booking, or a bookmaker, it could even be a surname. By observing how the subject interprets an ambiguous word, the reader can then follow up that particular meaning.

A common verbal trick is to ask questions in the negative form. No matter how the subject responds the response can be interpreted as confirming the statement made. For example, "You're not married are you?" If the subject answers "No," the reader replies "I thought not". If the answer is "Yes", the reader can say "I thought so". The reader is right every time.

Recap - this is where a reader uses information that the subject has already revealed. The reader won't acknowledge what is said there and then but but files the information away for later on.

Information reveal - most subjects are cooperative in readings and can be encouraged to reveal important information. A reader might begin by explaining that initial messages may be vague, but with help from the subject, they can understand together why they are important. From there, they can say something like,

"I'm seeing a name that starts with the letter P. I'm sensing that they have something to do with your mother, maybe they knew her?"

The subject then begins to fill in the gaps and, in effect, does all the work themselves!

Homework - or, to put it bluntly, cheating! There have been examples of famous readers being caught out doing this. A common method for big show type events is to ask audience members to send in questions in advance. These people are then researched. These days, even with just a name, you can learn a lot from a person's social media presence. Information can then be fed to the reader via an earpiece, such as was discovered with a famous "medium" in the UK not long ago

Outs - sometimes the reader will say something that is directly contradicted by the subject. When this happens, the reader has to come up with a plausible explanation for the apparent mistake.

These are called *outs*. One out is to blame the subject, perhaps imply that the statement is true but the subject doesn't realise it. For example:"You should ask your mother, she will be able
to confirm this."

The reader can also directly blame the subject for any resistance to statements,

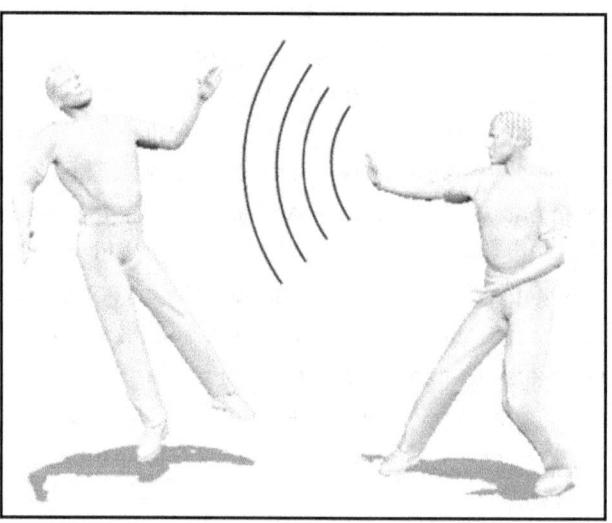

for example: "You must open your heart to these messages, my dear."

An alternative is to twist the statement. For example, "Your grandmother had a sister." No, she was an only child."

"Ah but she had a very close friend who was like a sister to her."

One other out is to blame local conditions! I remember our class once had a visit from a "no touch expert." He claimed he could use his "energy" to make people move. Nothing worked for him that night and he laid the blame on "dark energy spots" in the room.

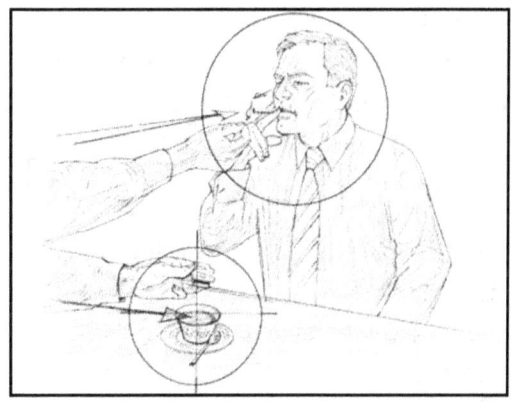

All of these methods are combined with the earlier deductions and pigeon-holing, plus observing responses. The accuracy of statements can be determined by seeing how the subject responds, using those indicators we spoke about before.

Now you know the tricks, re-visit the What's My Line drill from earlier and start adding in some questions and statements. Obviously, it's best to work with people you don't know well.

Incidentally, I touched on a side issue of cold reading there, with the mention of the "energy no contact" work. This type of "martial arts magic" has its own set of cold reading type principles, including peer pressure, gradual programming of students to respond in a certain way, bio-mechanics explained as mysterious forces and so on. As a simple example, have a group of people stand in a row, one behind the other, about a foot apart. You stand facing the lead person and begin waving your hand towards them. The first person will start to sway and that movement will transfer through the whole line. People may even stumble.

Nothing to do with energy, it's a purely physical and psychological response. People find it hard to stand still for a period of time, especially when a hand is moving towards them. Even slight body movement is copied and magnified in such situations.

MISDIRECTION

A fundamental skill of many types of routine is the ability to misdirect. In other words, your attention is directed away from where the actual trickery is taking place. I'm sure you are familiar with this, most of us had a relative who do the old "penny from your ear" trick or similar. Think, though, how this concept can be applied in different situations and on different levels. One tip is not not think of this skill as misdirection but as *attention management*. In effect, you are controlling the direction of attention of other people.

A simple example you can try. If you are talking to a group, after a few minutes, cough and look over at your bottle of water. Chances are, everyone else will also look at the bottle. The aim of managing attention is usually to create a gap or space that enables you to carry out some action. In crude terms, walk up to your partner and point, saying, "Look up there!". They look and you can easily hit them, they will not see your strike. Don't do this!

Pointing is a very strong method, it's difficult not to follow the pointing finger! Using eyes to indicate direction works well too, as I mentioned before. Did you ever do the trick that combines both? Where a few of you gather outside a tall building and look and point upwards? Before long a crowd gathers, all looking up and you all walk away and leave them to it. These are quite basic visual methods and we have already spoken a little about psychological directions, with the "asking a question" technique. The basic idea is to force the brain to focus on one thing while you do something else.

One component of attention management is the concept of leading. This is where you

subtly lead the person into making the choice that you wish them to. For a simple illustration, look at how a magician uses leading to force a specific choice. I have three cards, let's say the Jack, Queen, King of Clubs. I want you to choose the King.

So I hold up the three cards and ask you too choose two of them. If you choose the Jack and Queen, then great, I can get rid of those, we don't need them. Should you choose the King and Jack, then I discard the Queen and ask you to now choose one card. If you choose the King, we keep it, Jack, we discard it. In other words, whatever your choice, we end up with the card of my choice - though you might think you have chosen it!

Another aspect of leading is the use of words and gestures to gently nudge you in a certain direction. Another basic trick that illustrates this is to place a card face down on the table, then ask someone to think of a specific card. The patter goes something like this:

"First, when REDy think of the colour of the card, something NICE AND BRIGHT that you can VIVIDLY imagine in your mind, you can almost feel it in your HEART it is so BRIGHT (make a brief heart shape with your hands). Okay, now we have a colour we should think of a suit, this could be hard to BEAT (touch your chest) there's a real ART involved in this (flash the heart shape again). Last, we need a number, I want you to visualise that suit and the number (here you jab your finger out three times in a vertical line). I hope this isn't seeming too ODD for you. Remember this is a FREE choice on your part (subtly hold out three fingers)." Three of hearts? Ta-da, you reveal the card on the table as the three of hearts.

This is a slightly shortened version of this routine but give it a try, see how many times you can get someone to choose the right card. The trick is to be obvious enough in your leading to influence but not too obvious. Much like the mirroring and similar principles we discussed earlier.

If all else fails, there are certain tricks and gimmicks that make sure you are never wrong! But this first method is nice as it is purely psychological.

Once you understand the leading concept you can see how it is used in everyday life. Advertising is a prime example, something that we engage with hundreds of times every day, often unnoticed. Take some time to actually watch an ad and see how many principles of leading and persuasion you can spot.

Politicians are another prime example, where conversations and questions are steered towards what the person wants to answer rather than what the actual question was. Also watch their body language and how they employ all the tricks of public speaking - the use of the hands, pauses in certain places and so on. This is all learned behaviour on the part of public figures, though the best make it look very natural. Once we get into this area, we could also start to investigate methods used by smugglers, the tradecraft

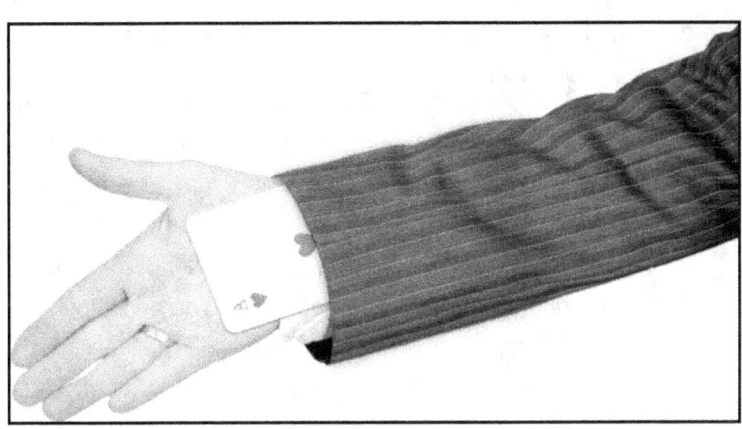

used by spies and similar, we could also get into the areas of hypnotism, influence and control mechanisms, but we will conclude this section with a look at an a rather more common activity.

PICKPOCKETS

Pick pocketing, or dipping, is generally a criminal activity but watching an expert in action is a master class in attention management and stealth. Take a look on Youtube at a guy called Apollo Robbins, for example. He is an entertainer and openly explains how he performs much of his routine. Interestingly, he also talks of zones of awareness and how the attention is like a torch beam.

Now, I'm not into training up pickpockets, like some modern day Fagin, but we do occasionally cover this type of work in class. It helps develop skills from the dipper's perspective but, primarily, it helps educate the target as to how pickpockets work and what to be on the lookout for to prevent yourself being robbed. So here's a few tips.

Location - dippers are more likely to work in crowded areas where proximity is not an issue. So trains, crowded streets, tourist areas and so on.

Where's your wallet? - A favourite place to stand is close by signs on the underground that say "Beware pickpockets." When you read the sign there is a natural tendency to tap your wallet, to check it is still there. You just told the thief where your wallet is.

The jostle - one tactile sensation can be masked by a greater one. So a hand in your pocket may be felt on its own. In conjunction with a jostle or push, though, you won't notice it. Check yourself immediately. The difficulty now is that the dipper has likely passed your item to an accomplice moving in another direction.

These people work in teams!

By the door - on the tube a pickpocket will often position themselves by the door. They can grab as the train enters the station and be off and away as the door opens.

What and how are you carrying - it makes sense to keep items safely tucked away and close to you. However, do not think that an inside pocket is safe. A good dipper can access it as easily as anything else. A buttoned pocket our buttoned up coat is much more of a challenge. Handbags should be closed and held tight under the arm. Some people attach a small bell, similar to what you might find on a cat's collar, to their purse. If removed from the bag, the bell is tinkled as an alarm.

Got the time - while not becoming paranoid, if we get stopped and asked the time, or similar, become extra aware of anyone else around you. It's a classic distraction technique.

Money belt - if carrying a lot a cash or documents in an unfamiliar place, consider a money belt. Some people also like to carry a dummy wallet, a cheap one with very little in it.

Don't display - I've been on a train where the person opposite sits down, pats their pockets, gets out their wallet, phone, keys, diary, etc. Maybe they are looking for something, their ticket perhaps! In any case, they have given a nice display of their wares, sometimes even placing them on the next seat while they search for whatever they are looking for. Likewise, be aware at places where you have to take your wallet out - cashpoint machines, ticket kiosks and the like

Bag slashing - a less subtle method is to cut open a bag or sometimes cut the straps. Backpacks can be especially vulnerable to this as, when worn on your back, you have little tactile awareness of them.

Major distractions - a question is one thing, other ways a dipper can get close is by asking you to sign a petition or similar. There's also an old scam called the mustard trick, where someone throws a little mustard or similar on your back, then says, "Hey, you have some mustard on your jacket there, let me help you!". I some cases, before you know it, you have even

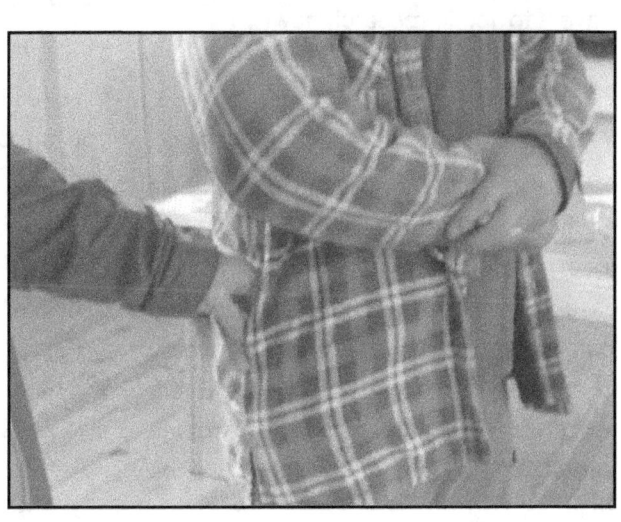

taken off your jacket!

So these are few ways in which thieves can work. In short, if in a known pickpocket area, stay alert and guard your valuables!

TAKE THE PAPER

If you want to develop some dipping skills - purely for educational purposes! - there's a couple of simple drills you can start with. One is to give everyone a strip of paper wit h a fold in the top. The paper goes in the trouser pocket, with the fold holding it in place so the paper is just poking out. This allows anyone who gets close enough to be able to take the paper from your pocket. Run whatever other drill you are doing and, by the end, see who has picked the most piece of paper.

Along similar lines, have everyone wear a jacket, carry a bag and so on, see how many items can be filched. With a bit of practice you can even take a watch from a person's wrist without them knowing. I'll leave it to you to research how!

PASS THE KNIFE

This is a good observation drill and also gets people used to working with objects on the move. You need a group of, say, 8-10 people. They move in and around each other. One of the group has a training knife. They have to pass the knife covertly to another member of the group. Every now and then, call a halt and ask everyone to point to the person they think has the knife.

If you wish, you can add in another option for the knife holder, to randomly attack another person. This can be just a simple stab or slash which the target must avoid. For further variations, add in more people and/or more knives

SECRET SQUIRREL

The difficulty with running any type of misdirection type drill is that as soon as you announce what the drill is about, everyone becomes hyper-vigilant! A way to get round this is to brief only one or two people on a task and to drop them into a more conventional drill. For example, run a drill on moving and striking in a crowd. Give a couple of people the task of passing an object between themselves. After, ask the other participants if they noticed anything unusual.

Given time and resources, I'm sure you can come up with more layered and complex scenarios but the basic principles can be practised in most classes.

PRACTICING SOFT SKILLS

Much the same applies to all aspects of what we might term "soft work." So, as with the above, it is up to you to work these aspects of training into the more physical drills. The aim, of course, is to fully integrate all of these skills into a coherent whole. This is really something that defines Systema as being a method of behavioural training rather than a martial arts "style." Our work should develop us as a complete person, not just a person who knows a few cool moves to pull out of the bag in a sticky situation.

How you implement this depends on how you run your classes. My personal approach is to start with quite simple exercises and drills and gradually add in more layers as the class progresses We then conclude with an opportunity to put all those layers together in as freeform a style as possible.

One way to do this is to set up drills that are somewhere between free sparring and a scenario. Without developing a full blown scenario, give each participant a simple goal. It might be "get through that doorway within two minutes." In other words, there is enough freedom in the situation to give participants scope to use their range of skills, with enough guidelines to keep things focused.

How intense these drills are is up to you, depending on the experience levels of those involved. In some cases, it may be a goal for one person to goad another and actively try and spike their nervous system. Sometimes you may find that having a person applying physical resistance will prompt an emotional spike in one or more participants.

That means you should always be ready to step and calm the situation, if needed. Sometimes it is good to let these things play out a little. Again, don't be afraid of strong emotions in training. As long as everyone goes home friends!

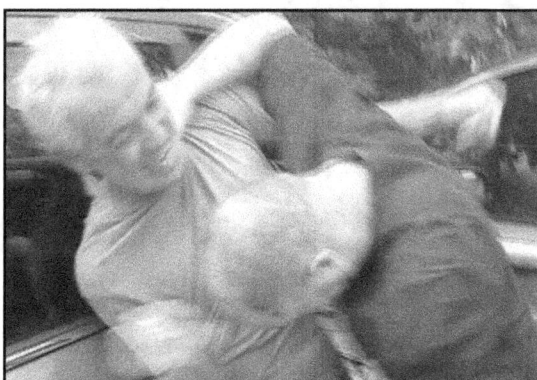

To that end, I advise that you put everyone through the earlier "emotional" drills, such as the name calling, pain control, taking slaps and the like, as well as being sure they have a decent understanding of how to use their breathing to maintain emotional control.

CHAPTER SEVEN
SITUATIONAL AWARENESS

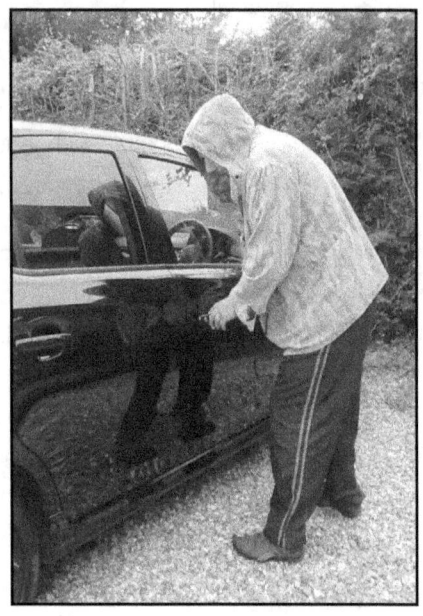

Many years ago I was on holiday in Majorca with my girlfriend. One evening we went into a nice local bar for drinks after our evening meal. About ten minutes later, a group of around six men came in. They were older than us, maybe in their 40s. Something about them drew my attention straight away. They were being quite loud and made a big fuss about where they were going to sit. When the waiter came over they began racially abusing him, the same again when he returned with their drinks. The loud behaviour continued, including comments directed at other patrons in the bar. I said to my girlfriend "drink up, we're going somewhere else." She asked me why?

It was interesting to me that she hadn't really noticed any of the above behaviour at all, until I pointed it out. Anyway, we moved on to a bar over the road and, sure enough, fifteen minutes later, sirens announced the arrival of the police at the first bar to deal with the big fight that had broken out.

There are two things to take from this. The first is picking up on things before they happen. The second thing is, having got that information, acting on it. In that particular case, I had no real reason to stay in the bar and get involved. I had a friend with me, who I would not want to get dragged into a situation. The bar owner and staff were well equipped to deal with the situation. So, I made the decision to leave.

If circumstances were different, then the decision would have been different. What if I owned the bar? What if we had been directly threatened? What if those guys started beating up another person? The point is there are no "one size fits all" rule when it comes to situational awareness. As I am so fond of saying, context is key! However, there are some general guidelines, so let's look at those before going into more detail.

GUIDELINES

Establish a baseline - it helps if you have at least a rough idea of what is normal and regular for any give place or situation. At a nightclub, for example, you would expect noise, drunkenness, dancing. That would all be out of place at a business meeting. Once we have that baseline, we should be able to spot anything unusual much quicker.

Utilise all your senses - we rely on our vision a lot but, as I hope this book has shown, all our senses should be utilised. The sound of a car at high revs, the smell of something burning, a sudden drop in temperature, all may be indicators of a potential problem.

Know where you are - if you are working your awareness properly, you should always know a couple of things, namely, how to get in and out. Where are the exits? How are people moving into the space? What are the likely choke points? Outdoors, which direction leads to safety?

What is the best path through the terrain?

Understand behaviour - in the case earlier, my radar was pinged by the loud behaviour of the other group. Now that in itself doesn't mean trouble. Think about cultural issues, for example. Some people like to talk loud, maybe with large gestures. Yet it is all friendly! However, if the loudness is accompanied by tension, insults and so on, trouble is likely not far off.

Watch also how people cluster. Tension draws attention! People gather around, either to participate or to watch (or, these days, to film on the phone!).

That's humans - how about animals? If you are in the wild, you should have at least some prior knowledge of the behaviour patterns of any wildlife you may encounter. Should you "go big" or play dead if a bear appears? Are there young in the area? Animals are unlikely to attack without a reason or provocation.

Local knowledge - as well as those cultural issues mentioned earlier, think on other local customs too. Clothing, behaviour, expectations may be very different if you are away from home. Think also about social structures and how they influence human behaviour.

When I was working the doors, it was very important to know "who was who." Treating the wrong person in a certain way could result in consequences. That meant difficult decisions at times, not to mention good diplomacy skills!

A quick example, told to me by a friend of mine. A young man was in a nightclub and was asked to dance by an attractive older woman. They danced and were getting on very well. Nothing further happened but the lad found out later who the lady's husband was - a local mobster, not a person you wanted to upset! The lad immediately went to see the man in question and explained what had happened. He hadn't known, it was all innocent on his part. The man accepted the apology and respected the fact the lad had come to see him. No further action was necessary. So the situational awareness here extends beyond the actual event and into possible future consequences

Observe and assess - take note of what is going on. Don't just look, assess! Draw conclusions and look for motivations for the behaviour you see. Again, that may be human behaviour or it may the weather. Imagine you are out hiking and a there is suddenly heavy cloud forming ahead. What does this mean? Should you continue or head back?

Position - are you in a place where you can maintain good awareness of what is going on? The old "never sit with your back to the door" advice is not far off. It doesn't mean you have to be paranoid wherever you go but neither do you want to be sat facing the corner when potential trouble is brewing behind you.

Have a plan - this doesn't necessarily mean you have a meticulous plan for every single, possible situation. That would be impractical! However, as the saying goes, *be prepared to be prepared*! You can have general procedures in mind for particular circumstances. If with family, for example, designate a particular spot to meet if you get separated.

In more extreme circumstances, such as an active shooter, you may run some training drills in order to work out a survival response. Run? Hide? Fight? Explore the options in training in order to be prepared should the worst happen. There is a reason organisations run extensive training in emergency response. And even though, as the old saying goes, "no plan survives intact contact with the enemy," there is, at least, a plan in place to begin with.

Have the right kit - make sure you have appropriate clothing and kit for the environment. Take changing conditions into account. The rescue services have to endlessly deal with hikers who, on a sunny day, decide to trek up into the hills in shorts and flip flops. Of course, as they get higher

up, the temperature drops, fog rolls in, the terrain is more treacherous and they get into difficulties. In other types of circumstance this may mean having a ready bag, a first aid kit, or so on. In a potential fight situation it may mean picking up a bottle or heavy ashtray!

Respond rather than react - another concept that bears repeating. I've seen a few occasions where, when something "kicked off", people froze on the spot. They may also scream or cover their eyes or ears in denial at what is happening. Our training should offset that and allows us to respond in the appropriate way.

I've heard two versions of the "three reactions" rule. The less formal one was split into:

- people who see what is about to happen
- people who react to something happening
- people who ask "what just happened?"

The second version was, I think, following research carried out by an airline company. They also divided emergency response into three categories:

- people who sit quietly and wait to be told what to do
- people who panic
- people who quickly and calmly carry out the required action

Trigger points - people generally misbehave for a reason. It may not be a good reason, but certain actions my be triggered by something. In pubs and clubs, chucking out time was often a trigger for trouble In some establishments, staff were quite vigorous and none too polite in asking customers to leave. Added to that, you have a group of drunk people all being moved through a smallish space en masse. No wonder tempers fray and fights break out.

People who know how to manipulate a crowd will develop their own trigger methods. I saw this in the early 80s when on political marches. You could spot agitators, some perhaps planted stooges,

who would try different things to stir the crowd up and incite them to violence

Get involved, or not - if something happens you have to make a decision to be involved, or not. In a major event, you may not have any choice. However, the choice tends to boil down to "stay or go." There are so many factors to take into account - perhaps you have young children with you, perhaps a vulnerable person is being targeted, perhaps it's your job, perhaps someone else is intervening. All these and more are possible factors to influence your decision. But once the decision is made, implement it without delay - don't waver!

Gut feeling - finally, in some ways the best indicator! If something doesn't feel right, it probably isn't. This may be the result of sub-conscious signal from your senses, it may be the result of previous experience. You can get a feel for a crowd's mood and you can begin to sense when that mood is on the change. Once again, listen to your body!

Having covered the generalities, let's look at some specific concepts and methods to assist our situational awareness.

COLOUR CODES

I've not used this method myself but it is quite common in some approaches so you

might like to experiment with it. I believe this model was developed by the US military and later refined by Jeff Cooper, USMC. The basic idea is that our awareness is in one of four modes, or codes. They are:

Code White - unaware

Involved in looking at your phone, reading a book and so on.

Code Yellow - relaxed alertness

What you might call everyday awareness, our default position. There is no specific threat but you are generally aware of what is going on around you.

Code Orange - focused alertness

A specific activity has caught your attention. This may represent a potential threat and so "blips" on your radar. This may trigger an evasive response or it may mean you continue to monitor to gather further information.

Code Red - time for action

The threat has now developed and it is

time to take appropriate action. This is carrying out the action that we have prepared for in Code Orange.

So that is the Colour Code outline. There are some caveats with it, mainly that it was primarily developed in this form for specific use with police firearms officers. In that sense, given all our previous information, it may appear quite simplistic - though sometimes simple is good! Like the other models we have presented, you may find it useful in some circumstances or as a general teaching tool.

INTEGRATED AWARENESS

We have covered specific sense training, let's now look at integrating these senses together in order to expand our overall awareness. As we have seen, without actively shutting one sense down, to some extent we do this anyway. However, it is rare that we actively explore the extent of our senses, so let's being with that.

QUIET SITTING

Find a quiet spot, outdoors is good, where you will be undisturbed. Lay down and close your yes. We will begin with internal awareness, then expand outwards. Run through the usual Systema selective tension drill. Start by slowing your breath and letting the body relax. Next, work each muscle group in turn, inhale tense, exhale relax. You can work a whole limb, chest, stomach, etc or smaller muscle groups, calf, bicep and so on. Once you have worked round all the muscles, inhale and tense from head to toe, exhale relax. Add a short hold on each. Do this three times.

Finally go back into relaxed breathing. Feel your body relax and sink into the ground. Be aware of the sensation. Notice the air around you, the breeze on your skin, the feel of the sun on your face. Keep your eyes closed and start to focus on what you can hear. The wind in the trees, distant traffic, birdsong. Examine each sound in turn, then let them all meld into one.

On your next in breath, pick up on the scents around you. Again, take each one in turn then let them all meld. Start to move your body a little, twist and stretch. When ready, slowly sit up and open your eyes. Look down at the patch of ground in front of you. Choose something there, a flower, a blade of grass and study it for a few minutes. Notice its shape, its colour, how it moves. Does it have a scent?

Now widen your vision out to the wider patch of ground and notice all the things there, plants, insects and so on. Watch them, listen to them them, smell them. After that, raise your eyes and begin to widen out your gaze. Start with what is close to you, trees, bushes, etc then slowly expand out, forward and sideways, into middle and far vision. Do the same with your hearing and smell, try and pick up as much information as you can. Remain aware of the sensations in your body, your contact with the ground, your posture, your breathing. Now switch between that far vision and the near object you first looked at.

Once you've done this for a while, slowly stand, stretch and move a little but while maintaining that outward connection. Walk around and touch some of the things you have been looking at. Hug a tree, it's a nice feeling!

I can guarantee that if you spend time on this drill, you will walk away feeling much better and with a smile on your face. If I ruled the world this exercise would be compulsory for everyone once a week! It helps re-establish our connection both with ourselves and with your environment. One of the best experiences I had when doing this was the appearance of a muntjac (a small wild deer) who appeared to have a look at what this stranger was doing in his woods!

NIGHT SIT

You can run the above exercise in many different ways. Trying it at night gives an interesting experience. You can also work it, with slight modifications, in urban or other environments. A long plane or train journey is another opportunity to try it. You could add in observation of your fellow passengers. Take note of their specific movements, how they interact, have a guess at what their occupations and backgrounds might be.

HAPPY PLACE

The Quiet Sitting drill is also useful in the creation of a Happy Place. This is a mental construct that you can return to in times of stress or duress. Let's say you have to undergo an unpleasant experience. Recently I underwent dental surgery to remove roots of a broken tooth. Not nice! In the chair I used breathing to relax then, while the dentist was digging around in what felt like my boots, mentally transported myself back to the last time I did Quiet Sitting. It considerably reduced the discomfort of the situation. This is an example of reverse awareness, where you actively don't want to be fully cognisant of what is going on around you!

SLOW WALKING

Try the same drill while moving. Take a slow walk, as we did in the earlier chapter, and run a similar procedure to the Quiet Sitting. Go from near to far and back again, using sight, smell and sound. Be aware of your internal state, too. You might like to work in breathing ladders with this kind of work. This will help to make your breathing both more controlled and less conscious!

SCENARIO TRAINING

How can we being to integrate these skills and attributes directly into our training? One answer is in the use of scenarios. I covered these in detail in my book *The Ten Points of Sparring*, so will just give some

quick pointers here.

In short, a scenario drill is a training method set up to replicate a particular situation. As an example, let's use a road rage incident. First step is to set up the physical scene, I this case one person in a car, one outside, perhaps. Next set the situation - the person outside the car is angry because the car driver nearly hit them. Next, set a time limit plus some kind of overall guidance. Brief the pedestrian to be angry but non-physical, angry and violent and so on. Now run the drill and see how it goes. You can run it several times, working I different variations and switching roles as you see fit.

The downside of scenarios is that they rely on "role play" and so a certain amount of acting is required. In this sense, everyone knows the situation is not real. However, remember what we said earlier about "fooling the brain.". With a good actor and enough shouting and swearing this can be easier than you think!

A nice variation is for the victims, sorry participants, not to know they are in a scenario! I wrote about this in the book previously mentioned too, where we had some local "farmers" confront the group about being on their land. The adrenalin was very real in that one, though you may have to monitor the situation carefully!

POSITIONING

Let's say that a situation has developed and you are in direct confrontation with someone. How should you approach them/ How should you position yourself? Again, context is important but here are some methods I have found useful in the past.

The first thing is to revisit our work on moving quietly into someone's personal space. If you can achieve this, you are halfway there. I mentioned in that exercise about "lining up". This means that you position yourself in such a way that you have quick and easy access to the main target areas should you need to strike or grab the other person.

Incidentally, just a legal note. In the UK, the law as it presently stands, allows a person to take appropriate pre-emptive action against another person if they are in fear for their safety. In other words, if someone is in your face and being belligerent, if you fear they are going to attack you, you can legally act first. That might be pushing them away, hitting or throwing them, etc. However, your actions must be proportionate to the perceived threat. If a person says "I don't like!" and you shoot them dead, you may well be in contravention of the law. Likewise, if you continue to attack once the threat is neutralised, you will also likely be in trouble.

There were two recent cases here - in one a man was cleared after killing a burglar in his home. Another man was convicted after chasing a burglar out of the home and down the street, where he beat him with a cricket bat. These can be very blurred lines, especially when later explained in court, which is one reason in English law works on a case by case basis.

Legalities explained, let's go back to our positioning. Think about the message that your posture conveys. A rigid hands up

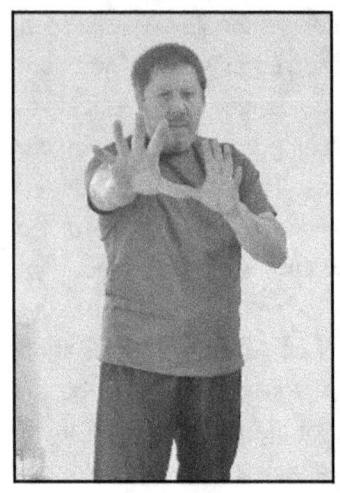  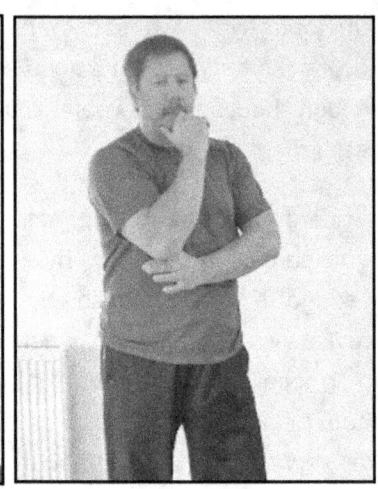

and out stance may form an obvious barrier, but to me it also conveys fear and tension and makes me feel annoyed and irritated. A bit like when people shout "relax!!" at you!

More subtle stances bring your hands up and ready but in less overt displays. Consider the crossed arm position. Note how the hands are not tucked in, for quick response. An old standard is the "conversation stance.". One arm across the body, the other supports the chin. Note, also, how the body is slightly bladed away and the weight is ready to shift. Don't plant the feet.

Those are a couple of posture ideas, but how about position? Ideally, I want to be close enough to quickly hit my priority targets - solar plexus, temple, carotid sinus, jaw. This takes us in quite close but allows for us to strike without giving the other person time to react.

One concept I use for this is the idea of *centreline*. Imagine a vertical line that runs down the front centre of your body. Now imagine a line extending out horizontally at chest height from the centre point. This is your "line of fire." Some people also call it a *Fighting Arc*, basically the space between your fists if you hold your arms up in front of you. Look at the photos opposite. If you stand face on to someone, both your lines of fire point at each other. But if you angle off a little, you can keep your line of fire on the other person, while theirs will miss you. That's the basic idea.

I then use that centreline as a kind of sight, to line up on whichever target is most appropriate. Through training, I know exactly where to place my hands from that position in order to hit the target. This also takes us back to our idea of not confronting or approaching head on, but blading off to the side. That should get us in position and with the right posture we can respond effectively. If your response is a strike, think back to our earlier work. Learn to hit with little or no tension or tells. This is something we will train in our next drill.

HIT FIRST

Stand in front of your partner and take your pose. Think back to our earlier Spot the Tension drill. This time, when you see your partner's tension, you strike. These should be light strikes of course, but work your reaction and position. Remember, real speed is all about timing and position! If your partner sees the strikes coming they should evade.

Two things to bear in mind - don't go down the route of always striking fast but "slappy". Make sure you work on hitting fast but with effect. The second is try not to become too twitchy with these drills, the aim is to stay relaxed.

SWEEP THE LEG

So far we have been working with the upper body, but here is something else to consider. Work to also take in your attacker's legs, in particular look at how they stand and how the legs are weighted. Taking out a person's base of support usually renders the hands useless. Plus it is a nice, quiet way of dealing with a person, difficult to counter when they don't know what is happening.

To train this, you walk alongside your partner, slowly. Try and match their pace and position, left, right, left, right.

At some point, just as they place a foot down, gently sweep it aside or brush it forward a little. Timing is key, you want to get the foot just as it is about to touch the floor. The weight is committed and your partner should at least stumble and most likely fall. Once you've developed that timing, start to work from different positions. Have your partner approach you, and sweep. Have them come in and grab you in some way. This makes life easier as, with a turn of your body, you can actually direct their step, so you know in advance where the foot will be placed.

At first, you will find that you are intently

watching your partner's feet. This is obviously not good from an awareness point of view, so we need to learn how to spot the feet with peripheral vision. To do this, you and a partner join forearms and, while keeping the gaze up and over the shoulder, try to step on each others feet. You can take it in turns or just both go for it.

WORK THE KNEE

Next, start to work up the leg. The best way to do this is for one person to sit or kneel and the other stand in front of them. Begin to work on pushing and pulling the knee and ankle. See how the joints work, which direction works best and how each can be disrupted or locked.

Work with your hand first, then your feet. Finally, transfer back into the standing drills, static and walking. As the lead foot touches done, gently tap the knee. Once again, with the right timing the person will stumble or fall. Please be very careful when applying force to the knee!

VERBALS

Remember our earlier work on asking questions to engage the brain? This is something else you can work into your pre-emptive drills. Also consider those ideas of pointing to direct the other person's gaze, or even odd behaviour to manage their attention.

The other aspect of verbals is talking our way out of situation, or calming a person down. For this, refer back to our work on moving a person in the previous chapter as many of the same principles apply - establishing a connection, being calm and clear in our intentions and so on. Remember also, how tone of voice is just as important as what we say.

Try this with a partner; see how many ways you can say the word "Hello" to them. See how each different inflection makes them feel. Now add in a hand gesture or body posture. This may match the spoken word, or be in opposition. A cheery "Hello! with a hand wave is one thing. A surly "Hello" as you turn away is something else. In short, match body language, tone of voice and posture. That may be genuine on your part, it may be that you use placatory gestures and words in order to get in position to hit someone. Context strikes again!

Generally it's best not to get angry and to keep emotion out of your voice. Any police officer or similar will tell you how some people like to try and "wind you up." We all have buttons that can be pressed. The better a person knows us, the more likely they are to score a direct hit on those buttons.

This is where our internal awareness comes into play, through the drills we described before on developing emotional control. An insult can be like a strike. The effect can be the same on the nervous system, we get spiked. Or we can absorb, deflect, shrug it off.

Having said that, never say never. At times it might be appropriate to show anger, or any other emotion. A loud shout has impact and putting fear into someone can assist at times. It's a two edged sword though, putting fear into someone, or something, can also prompt them to react. In fact, as I often say in class, putting the wrong kind of fear into a person can actually make them a better fighter, whatever their perceived capabilities may be. The instinct to survive is powerful and can be overwhelming, even in the most unlikely cases.

Another story from days gone by! I had some friends round, we were sat playing cards and having a drink. My partner came in to let us know she'd seen a mouse in the kitchen. Being tough, burly men, this was something we had to sort out. So the four of us began rooting round the kitchen, searching for the beast. We found it, and managed to usher it up into a corner on the worktop. Now it was trapped, we were going to put a cup over it, then release it outside. As we moved in, the mouse turned, stared us in the eye (I swear!), bared its "fangs" and leapt directly for us! I'm not kidding, four men went "aaargh" and dodged out of the way.

The mouse escaped, needless to say. My girlfriend rolled her eyes in despair and we resumed our card game, reluctant to make eye contact with each other. Point is, that when you rouse that pure survival instinct in anything, it has a physical and psychological effect on anyone else in the situation. We can ourselves become overwhelmed by what we have triggered. So be aware of that if you are using fear as part of your armoury.

We have covered a lot of methods of

developing our general awareness, so let's now look at some specific ideas for putting these into practice for our everyday personal safety. This doesn't mean creeping round like a ninja, or walking round in a state of permanent "alert tension." The best approach is simply to take a few precautions, plan head and generally be aware of what is going on locally. In terms of situational awareness, it makes sense to focus especially on those areas or places in which we spend a lot of time.

HOME SECURITY

According to the old saying "Every Englishman's home is his castle!" That may be true but even the strongest of castles can be breached and domestic burglary is a fact of life. The tips presented here are from a UK perspective, so it is important to check laws in your own area and be sure that you are complying with them.

The first step is to be aware of the main entry points to your home. Are they secure? A lot of burglary in the UK is opportunistic. Someone sees a back door open as they are passing and nips in quick to steal something. Stage one then, when you are out is to always ensure vulnerable doors and windows are closed and locked. Even be aware of this when you are in the house. Thieves have been known to knock at the front door as a distraction while an accomplice goes in through the back.

Are your entrance points hidden or overlooked? A doorway concealed by foliage or in a dark recess allows a thief time to work on a lock. One that is well lit and overlooked by neighbours is less attractive. You may consider getting motion activated lighting or perhaps one of the new type of cameras, which not only monitor movement but allow you to speak to the person in front of them.

Next, take a step back and look at your home in its setting. How easy is it to access your property? Being on the top floor of a block of flats is very different from having a house in the corner of a quiet field. Can people approach without being seen? Can they easily climb over your back fence and into your garden?

Having done that, can you take steps to harden your perimeter? Repair broken fences or replace them with something a little higher. Nature provides the best barrier, if you can, have a nice hedge with brambles in it.

Depending on local laws, vulnerable walls might be topped with wire or similar. Gravel makes a noisy surface to walk on. Maybe cut back any heavy foliage that is close to windows.

I mentioned earlier the Google street maps view of your house. If you feel it makes you more vulnerable you can have the view obscured.

Alarms are an obvious security precaution, though personally I've never used one. They can be expensive to fit and I've found that when they go off, people tend to ignore them! In fact, when I lived in London, car alarms, in particular, were a bloody nuisance! Having said that, if you can get a monitored system that suits your circumstances, then by all means go for it. Be sure to do your research first, or speak to your local law enforcement office. Speaking of which, in the UK you should have a local Crime Reduction Office at your main police station. They can give free advice and possibly even arrange for security checks, or free fitting of good locks in some cases.

Personally, I find the best alarm is a dog! We have two and while it can be a pain when they start barking at three in the morning, you know it is for a reason. Their senses are much sharper than ours and, of course, dogs are very territorial. Some people use geese or chickens to similar effect. "Alarm cats" is a concept yet to catch on though, to be fair, ours are good at catching small rodent intruders!

I know people who have done all the above, their homes are nice and secure. Then they announce on social media exactly when they are going on holiday, and how long for. Criminals gather intelligence just the same as police or military. These days, that will include scanning social media, taking reconnaissance drives around the area, or, a favourite local one here, daylight knocking on doors to see if you "have any scrap."

Doorstep traders may be genuine, they may also be scouts, or people on the look out for an opportunity. You can get "No Cold Callers" stickers to help cut down. If you feel vulnerable, it may be best not to even answer the door. If in doubt, call the police.

Having all your possessions on display is another issue. Some local people made FB posts, with pictures, about the wonderful "really expensive" outdoor lamp they'd just fitted to the front of their house. Guess what happened to that! But even on a pure visibility level, take a walk round the outside of your house and look in all the windows. What can you see? Consider net curtains, perhaps.

Speaking of holidays, when you go away, what should you do to make the house look lived in? Timer switches are good for keeping the place lit at night. Two other signs burglars will look for are piled up mail or papers sticking out of the letterbox. Have a neighbour collect them if possible, and also ask them to keep an eye on the place.

On the subject of neighbours, be aware of local issues and community. We know that some places are more prone to break ins than other, particularly in urban areas. It may be that a lot of that burglary is drug related, that is certainly the case where I used to live. Most burglars were not "professionals" but people who would smash in a door or window, grab your hi fi and run, all to fund their next fix.

In a different area, you may get another type of thief. Perhaps someone who targets specific people, those who might have a lot of jewellery, or someone who has an expensive sports car, for example. There is a trade in high end cars being stolen to order, so try and ensure any vehicles are housed in a secure garage.

So if you are moving to a new area, do some research on the crime stats. See if there is a local Neighbourhood Watch, or similar. The best "soft" defence against any type of crime is to have a strong community. Having people look out for

each other, particularly keeping an eye on elderly or vulnerable neighbours, makes life a lot more difficult fro criminals. Tie that in with your local police force and you have a major deterrent to criminals.

My own village is quite strong on this, particularly amongst the local farmers who seem to have eyes on everything 24/7! Rural theft tends more towards stealing expensive farm equipment as well as domestic burglaries, not to mention the odd cases of hare coursing and the like. A good network, whatever the setting, helps not only with crime fighting but also in building good social bonds too.

Home defence can be a contentious issue and, again, understanding local law is key. Generally speaking, in the UK, as we have said, if you feel you or your family are in immediate threat, you can take appropriate action. What you use and how you use it is another issue! The samurai sword or baseball bat are perennial favourites for home defence. Personally, I prefer items that are not quite so obvious but will certainly do the job required.

Once again, a little preparation goes along way. Do you have a family plan for intruders? Can you navigate around your house in the dark? Can you put your hand on whichever items you need quickly and easily? If you want to run some kind of

drills for home invasion, invite some Systema friends round and work through some scenarios. You could also ask them to approach the house from a burglar's perspective. Can they get in easily? Leave a window open and see if they can sneak in. Just be sure to let your neighbours know what is going on!

VEHICLE SECURITY

Much of the above also applies to your vehicle security. Make sure your car is locked and you have a decent alarm fitted. Don't leave expensive items in plain view. Consider tinted windows. Commercial vans are often targeted for their tools, be aware of this. For high end cars, trackers and the like are available.

Never leave your car running while you are not in it! Every winter, there are car thefts from people who start the car, then leave it to run on their drive while it defrosts, as they pop back in the house. An absolute gift to a passing car thief!

Consider where you park your vehicle. Is it well lit and busy? Are there cameras or security patrols? Be extra aware as you come back to your parked car. Are people hanging around? Can you get in and away quickly?

Of course, there are such things as professional carjackers, kidnappers and the like. Countering those is more specialised work, more along Close Protection lines, something which Systema can also teach us. For now, though, we will keep things "everyday."

So when driving, keep doors locked. If your windows are open, don't have a bag on the passenger seat, put it on the floor. Be aware at traffic lights and junctions of anyone approaching your vehicle. If possible, always leave some space between you and the car in front. If you can see that car's bumper, you should be far enough away that you can turn and drive out.

Shunt and claim incidents were increasingly common a while back. This is where people would hire a car and drive in such a way that you knock into the back of them. They then claim for whiplash, emotional scarring, etc. Having a dashcam can help in these cases, along with having a general record in the case of any genuine accident or other incident.

Speaking of scams, here's one that I experienced a few months back. A guy was parked on the side of the road and flagged me down. I pulled over and he came to the passenger side window. I wound it down a few inches (never open your window full if you don't know who it is) and he told me a story about having run out of petrol and not having any cash to buy any. The punchline was, if he gave me his expensive watch, could I give him twenty quid so that he could walk to the nearby garage and buy some petrol?

None of it rang true. He showed me the

watch but I don't know a Rolex from a Bolex. I drove off. I checked with my wife when I got home. Apparently this was a current scam doing the rounds locally, the police were aware. The watch is virtually worthless, it's a pure con. This does highlight another method that bad guys will use, the use of someone in distress, an appeal to the Good Samaritan in all of us. So if you do find yourself in a similar situation, be aware!

Other general driving considerations are to be aware of weather conditions and be prepared should your vehicle break down. Do you have cover from the RAC or similar? If it is could do you have a blanket in the car and so on. Before a long trip make sure your phone is fully charged. Be aware of changing weather conditions when driving and modulate your speed accordingly. If you are feeling tired, pull over for a nap or a walk in fresh air.

BEING PREPARED FOR VIOLENCE

I find it interesting that violence forms such a huge part of our entertainment, whether it be in TV shows and movies or in watching two people fight. There is obviously a thirst in us to see such things and experience them vicariously. Real violence, of course, is shocking, brutal, deeply unpleasant, potentially life changing or life ending and emotionally damaging. If we are training in Systema from the perspective of self defence or professional work, how do we deal with the issues that violence can bring?

The first issue to address is our own personal response to violence. This depends very much on our background, previous experiences, social values and so on. If you have grown up around violence, you may be more immune to some of its effects than a person who has never been near a real fight let alone in one. We should then consider, though,

the types of violence involved. For example, I grew up in a time and place where fights at football matches and in pubs and clubs were very common. Mostly young men involved in what you could call "tribal disputes." Generally fists and kicks, usually in a group or crowd. Occasional use of bats or knives. It was rare to see a gun, though it did happen now and then. Also a lot of posturing and verbal aggression.

That is very different from some who has grown up in war zone, living with the threat of bombing, enemy troops, shortages of food and water and so on. Or a person who perhaps grew up in an abusive household. To some extent, we are all products of our past. But how much we allow our past to mould our present and future is up to us. We should also consider our current environment and needs.

How deep do I need to go into some aspects of training, how much do they relate to my present life and activities? That is not to say that just because you work in an office, say, you should avoid all types of "professional work" training. What I mean is that we have to be honest about our needs, our expectations and our capabilities. Doing a bit of "weekend warrior" training does not make me a special forces soldier.

However, if approached from another angle, that training might well put me in better touch with myself, and allow me to go further and deeper in my regular training and activities. I mention this because sometimes people see camo gear or people with knives on Systema videos and draw the conclusion that we are all wannabe commandos. That is far from the case (though some Systema people are real commandos!) I also want to draw a distinction between our kind of work and the sort of macho "tough guy" posturing that some put forward. We aim to work from a place of intelligence and humanity, not from a place of ego and fear.

People not used to violence can easily become overwhelmed by it and that applies to all of us at some point. I hope that the drills presented here, as well as from other good resources, go some way into fixing that "freeze" reaction and form a good base for you to build on should you wish to take this work further. There are other ways to expose ourselves to violence. These days we can easily find "fight clips" all over the internet. They may be various types of sports matches, or CCTV of actual attacks and incidents. There are even websites posting even more unpleasant things. Watch these things by all means, but make sure you don't get too drawn in by them.

If you want to experience a safe fight, you might look at taking part in for some form competition - boxing, grappling contests, and so on. It is usually possible to access these at different levels of ability and most decent clubs will be welcoming to beginners.

A less safe method is go to places where you might see or even be involved in violence. You've seen the movie *Fight Club*? A method that comes with a health warning, not to mention any legal consequences of being involved! On a more positive note, you may also do that by becoming a volunteer of some sort, a community police officer or paramedic, for example.

There's nothing to stop you combining any or all of these methods, along with the testing available from good Systema training. And whether you are concerned about how you may deal with violence, or if you want to overcome the effects of previous situations, I think you will find the Systema methods of stress and fear inoculation to be among the most effective all round. Not only in terms of confrontation but in the deeper and more long term aspects of dealing with all aspects of human nature.

CHAPTER EIGHT
CONCLUSIONS

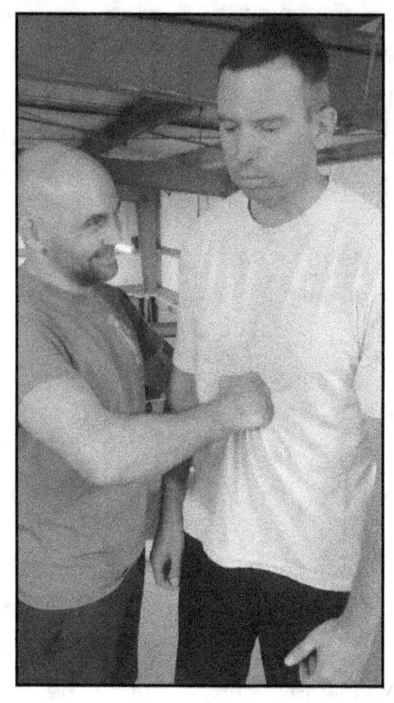

I hope that this book has given you some good training ideas, or, at the very least, make you think a more deeply about awareness in general. We have covered quite a lot of areas but, in some respects, we are still only scratching the surface, especially in the more specialised subjects.

With that in mind, I highly recommended you carry out further research as well as, of course, train with the top teachers whenever you can. Have a look around locally for further resources. Perhaps you can access woodcraft instructors, communication experts and the like, people who can help you deepen your knowledge. This type of work really is a never-ending learning experience and, like Systema itself, spreads deep and wide.

Please don't think that being aware means that you are in a constant hyper-alert state. There is a saying that "absolute paranoia is absolute awareness." There may be something in that, but paranoia is a debilitating mental condition, not a state to be aspired to. Mikhail says it best, when he says our work should be like "buttering toast." This applies to all our work, from the physical to the psychological.

Also, don't make the mistake that I heard of recently, of putting the cart before the horse. This was from a well known martial arts podcaster who was referencing Musashi's advice on "battle mindset." The gentleman in question seems to have taken this to mean we walk around in a perpetual crouch, hands ready, war face on, grimacing at everyone that comes near. To my mind, this is a total misunderstanding of what Musashi was trying to say. In battle, we aim to be as clear minded as in our everyday activities, exactly what Mikhail and other professionals tell us hundreds of years later.

This is symptomatic of an issue around modern martial arts. They have become primarily a visual activity, based around supposed "Alpha male" behaviour (another flawed concept not backed up by science.) The vast majority of people access martial arts visually - films, martial art demos, combat sports. The primary sense used is sight; they want to see the tension, see the cool movement, see the drama, sweat and action.

Systema, especially, is built much more on feeling. Tactile, emotional and so on. It is difficult to transfer that over into a visual medium. We see a guy hit with barely a movement and the other person collapses in pain. Must be bullshit! Where's the power? Where's the tension? The proof, of course, is just like the pudding, it comes in the tasting. With feeling comes understanding but feelings don't look good on Youtube!

As Vladimir has often said, a professional looks at things with a different eye. That is true of anything. As a musician, I hear music with a different ear. I might notice the tempo slipping, or an interesting chord change. The same is true for artists and others, I'm sure. However, in a world becoming increasingly digitalised, visual-based and removed from direct human contact, perhaps such skills are receding? All the more reason, then, to share our work and experience.

ARE YOU HERE?

This leads me to an important observation on awareness, especially in light of advancing of technology. Don't get me wrong, modern technology is a marvel. It allows me to write this book! It allows me to communicate with people from all over the world. But there is a downside, one that is causing particular concern about young people. That is the notion of being drawn into the digital world at the expense of interactions in the real world. In extreme circumstances, that means cases of addiction, even of people dying after spending days playing a computer game.

At a recent workshop someone asked me a good question. "How can we best bring ourselves to be in the present?" It's an important issue for a number of reasons, quite obvious ones if we are talking about awareness. But what do we mean by being "in the present?" Sometimes, when teaching, I look around the room as I'm explaining a drill. Most people are watching me or obviously listening. Sometimes, though, you spot a person who is not looking and has a far away expression on their face. That person is "not here."

Where do people go when they are not here? Into either the past or the future. That person may be thinking about something that happened to them earlier that day. An argument at work, a driver who cut them up on the way to class. Or they may be thinking about something in the future, what they are going to eat when they get home, the long journey they have to make tomorrow. So the drill is explained and everyone partners up. The person in question will then invariably ask "What are we doing?"

Now, as humans, it is virtually impossible for us to live totally in the here and now and, let's face it, we wouldn't; want to. Memories are drawn upon for all sorts of reasons. Experience teaches us, memories comfort us or provoke emotion. Likewise, thinking ahead means we are able to plan for the future, to anticipate events and take appropriate action. Problems arise when, rather than visit past of future, we live there. It may be that we have suffered some bad experience in the past. The question is, do we allow that negative experience to shape and mould us for the rest of our lives? Are we to be defined by that experience, or can we move beyond it?

I'm not suggesting that this always an easy things to do. People who have undergone extreme trauma of some kind may need extensive professional help to move forward, but it is important that they seek it.

On a more mundane level, think back to our earlier example. Someone cuts you up at the lights on the way to training. So you bring that anger into class. Perhaps you hit your partner harder than is appropriate. Is that a good thing? No, you have transferred your anger to another person, that's all. Better, instead, to deal with that irritation there and then, on the spot, as quickly as you can. Leave it behind. Imagine every incident as a stone that you have to carry. After a week, you'd have a sackful to lug around.

Extensive worrying about things in the future, things that have not even happened yet, is a common aspect of neurosis. Here, a person tends to live very much in the conscious part of the brain and is perhaps prone to over analysing every situation. All well and good in its place but consider, again, how that can impact on our present actions.

In an emergency situation we may freeze as we consider which of the 15 options to choose and what might happen if we do this, or if we do that. So the question arises, how to be fully involved in the present? I hope that the previous exercises go some way towards answering that question. Simply take time to observe with and connect to what is around you, on every level. One key to this is to slow down a little, every now and then, take time to smell the roses as the saying goes.

More immediate methods are to work with a partner on something like taking strikes. This is, in my view, the single most direct

method of bringing the mind squarely back into the body! You have to deal with what is happening here and now, there is no escaping it. This work is very interesting beyond the obvious "fighty" applications, because disguised within that combative appearance is a very powerful method of helping people connect with their deeper inner tension and emotional issues. Not just connect with, but being empowered to release them, too.

This is a practice beyond the scope of this book, I refer you, of course, to the excellent *Strikes* book produced by Vladimir referenced earlier. Suffice to say, that an exploration if this work with an eye to dealing with past injuries and bad experiences is very interesting and rewarding.

For solo training, I recommend you do some falls and rolling work. Again, it is very difficult to be worrying about your phone bill when flying through the air. As a side note I often find that this is the most unpopular type of training in class (myself included). I wonder if that's because of that very reason? It forces us to be present with ourselves, with no outside interference, fully facing up to tour fears and tensions. Just a thought!

CHANGING PERCEPTION

Implementing the simple solo drills here should help you to be more attentive in your daily life. Not only of potential threats but of other people's moods, the weather, local conditions and so on.

Something we have to understand, though, is that our perceptions are filtered through many layers - social, cultural, personal likes and dislikes, expectations and so on. It is very difficult for us to look at anything without some form of judgement, particularly when it comes to other people! For the first job I had on leaving school, I had to wear a suit. Later on, I left that job and ended up, for a while, working as a council gardener. That meant wearing a donkey jacket, old jeans and workboots. I began to notice that in certain shops, I was getting eyed and followed by security. The same shops that I had gone into previously, with no problem, wearing the suit. I'm the same person, yet to the security staff I was now a threat.

This will not be news to anyone who lives in a society with a defined class system. Even in modern times, the saying holds true in the UK, that a person is judged as soon as they open their mouth. A "common" or regional accent does not carry as much weight as an "upper class" one. This is two way traffic. People get called "posh" for talking well. At one time, in the music industry, it was fashionable to be "working class", and the well educated began dropping their aitches and wearing torn clothes! There are a whole host of judgements made, positive and negative, for virtually every human characteristic you can think of, from skin colour to nationality to disability and so on.

These are all constructs, all learned behaviour. We should take care, then, that we try to mitigate the effects of these filters as much as possible in our awareness work. One way to do that is to consciously change your perception. No, I'm not talking "mind expanding" drugs, but something far more down-to-earth! Simply try this - change your viewpoint. That might mean thinking from the other person's perspective in order to gain an understanding of their motivations.

You bump into someone getting off the train and they give you a torrent of abuse. You respond in kind, you get into a tussle and end up rolling round on the platform. Or - you think, wow this guy looks really stressed, perhaps he just got fired from his job, he's on the way home to tell his wife they won't be able to pay the rent this month. You apologise and move on.

A homeless looking person comes rushing towards you, gesticulating wildly. You shrink away, turn and hurry off from them

Or - you wait as they get close, they return your wallet which you just dropped as you walked past them.

I'm not saying that you always think the best or the worst of people, just that you take all data and information into account before formulating a response. If that sounds like it may take some time, with

practice it won't because your primary indicator remains your gut instinct. Another method is to take yourself out of the situation completely and view it from a different place. Imagine you are watching the scene on TV. How are you acting? Can you see the other things going on around you?

Have you ever had a bad day, nothing has gone right, you're in a rush and the printer jams. You might stomp around, hit the wall, even throw something in anger. A printer once annoyed me so much I threw it out of the first floor (open!) window. Imagine how that looks on camera. Stupid! A grown man swearing at a machine!

So sometimes a simple switch in viewpoint can help give us another side to the situation. Help take us out of the emotional state, and consequent reaction, into a space where we can assess more calmly what is going on. Though if that means having a brief tantrum, by all means have one!

SOCIAL SYSTEMA

This self awareness is something my colleague Ed Phillips calls *Social Systema*. It's the little voice that tells you you are being a bit too loud in the conversation. Or that another person is not comfortable with what you are saying. Or that someone may be a bit shy or nervous, so you modulate accordingly. You can think of it as the psychological equivalent of knowing you

have a bit of spinach stuck to your front teeth. Why does everyone recoil when I smile?

Knowing ourselves and others should mean that we navigate the social jungle much more comfortably. Again, prejudgment and prejudice, positive and negative, can hinder that, so always try to take people as you find them, judge by actions and deeds rather than looks and words.

We should always bear in mind the phrase "true communication is only possible between equals." If you have a power over someone, or if you are in fear of someone, that will always colour the flow of communication between you. Studies have shown that once you get beyond a few tiers of structure or rank in an organisation, communication suffers. The people at the top don't really know the issues the people at the bottom face. This is applicable to many situations and should be factored into your awareness work.

HABITS, FEARS AND PHOBIAS

Another aspect of our make up is the formation of habits. We get up at a certain time. On Thursday we always have egg and chips for dinner. We have a routine. Routines are important, they help structure our lives according to our activities and needs. But they can also become stifling, we begin to stagnate.

The answer is simple - change your routine, try something new! It doesn't have to be major, maybe go to a place you've never eaten at before and try some new type of food. Get up an hour early one day and go swimming. Take up a new hobby, meet some new people. The thing is not to get stuck in ever repeating patterns of behaviour that, over time, become smaller and smaller. Life is for living, we are not machines. The best quote I heard on this was from English comedians Peter Cook and Dudley Moore. They stated:

"Always remember. If your life seems dull and boring…. it is."

Behaviour patterns include habits but may also include things fears and phobias. I imagine that phobias are another aspect of constructed behaviour, perhaps due to some experience in our early life. Phobias may also be a mask for a deeper issue. In any case, they need to be addressed as not only can they interfere with our general awareness, they can also have a detrimental effect on our lives in general. There are numerous methods of dealing with phobias. Some very much echo our Systema methods of fear inoculation training, involving incremental exposure to the stress trigger, alongside good coping mechanisms for dealing with the resultant tension.

Phobias are very obvious manifestations of fear, but long term stress and worry can be just as damaging. Prolonged exposure to even low level stress suppresses our immune system, making us more susceptible to illness and disease. Worries that get out of hand can over-shadow our whole lives, even to the extent of self harm or suicide. Again, there are numerous therapies available but there are also a few simple guidelines we can look to.

The first is to be aware of how and when

stress and worry take hold. Can we deal with the issue there and then? Are we able to change the situation in any way? If the answer is yes, then take the relevant action. If the answer is no, we have to ask ourselves if our stress and worry will have an effect on the outcome? If the answer is no, which it usually is, then what is the use of worrying? This is easy to say, less easy to put in practice, of course, but as a general principle, it stands.

It seems that no matter how "advanced" or well off we become as a society, deep levels of stress still exist. In my view, much of that is down to social engineering and the media, but that's another topic! Just be aware of how much worry is laid upon you from outside sources.

The second guideline is to take action against the symptoms of the stress. Deal with the tension as best you can. Do some training. Get a massage, take some time out for a nice, relaxing walk. In other words, give yourself some time away from the situation in order to reset your stress levels. It may not resolve the situation but you are protecting yourself from its effects.

If there is still an issue, then share your problems. Talk things over with friends, family, workmates. Worries that are held in tight tend to grow beyond all proportion. Others may be able to offer practical suggestions, or provide emotional support.

If the cause of the stress is an on-going issue, can you break the cycle? An abusive relationship, for example. A common frustration when I worked in the court system was sufferers of domestic violence who failed to show on the day of the trial. The perp would walk free, the other person would usually say "He said he would change, I've gone back to him." Six months later - back in court again the cycle repeated. Now, I'm very aware what a complex issue such a cases can be, with no easy answers. But at some point, we all have to take charge of our own lives and draw a line.

On a more flippant note, I used to frequent a combatives forum where the standard measure of practicality about any method was: "Will it work in the chip shop on a Saturday night?" My, I thought, not unreasonable question was "Why not just go to another chip shop?"

In short, be aware of solutions, not only

problems. Systema should encourage a problem solving mindset! We sometimes like to wear and display our problems for all to see. In extreme cases, they come to define us. But we are more than our problems.

KNOW YOURSELF

At the root of all our awareness training rests the simple phrase *know yourself*. As some of you will know, this was the original name chosen for Systema - *poznai sebia*.

In many ways, Systema is the study of pure awareness. Of ourselves, on every level of behaviour, of others and of how those two things intersect and interact. For these reasons, we try to keep our work fresh and perpetually challenging. Not just in a physical sense of "do more press ups", that's just training based on numbers. More with a sense of "how do I react to his situation. How can I improve my response?"

Incidentally, one important sense that I have neglected to mention is a sense of humour! As the saying goes, *take your work seriously but don't take yourself too seriously.* Humour is a great way to release tension, build bonds, cheer people up and spread a good mindset. Use it wisely! As I mentioned at the start, through self awareness and knowledge of our own shortcomings and frailties, I hope we can develop a deeper understanding of the frailties of others and that that, in turn, leads to greater tolerance and unity of all.

We are all human. We all face the same struggles, in most cases we all have the same common, base desires and needs. Food, family, friends. On a wider level, we are all sharing life and air on a tiny ball of rock spinning through space. Awareness of not only those we share the planet with, but also on our personal and social effects on the ecological systems of that planet, is another important issue that we should bear in mind.

Life is a wonderful gift, an amazing opportunity. What a shame if we waste that opportunity by spending our days living in stress, spreading anger, fear and hate. Especially when we have been given the means of always developing, always growing, of being totally present in the flow of life and reaping all of its rich rewards.

RESOURCES

Mikhail Ryabko
Systema HQ Moscow   www.systemaryabko.com

Vladimir Vasiliev
Systema HQ Toronto   www.russianmartialart.com

Robert Poyton
Cutting Edge Systema   www.systemauk.com

Instructional Downloads   www.systemafilms.com

RECOMMENDED READING

Strikes - Vladimir Vasiliev & Scott Meredith

Let Every Breath - Vladimir Vasiliev

Secrets of the Russian Blade Masters - Vladimir Vasiliev

The Systema Manual - Major Konstantin Komarov

The Ten Points of Sparring - Robert Poyton

Systema Solo Training - Robert Poyton

Systema Partner Training - Robert Poyton

Systema Locks, Holds & Throws - Robert Poyton

The Gift of Fear - Gavin De Becker

What Everybody is Saying - Joe Navarro

NOTES

www.ingramcontent.com/pod-product-compliance
Lightning Source LLC
Chambersburg PA
CBHW051404070526
44584CB00023B/3282